I Lived Inside the Campus Revolution

OTHER BOOKS BY *James Joseph*

YOU FLY IT

CAREERS OUTDOORS

INCOME OPPORTUNITIES

HOW TO START A SUCCESSFUL SMALL BUSINESS

I Lived Inside the Campus Revolution

William Tulio Divale
with James Joseph

COWLES BOOK COMPANY, INC. NEW YORK

Contents

Introduction: Inside the Campus Revolution

THE blackest day in my twenty-eight years was Tuesday, June 17, 1969. Early that morning, on a downtown Los Angeles street, I met my FBI "handler"—one of several federal agents who had been my contacts during more than four years of campus turmoil and confrontation.

I was hustled into a car. In silence, we drove a circuitous route to Los Angeles' monolithic Federal Courthouse Building, parked in a secluded stall in its subterranean garage, and entered the building through a back door. Other agents were waiting. We took a freight elevator to the seventh floor—and walked, for security reasons, to the eighth. Quickly, I was ushered into a courtroom antechamber. On the other side of its massive oaken door the five-member Federal Subversive Activities Control Board (SACB) had, only moments before, opened two days of hearings. Once I stepped through that door and into the courtroom, I would be revealed—as an FBI student undercover informer.

"Wayne," my FBI handler said quietly, using my undercover name, "are you absolutely sure you want to go through with this?"

I nodded. I had made my decision. More exactly, time and circumstances had made it for me. Nonetheless, it had been made. I would testify.

My handler's concern—as both of us very well knew—was mere stage business in what, for the government's scenario writers and directors, has become a smash succession of sociocomedies. For want of a better name they are called "surfacings."

Their scripts have the look-alike sameness of Xerox copies. Their settings are likewise. The play is called to curtain by a sergeant-at-arms. As the house lights dim, and those onstage go up, Act I opens to a courthouse scene.

Center-stage sits a panel of elders. Before them are arranged two other tables. One is for the government's Prosecutor, the other for the Defense. As though contrived by an allegorist, the Defense table invariably is to the left of the Prosecutor's, and even farther to the left of the panel of elders. Were a placard to mark the Defense table, it would read: "Youth Generation."

Now the eldest of the eldest, in descending order of social conscience, summons the actors to cue.

"Will the clerk call the first witness."

A gasp of torment, audible and malignant, believing but incredulous, goes up from the spectators, most of whom are no older, nor any more guilty or more guileless, than their peers who sit at the Defense table.

On trial is not one youth or two, or even a hundred. On trial is a global generation. It is a generation that knows no national boundaries and less of the world of their elders who, knowing even less of the new world of youth in the sixties and seventies, presume to sit in their judgment.

I had come to bear witness against my peers, for I was of their generation. I was to be that first witness. My time to "surface" had come.

I knew and had carefully weighed the risks, both personal and philosophical. Step through that massive oaken door and into the hearing room and I would forever be branded and despised as a "fink," or worse, by my campus peers—the people I had led, worked with, spent endless hours in conference and discussion with, and had counted, until that moment, as my friends—my closest friends— through nearly five tumultuous school years.

I had lived inside—and helped lead—the campus "revolution."

Yet, through it all, I had secretly worked under cover for the Federal Bureau of Investigation.

In time, perhaps correctly, the FBI would come to list me among its "most valuable" student informers. I had filed nearly eight hundred undercover FBI reports, 602 of them written or recorded transcripts, the rest verbal—in telephone contacts with Bureau agents in the half-dozen cities (New York, Chicago, Washington, Montreal, San Francisco) I had visited as a student activist and during secret once-a-week meetings with my FBI handlers in Los Angeles.

My undercover file for the Bureau ran to thousands of pages, documenting day by day, meeting to meeting and over a perspective of years, the campus' evolution from social democracy to radicalism and on to revolution. I had named names—the names of perhaps four thousand activists with whom, from one end of the nation to the other, and across international borders, I had worked or had become acquainted. My value to the Bureau lay in the increasingly active role I played within the student "revolution." I was a leader, not merely a follower. My perspective was that of an "insider"—from the top of the pyramid of dissidence rather than from its more populous base.

In many ways I was a product of the Federal Bureau of Investigation. The Bureau had "recruited" (solicited) me when I was a political virgin. At the time I had no politics of my own and little of anyone else's. It was the FBI that pointed me toward membership in the Communist party, urged me to penetrate the W.E.B. DuBois clubs and to infiltrate SDS (Students for a Democratic Society). It had molded me to political consciousness. Once that consciousness was fully matured, I had "turned"—"soured," the Bureau was to say. I came to see the Bureau not as the defender of "democracy," but as the keeper of the status quo—not as an instrument of orderly change, but as the handmaiden of reaction and the tool of entrenchment. My break with the FBI was inevitable.

During much of those nearly four and a half years under cover, I was a trusted member of the Communist party. I sat on the party's forty-member Southern California policy-making "central" committee, served as chairman of one of the party-sponsored student W.E.B. DuBois clubs, demonstrated against the draft, and marched as a bearded New Leftist on the protest lines—for peace (in Vietnam), for war (against the Establishment and America's growing imperialism), and in behalf of the "struggle for liberation" for black people, not the least of them being the black students' demands for black studies programs taught by black professors.

At the FBI's (and, ironically, also the party's) urging, I had joined SDS. Along with other top campus Communists (philosophical Marx-

ix

ists as well as party members), I had helped spearhead SDS in its on-campus confrontations—against napalm (and Dow Chemical Corporation, then napalm's chief supplier); against the ROTC; against the police and my college administration's hardening stand in the face of escalating dissidence.

My credentials for party and SDS leadership were the envy of johnny-come-lately campus activists. I'd once been turned down for a scholarship because I refused to recite the Pledge of Allegiance. Later, in a melee of fists, I helped prevent campus counterinsurgents (rightist students) from desecrating—and burning—the Soviet flag. I was co-founder of SDS at one of the colleges I attended and led the fight to get it accredited there.

I was—and remain—an admirer, though not a disciple, of Marx and Lenin. I believe the Vietnam War is immoral. I would refuse the draft were I called. And I would march again—as I have marched countless times before—against all the evils of this society, from racism to puritanism. But, like the vast majority of equally concerned students (I am now a graduate student), I march to correct the wrongs of the American society, not to destroy it.

This was the reason I decided in June of 1969 (and scarcely a month after my return from the Communist party's national convention in New York City, to which I was a student delegate) to do more than simply break with SDS, the party—yes, and with the Federal Bureau of Investigation—but to come forward, openly, to tell it like it really is.

Adult Americans—the parents of today's youth generation—already know in the depths of their hearts, I am certain, how it really is and why it really is that their sons and daughters are rebelling. And why they are repudiating the very dream which they and their fathers and their fathers' fathers scrimped and worked and saved to achieve: the *American Dream*.

For today's adults—the parents of today's young rebels—having achieved or having come within reach of achieving the American Materialistic Dream, have discovered it is not worth the achieving. It has failed to bring them the security, the peace of mind and, above all else, the happiness which, as the most huckstered and ballyhooed product of the American society, it was so loudly and so long advertised as bringing. Like so many other products of this society, even the American Dream was built in with obsolescence, glossed over with a thin veneer of virtue which too often flawed and faded, and whose luster—upon close inspection and when balanced on the immutable scale that weighs the quality of life in any society—was more in the mind of the beholder than in the world of reality.

The American Dream for these millions of adult Americans was found to be something other than as advertised.

Perhaps it was not so fraudulent that the Federal Trade Commission would prohibit its future achievement. Perhaps it was not so injurious that the Congress would seek to have it labeled with a warning, "Achieve It At Your Own Risk." Perhaps it was not so overpriced in terms of physical and psychological outlay as to compel a Senate committee to investigate its true cost to the achiever. Nevertheless, it was deceptively packaged, mislabeled, and short-weighted.

Yet from a distance—from the perspective of the depressioned thirties, the war-torn forties, and the early unsettled fifties—they could not perceive the deception toward which, with all their life's energy, they were striving.

Not until they had achieved the American Dream did they come to realize that they had become slaves to its attainment and, having attained it, lifelong chattels to its perpetuation.

Not so, however, vow their children—the first generation born to the American Dream.

It was theirs, by inheritance, from birth. They had been born to it through the sweat and strain and self-sacrifice of their parents. They had come of age in an era (the late fifties and sixties) when the American Dream of abundance was no longer a distant dream but, for many, and especially the middle-class youth of the campus, a taken-for-granted reality.

But as youth looked first to their parents and then at themselves and then to the materialistic trappings of what their parents believed —or at 'least told them—was "it," the American Dream, youth began to question.

If this was "it" then "it" was sham and hypocrisy.

xi

For all their affluence, their parents led small, often grubbing and frequently miserable lives. They had succeeded in the business of abundance but had failed in the business of life.

Their mothers had entered into marriage chaste ("virginity" was just another item of worldly goods; it was a prized possession) only to find themselves doomed to a life of marital frustration. Their fathers, no less disillusioned, lived out their lives as cheaters (and took comfort in Kinsey, whose statistics reassured them it was only "normal").

One couple in every four (the parents of these youths of the fifties) publicly conceded their marital failure: they divorced. Of those who did not, many lived in estrangement. They had made their compromise with life—for the love of their children, for the love of God, for the love of money, for the love of security, position, or corporate status.

Though "failure products" of an outmoded cultural and economic ethic, they admonished their children to follow them lemming-like into a life (some might say "into death") doing service to the very same social restraints and material goals that had foredoomed their own happiness.

The ethic they offered was a cop-out to life.

It was an ethic that rewarded conformity with patronage: a flanneled gray niche in the economic and political structure. It was an ethic that preached the gospel of social equality on Sunday—but closed its eyes to prejudice, bias, and bigotry every other day of the week. It was an ethic that revered honesty in public and private affairs, but which thought "deception" a normal business practice, shrugged when cops and criminals were found in cahoots, condoned cheating on exams as a way to "make it" in school—and as a shortcut to success in corporate life.

But above all, what decided the minds of youths of the fifties that the American Dream and its material superabundance wasn't "it" was the terrible price they saw their parents paying.

They were eyewitnesses to their parents' self-enslavement—trapped by suburbia's lifelong mortgages; by their struggle to stay abundantly abreast of "the Joneses"; and their shameless surrender to Madison Avenue and its pitchmen to buy yet a second car, a first

xii

boat, or a flight to somewhere if only momentarily to escape from the treadmill of their own existence.

To stem the tide of bills, charge accounts, credit buying, house payments, insurance premiums, and ever-rising taxes—all accouterments of the American Dream—their fathers (and often also their mothers) were frozen in jobs they loathed, forced to moonlight (in an era of the supposed "forty-hour week"), and, though earning middle-class incomes or better, seemed scarcely able to find time to enjoy the very objects of their materialistic affection. Like horses freed from the traces only after they'd turned lame, they could look forward to freedom only when they retired at sixty or sixty-five. By then, life had passed them by.

Thus it was that youth—a thinking but influential minority—saw in their parents the hypocrisy of the American Dream.

"Let them have their dream," these perceptive youths—the precursors of the sixties—were saying.

By the mid-sixties, youths on hundreds of campuses would be saying the same thing. They would be telling pollsters they did not want to follow their fathers into business; they did not seek the security of a flannel-gray corporate niche; and they could get along with less to be able to enjoy life more.

Yet if youths in the mid-fifties were rebels—and not many of them really were—they were rebels without a cause. It was a motion picture by the same name—starring the late James Dean—which in 1956 mirrored the disenchantment of America's youth. In it, Dean played a juvenile delinquent rebellious against his parents—and their implied greater parental delinquency against him.

Youth's identification with the alienated James Dean was instantaneous. He was playing it like it was—as it was in their own lives and homes. In life as in death (Dean died that same year, at twenty-four, in a sports car accident) he was cut to the pattern of the beat generation—the rebels without a cause.

The "beat" life was typified by the beatniks in America and the angries in England. But though rebels, they weren't really interested in—or even looking for—a "cause." They'd simply dropped out of the hassle of their parents' society. They turned their backs on whatever it was society had planned for them.

Their drop-out had no noticeable effect on most youths of the day—with one explosive exception: *they looked to their peers as their cultural and behavioral models.* Doing so, they broke with the past, with established traditions—and with their parents and the world of their parents.

Born was the "generation gap."

No single phenomenon of the fifties and early sixties is more significant than this new cultural intradirection of peer to peer—of youth patterning itself after youth. This is the fact of life in the seventies which, contends anthropologist Dr. Margaret Mead in her new book, *Culture and Commitment*, differentiates youth of today from the youth of the past. And from any youth, ever. It is an age, as Dr. Mead points out, "in which peers are more than ever replacing parents as the significant models of behavior."

When youth ceases to take its example from its parents, but rather from one another, the break between the generation of the parent and the generation of the child becomes fundamental. Between parent and child there no longer exists either a cultural continuity . . . or even a commitment. For youth, having decided that his future lies with his peers, has in effect repudiated his parents, their culture, their way of life, and their values.

This is the impact of "peer modeling"— a phenomenon of the pre-sixties, which has been carried by the youth generation into the seventies.

"Peer modeling" is no mere abstraction of the anthropologist. It is the underlying stuff of today's youth rebellion—and the lyric lure of the Movement itself. It explains the ever-widening generation gap. And why American parents have *lost* their children; and how their children came to *find* their freedom. It explains as no single other cause how the Movement came to be, why it developed and how it evolved.

In 1960, a handful of alienated youths from the campuses who, even then, were forming the Students for a Democratic Society, would declare, *"We are all Social Democrats—dedicated to orderly change within the American society."*

By 1970, a fleeting decade later, some of these same SDS founders would declare, *"We are all Marxists—dedicated to the total destruction of the Establishment and the American society which perpetuates it."*

How had SDS—the philosophical soul and physical heart of the campus revolution, which is no longer confined to the campus, and of the New Left, which no longer really exists—come to so violent a philosophical turn of mind?

This was the question I attempted to answer in my voluminous reports to the FBI. It was not enough, as I saw it, merely to report the Movement's visible actions—its confrontations, conferences, and meetings. Far deeper—and often all but invisible even to its own membership—ran a philosophical strategy whose twists and turns, backtracks and steps forward motivated the visible part of the Movement, the part that made headlines at Berkeley in 1964, at Columbia in 1968, at the Moratorium marches of 1969—and, in 1970, as the aftermath of the "Chicago 7" trial and Richard Nixon's Cambodian venture.

In a single decade the campus rebellion had evolved from social democracy to revolution. It had moved from a quiet rejection of Jean-Paul Sartre and Albert Camus to a violent embrace of Marx, Mao Tse-tung, Debray, and Ho.

Understand this philosophical evolution and you understand the revolution itself. For this is the real "inside" to the youth rebellion. It is a political transformation which has no parallel in American society.

Power—first with a small "p," later with a capital "P"—was, from the outset, the salient thrust of the youth generation. Without power youth could not work the changes in the American society which at first it desired and would later demand. The problem for the young was how to wrest power from those who possessed it and, once having a little of it, use it effectively to gain still more power.

In the halcyon days of the fifties—when its rebels were without cause or causes—alienated youths had no hankering for power. They wanted nothing whatever to do with it or with those who had it— their parents, the university, the courts, big business, or bigger government. It was from those who held and wielded society's power that the alienated youths of the fifties fled. Abandoning society, they abandoned its power structure—and the power it had held over them. They espoused to change nothing, not even themselves.

xv

With the beats (as with the latter-day drop-outs, the hippies), life was inner-directed—a personal thing. And so beatdom took as its philosophers those who attempted to explain man (and the beat) to himself: *Kierkegaard,* the father of existentialism, who argued that the all-important fact about man is his mere *existence,* his simple state of being; *Jean-Paul Sartre,* the left-winger, atheist, existentialist, who declared that life, in the final analysis, is meaningless; *Albert Camus,* whose God-does-not-exist premise led him to the conclusion that, because death is really life's only certainty, life itself is not only ridiculous, but absurd. To alienated youths, these philosophers and others (including beat authors Allen Ginsberg and the late Jack Kerouac) mirrored the conclusion to which they themselves had come: that though life in the society from which they had fled was meaningless, they had neither the means nor the power to change it—to make it more meaningful.

But even while beatdom's rebels without a cause grubbed in their meaningless, powerless jungles of escape, other youths—no less alienated—were fighting the "southern wars."

There in the South these former rebels without a cause had found one: *civil rights.* In finding it, they discovered what all along they had had, but had never known they had: *power.* What led them to discover both was their own *activism.*

SDS was founded in 1960 by veterans of the "southern wars," who, unlike any American youths before them, had come to realize that in activism lay youth's potent power to change himself and the society in which he lived. But not by the ways or means, or the philosophies, of flat-on-your-back negativism. They rejected the existentialists as freedom-of-choice philosophers who failed to spur their adherents to action. For activism meant action. What the new youth reached out for were philosophies that bade youth to stand on its own two feet, pointed him in the direction where the action (and power) was—and said "sic-'em."

It was C. Wright Mills, the Texas-born Columbia University sociologist (his death in 1962 at the age of forty-five came two years after SDS's powerless birth), who pointed—in his book, *The Power Elite*—to the interlocking self-interest of America's industrial-military-political "'directorate," as the seat of All Power.

Born was the "Establishment," against which the New Left's hardened-to-activism young leaders would point the campus cadres.

Hand in glove, Mills had said, and often with hands in one another's pockets, the triumvirate of America's power structure perpetuated themselves and their own power: government's big spending —military, scientific, and social—fattened big industry whose corporate executives served as government administrators only to serve themselves. The spending programs devised by the power elite, who moved effortlessly from the executive suites of big business to the administrative suites of big government, perpetuated the military and profited their own corporations (and, ultimately, their own portfolios of power, status, and stocks).

The monster of power in America, as the young leaders of the New Left came to perceive, through Mills, was the Establishment. Since it held most of the power, it was from the Establishment they would have to wrest what little power they actually wanted and needed in order to move America out of its self-alienation.

Nor to grasp that power, as some of the New Left's theorists quickly saw, need they necessarily knock first at the door of the Pentagon or march down Pennsylvania Avenue (as during 1969's Moratorium demonstrations they ultimately would).

The Establishment was entrenched on their own campuses!

That it was—as University of California president Clark Kerr unwittingly showed them—was evidenced by what Kerr labeled the "multi-university": the educational factory whose end products were molded to serve the Establishment (to provide it with technological and scientific muscle and management minds). And whose production lines were bound to the Establishment through prodigious research grants, the corporate ties of many college administrators and regents, and the consultative fees paid the university's brainiest for their allegiance to the Establishment.

No, to get America moving, reasoned early New Left thinkers, students at the outset, at least, wouldn't need to move off their campuses. The Establishment could be confronted in a student's own classrooms. Thus, one question was answered—the locus of the society's power.

Still to be answered was another question: What was the root cause of the new youths' alienation—from their parents, from the society of their parents, and from the university itself?

The life-is-meaningless philosophers of the beat generation simply turned the New Left's activists off. Life to them was meaningful—and amenable to change providing they could find the power to change it. Resignation wouldn't change it. Activism would. The alienated New Left turned for an explanation of its own alienation to the most "activist" of philosophers: Karl Marx.

But piecemealed and improvised as was the philosophy of the New Left (which borrowed words and phrases as easily from Dwight Eisenhower, the reluctant militarist, as from Michael Bakunin, the eager anarchist), it didn't—and couldn't—take Marx either in whole or even in part, but only just a bit.

The bit the New Left took from Marx as an explanation for its own alienation was Marx's concept of "estranged labor."

Marx was talking about the working man who, because he did not receive the end product of his labor, but only payment for it, was "estranged" from his work. New Left theorists applied Marx's "estranged labor" concept to their parents and to themselves as students.

They saw their parents' lives as meaningless largely because they were estranged from their labor. To succor their alienation they "bought happiness." While the abundance their parents bought might bring momentary sensual pleasure, or even a moment's dealienation, it failed either to give them a deeper purpose in life or, ultimately, to buy them happiness.

New Left theorists saw their own campus experience as a similarly futile buy-off—and just as meaningless. The reward of a prescribed and often ritualistic curriculum of study wasn't a deeper understanding of themselves, of society, or of life—but merely vocational training to prepare them to serve as the technicians and managers of the Establishment. The final reward of four years of college was not the product of their campus labor—knowledge, and the wherewithal to comprehend life—but a paycheck. Like his own father's estrangement from his work, the New Leftist felt similarly alienated from his—the university.

Neither a bead on the Establishment as the seat of power nor "estranged labor" as the reason for their alienation were really "activist" philosophies. These were concepts that defined conditions. What aimed at changing the conditions was "participatory democracy" and the concept of the "new working class." Both were made-in-America philosophies. Both were innovated to get done what the New Left wanted done. Taken together, they made the New Left *the* "New Left"—a new, vital, philosophical entity.

"Participatory democracy"—which SDS propounded in its founding document of principle, the "Port Huron Statement"—was at the heart of what the new youths felt and were saying: In a democracy the individual ought to have the right to help formulate those social decisions which most directly affect the quality and direction of his life. He ought to participate—and have a decisional hand—in charting his own future life and happiness.

If youth is called upon to fight in foreign wars, then youth should sit in the councils of those who decide draft laws and, ultimately, in the war room with those who make war—and formulate war policy.

If, as every New Leftist agreed it did, the university shaped the quality and direction of their lives, then they ought to have a hand in university administration and in shaping curriculum.

If adult law forbade the smoking of marijuana, though it was youth who used it and were arrested for it—an arrest and subsequent confinement that might change the direction of their whole lives—then youth ought to help make the laws society expects young and old alike to obey.

In short: The big "quality of life" decisions should be moderated, if not made, by those they most directly affect.

It was the new youths' attempt to speed the implementation of "participatory democracy" that brought New Left philosophy to its zenith—with the concept of the "new working class."

By then, 1966–67, SDS's search for allies in its struggle for power had proved largely disappointing. As prospective off-campus allies, it had all but written off the worker, the poor, the indigent, and the blacks (who at the time were championing a separatist kind of militancy, though eventually they would again look to the campus for support). The New Left was forced to devise an ally-to-power of its own making—"the new workers"—whom it envisaged as the honed-to-activism collegians, graduated from the campus and into the upper strata of industry, government, and the military, who could be relied upon as the broad revolutionary base envisaged by the New Left philosophers.

Largely it was the "new working class" concept that spurred SDS to organize the high schools (in order to raise the level of student consciousness a full four years before college); to work within the military (radicalizing GIs bound for college or those already in upper-echelon enlisted careers); and to establish the REP (Radical Education-tion Project), organized in 1964, and MDS (Movement for a Democratic Society)—both postgraduate organs of activism. And both designed to keep a revolutionary hone on former New Leftists and SDSers who had found their way into government or industry, and now comprised the new working class.

The new working class was to become the key to SDS's solicita-tion program for off-campus allies—and power. How vital the new worker might in time become has been spelled out by Carl Davidson, one of the New Left's leading theoreticians. Davidson wrote:

> If there is a single overall purpose for the student power movement it would be the development of a radical political consciousness among those students who will later hold jobs in strategic sectors of the political economy. This means we should reach out to engineers and technical students rather than to business administration majors, education majors rather than to art students. From a national perspective, this strategy would also suggest that we should place priorities on organizing in certain kinds of universities—the community colleges, junior colleges and technical schools, rather than religious colleges or the Ivy League.

There you have it: a philosophical glimpse into what the "New Left" was up to in mid-1968. After that, everything changed. All that was distinctly "New Left" was abandoned. And the "new" simply reverted to the "old"—to the old words, the old phrases of traditional revolutionary Marxism. If, after 1968, there remained anything "new" about the New Left (which, in fact, was no longer either practiced or preached), it was simply its orientation toward the "new" Marxists (Mao, Ho, Castro, and Che) rather than toward what SDS theoreti-cians had taken to calling the "revisionists"—Marxism of the older

Marxist–Leninist strain, as practiced and largely led from the Soviet Union.

I should know. My own Marxism is of that "revisionist" strain, although I prefer—as any intellectual Marxist—to take mine directly and unadulterated from its philosophical sources, the works of Lenin, Marx, and Engels.

Should the complex of theory that comprised the New Left surprise adult America, it may well surprise their campus activist sons and daughters as well. Only a handful of the more perceptive campus activists followed, much less were conversant with, the twists and turns and the nuances of New Left logic. Plain and simply, most were too involved in being active to ponder philosophy.

I can recall only a handful of campus SDS or DuBois club meetings—and I attended hundreds of them—where a planned confrontation was even discussed in its broad philosophical terms as to whether or not, and in what direction, a given planned campus action (a sit-in, protest, or demonstration) might "advance" a particular philosophical line.

The philosophy? Largely it was worked out by a handful of leaders before the action was even planned. The action was carried into the SDS or DuBois meeting, not the philosophy.

Thus has grown up a dichotomy between the activist who participates and the activist who ponders. The contrasts between the two are often sharp—and revealing.

In late February, 1970, rioting students at the University of California's Santa Barbara campus raised the level of the campus struggle a couple of notches by burning to the ground a Bank of America branch.

Interviewed by a radio reporter, one of the activists among the rioters gave as a reason for the attack, "The bank was a symbol of the Establishment."

But an SDS leader on campus, asked to discuss the same incident, had an entirely different—and philosophically far broader— view.

"It was a good thing," he said, referring to the bank's burnout. "It raised the whole conscious of this once sleepy campus to struggle."

One saw the building as a concrete-and-mortar symbol of the

enemy—the Establishment; the other, as an escalation of the struggle nationwide and as an awakening of yet another campus (which heretofore had never experienced a really major riot) to the aims of the youth generation. But the riot and burning had done much more. It had honed to activism hundreds of students to whom, previously, the campus "revolution" had been distant, obscure, and elusive. In a dozen hours' time they had learned to call police "pigs," how to bait National Guardsmen called to put down the fracas, and the dozen other little tricks which the U.S. military (for its purposes) teaches in basic training but which the Movement teaches in the streets.

Or consider an Ivy League incident of May 2, 1969. A Harvard student, employed as a strike-breaking driver for a linen company, was attempting to deliver linen to Harvard dorms. Forty SDSers set upon him, roughed him up, and scattered three hundred bundles of linen in the street—each of which they systematically broke open. A couple of SDSers concluded the job by pouring maple syrup into the truck's gas tank.

One SDS rank-and-filer told police, "The driver was breaking a strike at the linen plant and we were out to stop him."

A Harvard SDS leader saw it differently. "We were firming our alliances nationwide with the mostly black linen workers' unions."

Behind such differing perspective lies the seldom-recounted adventurism of SDS's reach beyond the campus for alliances and allies in its quest for student power and, ultimately, for national power. It is one of the youth revolt's most fascinating—and forlorn—sagas.

From the very outset, SDS's leaders faced the realities inherent in any student movement. The realities were dismal. What made them dismal was the distance and isolation of the campuses from the Establishment's principle power base: corporate industry.

When industrial workers struck and walked off their jobs, industry stopped. When students struck the campus, nothing stopped. Tactically, students simply weren't "where it was at" when you were talking about power in American society. And no matter what individual rebels on campus might be talking about, SDS was talking—in its councils of leadership—about raw, gut power—the kind it takes to remake, shape, and move a society.

SDS's alienated leadership believed that participatory democracy —if implemented in society—would eliminate the alienation they felt. But how was it to be launched into society from the powerless base of the campus?

The problem was basic. Students were a minority in society. And because they had no vital connection with society, or with its places of power, they were helpless to effect any immediate change.

Obviously, the New Left would need a new—or at the least, a broader—base from which to launch its planned attack on American society.

One by one, SDS's leadership considered the possibilities for future alliances with the traditional agents of change, among them the working class. But by 1960, when SDS was founded, the American working class was all but unrecognizable in the revolutionary context of a "working class"—the industrial working class—upon which Marx had relied for revolution.

For one thing, the industrial (craft) class of worker was shrinking numerically. Automation and industry's need of higher-echelon skills (from computer operators to systems designers) had decimated the ranks of the traditional blue-collar worker. Moreover, most American workers no longer considered themselves "workers" or even as belonging to the "working class." They had climbed—and some had leaped—into the middle class. With every step up the economic and social ladder, yet another spark had been snuffed from their revolutionary fervor which in the twenties and thirties had flamed on a dozen industrial battlefronts.

America's middle-class workers weren't buying revolution. They were buying new cars and boats and homes in the suburbs. Heedlessly, they were still in hot pursuit of the American Dream. The campus's alienated, who already had it because their parents had it, knew it to be false. But until the American worker had made the discovery himself, there would be no stopping his overtime striving toward disillusionment. And SDSers weren't about to try.

Far worse, from the viewpoint of SDS's veterans of the southern wars, the American worker—and his union—were racist. It was the middle-class union worker who was roadblocking black equality—in the streets of Chicago and Cicero in 1961, at factory gates in Gary, and in their very unions, many of which virtually barred blacks from apprenticeship training.

SDS wrote off as a prospective ally the American working class. The workers, SDS's top leadership concluded, had sold out. They had sold out to—and had been corrupted by—the Establishment. The Vietnam War would bolster SDS's conclusion. Union leaders were hawkish. War made jobs for their rank and file.

Remaining to the New Left youth were two great potential bases for alliances: the white poor of the slums and the black poor of the ghettos.

Both, in SDS's analysis, seemed ready to reach out to the campus for leadership, just as the campus was ready to reach to them for allies. Moreover, America's poor—black or white—had not yet been corrupted as had the American worker. For the poor and deprived of the urban ghetto had none of the trappings of the American Dream that had bought off the worker.

In 1964 and 1965, SDS launched an ambitious nine-city (Boston, Newark, Trenton, Cleveland, and Louisville, among others) community organizing program. By "organizing," SDS meant "radicalizing"—raising the poor's social awareness to their own innate power. SDS's aim was to show the poor how to "fight City Hall," how to protest for community needs: better street lighting, cleaner streets, more parks and swimming pools. Rent strikes were another issue around which SDSers hoped to organize, to radicalize, and eventually to coalesce the uncorrupted poor into an off-campus bastion of student strength—for a direct attack on the power structure.

Two of SDS's better-known community organizing projects were in the white slums of Cleveland and the black ghetto of Newark. Tom Hayden, SDS's second president and one of the convicted "Chicago 7," headed the Newark project which in a single summer brought 2,500 campus activists into the ghetto.

SDS's aims were outlined by Hayden himself in a critique on the Newark project.

"What does it take to involve the poor in social action about their own lives?" he asked. And answered himself, "They (the poor) must become willing to act on the knowledge of their exploration, instead of remaining paralyzed by what they are supposed to think: 'You can't fight City Hall' . . . They must learn to shift the blame from themselves to the power structure."

But student activists failed miserably in making allies of the poor. The upper-middle-class kids from the campuses found they simply could not communicate with the really poor, nor the poor with them.

"Who are these people," the poor said in Newark, in Cleveland, in Trenton, and elsewhere, "to come in here and tell us how to organize our lives?"

Remorsefully, SDS wrote off the poor as allies.

In another fitful quest for alliances, campus New Leftists borrowed once more from Marx. This time they reached for society's dregs, those Marx had called the "Lumpen proletariat." These— the unemployed, the petty thieves, the prostitutes, the dope pushers —were, by any definition, a classless lot. But SDSers, though they gave it the old college try, got no further with society's "Lumpens" than with its uncorrupted poor.

In desperation—for it still lacked an off-campus power base— SDS devised its concept of the college-trained, honed-to-activism graduate who would penetrate the Establishment as the "new working class." From 1966 through 1968 the "new worker"—and how to organize him as a political force in society—occupied much of SDS's off-campus effort.

But by early 1966, SDS itself was being secretly infiltrated by a virulent new breed of student radical—the fiery followers of Maoist revolutionary Marxism who held almost mystic faith in inevitable revolution through a worker-student alliance. The Maoists placed the worker first in their hyphenated thinking because they saw workers— especially the black worker, not students—as the power base for war on the Establishment.

The worker-student alliance remains today the main power thrust of a schismed SDS. It explains SDS's embrace of the Black Panthers, its firm alliance on campus with the Black Student Union and its championing of the black worker both on campus and off.

Recently, both at Harvard and UCLA, SDSers made headlines for what, to the casual reader, must certainly have seemed a protest wholly unrelated to the campus revolution. In the one case, Harvard

SDSers halted a campus construction project, demanding that the contractor hire more black workers. In the other (more puzzling yet to adult America trying to understand the campus rebellion), twenty-seven UCLA radicals staged a seven-hour sit-in in the office of a campus official, protesting the university's firing of a black food service employee.

Though incomprehensible to the average American, the sit-in was superbly logical in the context of SDS's drive for worker-student alliances. What was more logical than to bulwark those alliances nationwide by a widely publicized alliance with a worker on the students' own campus? It was part and parcel of SDS strategy.

Does all this mean that the campus's youthful rebels are Communists? It does not. Very few of them are and they'd be the first to tell you so. What it does mean—and if you've been reading SDS's factional weekly, *New Left Notes,* you already know—is that most SDS leaders are Marxists. They boldly say so.

But campus discontent is not SDS. The Movement, though SDS has long been its heart and philosophical soul, is bigger than any of its parts. Regardless what direction SDS goes (and it has plainly gone Marxist), the basic alienation of millions of youth, on campus and off, remains. Calling them Communists won't make the rebellion go away or its rebels any less alienated from society. The root cause of the campus revolution is not communism or Marxism. It is America's alienating society.

And so SDS and the New Left have seemingly run full course.

The philosophy that would come to be tagged the "New Left"— the name attached to it by SDS itself in the "Port Huron Statement" —was a ragtag of something old, something new, and much of it borrowed. From the very outset, SDS—like the New Left itself, of which SDS was the philosophical epicenter—was a contradiction unto itself and a bafflement to outsiders.

While early SDSers rejected Marx out of hand, they nevertheless took from Marx the explanation of their own alienation from society.

While calling themselves "young people of the Left," they rebuffed the Marxist–Leninist Old Left (the very term, "New Left," was a rebuke to the Old), and sternly decreed in their constitution that membership was open only to those "who share the commitment of the organization to democracy as a means and as a social goal."

While decrying militarists, they borrowed from Dwight Eisenhower, who coined it, the term "military-industrial complex"; forced Dr. Clark Kerr's resignation from the presidency of the University of California—but retained his analysis of the "multi-university"; championed the poor, the black, and the downtrodden yet remained essentially a membership of upper-middle-class white Americans; shrank from the employment of force by others (especially in Vietnam and Cambodia), but in time would become expert in the use of violence; and though so seemingly disorganized it was often difficult to sort leaders from followers, planned 1968's bloody confrontation at the Chicago Democratic National Convention fully five months in advance and even had Movement doctors on hand to bandage the injured and a committee of lawyers standing by to free the jailed.

Were all this not confusing enough to adult America straining to comprehend its children, and to understand the New Left and SDS—and where they and America might be heading—consider the two greatest contradictions of all:

Neither the New Left as a viable philosophy of political change nor the Students for a Democratic Society, as a viable entity, any longer exist.

The philosophical New Left reached its zenith in 1968—and was abandoned by those who had once called themselves "New Leftists."

SDS itself ceased to exist as a whole after its June, 1969, national convention in Chicago, when the organization split into five widely divergent factions.

What remains is neither "New" nor simply "Left." It is "Old"—meaning "Old Left" Marxist—and almost wholly revolutionary.

I Lived Inside the Campus Revolution

1. Making of a Fink

WHEN the knock came at the door that Monday afternoon, April 5, 1965, I answered it in my stocking feet. I had a Coke in one hand, and in the other the hamburger I'd been making myself for lunch,

I don't know which of us was the more surprised. He, at the sight of me (I weighed nearly 250 pounds then and at 6 feet 4 inches looked like what I'd been through most of high school—a varsity lineman). Or me, at the sight of him, standing trim and impeccable in a single-breasted charcoal-gray suit with an attaché case snugged under one arm.

My first thought was that he had the wrong address. Or, more likely, the wrong part of town. He seemed strangely out of place in that Temple City, California, factory workers' neighborhood where my brother, Robert, two years my junior, and I shared a students' apartment.

At that moment—as usual, to be perfectly honest—the place was a shambles. Two days' dirty dishes stood in the sink. Half empty Dixie cups and last night's take-out pizza cartons littered the floor. Somewhere beneath a mountain of books and papers (I was cramming for an exam at Pasadena City College, where I was a sophomore) were a couch and a couple of chairs, if you could find them. We didn't often try. The floor and the beds were our natural abodes. And bills were our natural enemies. A stack of them—most stamped "overdue" —were stashed beneath a table lamp which for the moment served as a paperweight.

Prospects for an insurance salesman—what I immediately took him to be—we definitely weren't, and I was about to tell him so when,

1

as if reading my mind, he thumbed open a little leather wallet, flashed his identification, and introduced himself.

"Hello, my name's Wayne Shaw," he said. "I'm with the FBI. I'd like to talk with you, if I may."

"Ohhh," I gasped, inviting him in, and hoping my panic wasn't showing.

As he stepped into the place, I just came apart inside. My mind scurried away in a dozen directions. Frantically, I tried to recall what, over the past couple of months, I might have done to get myself into a jam like this. There was that book club thing. I had joined a book club, signed up for a first book and though half a dozen more had come along, I had never bothered paying for them. "Mail fraud," my mind hammered. Or maybe it had been something else . . . a bounced check, something like that. Offhand, I couldn't recall any recent ones I'd written that had.

More likely, I concluded, it had to do with marijuana. I suppose —if he had a nose for grass—he could smell some in the apartment even then, left over from a couple of nights before. My brother and some of his friends were high for joints. I didn't much dig pot myself, though I'd smoked my share.

For a long moment he stood there in the center of the room, a pizza carton at his feet, looking around, taking everything in but not saying a word. He turned then, sensing my shock, and said quickly, "This doesn't concern you directly, at all, Mr. Divale. It hasn't anything to do with anything you're supposed to have done . . . nothing like that."

Inside, my heart dropped down a couple of gears from the two hundred it was doing to maybe just 150 beats a minute, still high, but not threatening to burst right out of my chest.

"Tell me," he said, "do you know of . . . or have you any relatives or friends who are members of the Communist party?"

The thing struck straight out of the blue. I mean, had he asked about girls—I'd been pretty much on my own since I'd been fifteen and by now, at twenty-three, I'd had more than a passing acquaintanceship with the dolls, in assorted sizes and shapes—maybe I'd have had to think twice before answering. But when it came to politics, I'd scarcely

2

passed puberty. Really shocked, I blinked ("this guy," I told myself, "has just got to be joking") and told him truthfully: "No, I don't know any Communists . . . not friends, relatives—nobody."

Saying it, I had a flash of my grandfather, my mother's father, an Italian immigrant. Grandfather Viola, who, now well into his eighties and still living in the four-unit Bronx apartment that his small produce store—"Viola's Produce"—had bought and paid for over the years, was one of those emotional patriots.

When the television signed off at midnight with the National Anthem, my grandfather would rise from his chair and come to attention. He'd stand there quietly, facing the tube those three to four minutes, keeping his own counsel. He didn't demand that anyone else join him. With Grandfather Viola it was a personal thing. His father and his father's father, back as far as anyone could remember, had been farmers near Naples under the *mezzadria* system: the whole family farmed for a landowner and when the crop was in, they split. If the landowner liked you, the split might be 50-50. If he didn't, it was often a lot less.

In my grandfather's part of Italy—the southern half of the "boot" around Naples—things really hadn't changed since the Middle Ages. Where, in much of the rest of Italy, the landowner was apt to be just a rich man, perhaps one of the rising new generation of industrialists, the land my grandfather—and generations of Violas—had farmed still belonged to a baroness whose titled family had held it for centuries.

Grandfather was in his early thirties when, just before World War I, he'd first come to America. He came alone, leaving his wife— my Grandmother Pasqualina—behind until he earned money enough for her passage. When war broke out, grandfather was drafted into the Italian army. He returned to Italy to do his duty. My mother— Josephine, his oldest child—was born in Italy in 1918.

After the armistice, he returned to America, this time bringing his wife and their firstborn—my mother, then a child of three. Five other children—four daughters and a son—were born here. Often my grandfather told me, "In Italy, I would yet be a peasant. Here, I am a landowner." He meant the 2 by 4 Bronx lots on which his two modest apartment buildings stood.

3

Grandfather was the first Viola ever to own the land he lived on. I was the first to attend college. So far, I'm the only one of his eighteen grandchildren to have earned a college degree. Long before I decided to get my Ph.D. and make anthropology and teaching a career, Grandfather called me "the professor." Even when I was a lowly freshman, I was Grandfather's "professor." I still am. He always considered education a made-in-America wonder, even though he could not afford it for himself or for his own children—my mother and her four sisters and brother.

Perhaps that was why he so often stood silently before the TV. When the last glimpse of the flag and the final strains of the National Anthem faded from the screen, he'd flick off the set and say to my grandmother, in Italian, "Pasqualina, it is time now for bed." For my Grandfather Viola, that every-midnight vigil of patriotism was a kind of nightcap.

"Mr. Divale," agent Shaw was saying, "I think you should know why I'm here. Your name has been mentioned in Communist party circles as a possible candidate for recruitment."

I was dumbstruck. "I don't understand," I told him. "Somebody is thinking of asking *me* to join . . . the Communist party?"

"Something like that," Shaw nodded, "although 'asking' probably isn't what they have in mind for the present, at least. Your name simply came up as a possible recruit. Frankly, I don't know all the specifics. But that's the word we've gotten . . . through Party channels."

I told him straight off he must mean somebody else. The FBI, I wanted to say (but didn't), must have gotten its wires crossed. Still, with my senses better in mind, I questioned him sharply. How, I demanded to know, had my name come up, and where? How had the FBI come by its information? He repeated that he really didn't know.

"I think you're aware," Shaw said, a glimpse of a smile on his face, "that we have a rather complex organization. Often one of our sources learns something and it's passed on to whatever office it concerns. That's the first we hear of it."

Afterwards, I came to realize that Shaw, who was agent-in-charge of the Pasadena suboffice, attached to the Federal Bureau

4

of Investigation's big four-hundred-agent office in Los Angeles, was probably telling the truth.

Somebody at a Party "Youth Club" meeting (in the pre-McCarthy days they'd been called "cells") had probably mentioned my name.

Likely, it had been raised only in passing. Perhaps the club's chairman—a student from one of the Los Angeles area campuses—had merely noted that the club was ripe for recruits. One member might have spoken up.

"Bill Divale, out on the Pasadena City College campus, talks a good liberal line. He might be somebody we could interest."

If an undercover informant were present (which would hardly be unusual), a report of the club meeting—who was there, what was said and by whom—would have duly gone to the FBI's Los Angeles regional office. The agent concerned with Party youth would routinely have plucked my name out of the report and, without further explanation, notated it for transmission to the office covering the area where I lived, or, perhaps, where I attended school. Both, in this case, were covered by the Pasadena suboffice. Shaw himself would have no idea how the Bureau came by its information. On his dispatch teletype, the thing might appear only as a random few sentences:

"William Tulio Divale, 23, student, Pasadena City College; home, Temple City, Calif., mentioned 3/10/65 as possible recruit, CP/USA."

CP/USA was, of course, scriptise for the Communist party of the United States of America. In time, Shaw or one among his three-agent staff would run a routine check. The thing might stop there. Or it might lead to something more. In my case, Wayne Shaw had something more in mind.

"We were wondering," he said, "if you'd be willing to work for us . . . join the Communist party, perhaps, and report to us on Party and related activities?"

I guess my eyes flew open in astonishment because Shaw smiled. I mean, this was TV stuff, straight out of one of those corny scripts—you know, this nattily dressed perfect stranger raps at your door and straight off he asks you to be the "who" in a whodunit.

5

The proposal, so seemingly abrupt, wasn't as casually made as it appeared to me then. Shaw had checked me out thoroughly.

"Of course," Shaw said as he turned to go, "we wouldn't expect you to do this for nothing. We'd be willing to pay you."

I hadn't dreamed he was making a business proposition, or that his suggestion that I might "work" for the Bureau was quite literally that—as a paid undercover informant.

"Think it over," he said at the door, handing me his card. "I'll get back in touch in a day or so. And, of course, whatever your decision, our conversation here was strictly between the two of us—confidential, you understand?"

The whole thing hadn't taken fifteen minutes.

When he'd gone, I shut the door tight and sank to the floor. I sat there cross-legged, surrounded by those spent Dixie cups, pizza boxes, and books, trying to piece things together.

The only FBI agents I'd ever seen—other than on TV or in motion pictures—had been investigating a bank robbery a few blocks from where I had previously lived. I hadn't spoken with them, just stood watching, along with the other neighbors, as they came and went from the bank. Now the FBI had come to my house, had sat in my living room—and had suggested I work as an undercover agent.

What troubled me most was how I'd ever come to the FBI's attention, much less that of the Communist party.

I recalled one incident in my cultural geography class earlier that semester. We'd seen a film on Red China made by an English newsman. It was a cultural thing, showing life in Communist China. During the discussion that followed somebody commented that what the film hadn't shown was Communist China as it really was: just one big slave camp.

"That's nonsense," I spoke up. "If you're going to study the communist countries seriously, I think you've got to start from the presupposition that their governments are trying to do the best they can for their people . . . in terms of how they see themselves and the world. After all, they're human, too!"

From the back of the class somebody snickered, "He must be a Communist." He said it loud enough for everybody to hear. Perhaps, I reasoned, somebody had called the FBI.

"Say," he might have told Shaw or one of his agents, "there's a goddamned Commie in my class out at PCC."

Shaw would have made a routine check, figuring that here, perhaps, was somebody they'd slipped up on. There weren't many, I was to learn—either at the nearby California Institute of Technology, the "MIT of the West"; Jet Propulsion Laboratory, the huge space complex; or at Pasadena's myriad defense electronic-optical complexes—that the Bureau hadn't checked out. They'd found me clean. In checking, the Bureau had apparently decided I had the qualifications they were looking for and that, just possibly, I'd be interested in doing an undercover job for them.

Looking back, I suppose one way or another I was more conspicuous on the Pasadena City College campus than I might have wished—or had suspected. My politics weren't to blame. I had none. It was simply that the politics I *didn't* have weren't, for most PCCers, the right ones *not* to have. While I wasn't actively against the campus's patron saints—almost all of whom were frocked in the conservatism of the GOP—neither was I either their vocal or silent worshipper. That, in itself—at PCC—was political heresy.

The truth was that anybody much to the left of Goldwater-right showed up pretty conspicuously on the campus of Pasadena City College (a two-year junior facility). The majority of its eighteen thousand students came from rock-ribbed "Republicans-ville," as some of us called Pasadena and its entrenched environs: San Marino, Altadena, La Crescenta, Arcadia, and La Canada.

The John Birch Society maintained its West Coast offices in San Marino. Daily, from studios in Pasadena's arch-right Ambassador College, Garner Ted Armstrong—the voice of evangelical Americanism—beamed his conservatism to a worldwide audience via a net of more than three hundred radio and TV stations.

Henry Edwards Huntington, nephew of the founder of the Southern Pacific (Railroad) System and a rail-and-utility magnate in his own right, had in earlier years held virtual suzerainty over the town by virtue of one of the most adroit mergers of the twentieth century. He merged the family's fortunes by merging, in marriage, with his uncle's widow. When Pasadena's yacht-and-mansion crowd put up their palatial places for sale, it was more likely to be in the

7

Wall Street Journal than in Norman Chandler's *Los Angeles Times,* although the Chandlers were among the Pasadena area's first families —and top-rung on its vaunted society list.

Getting a phone number from some of PCC's campus cuties was tougher than cracking the Soviet war code. Invariably, their home numbers were unlisted. Half of those kids' grandmothers were the little-old-lady-in-tennis-shoes types, just as they and their mothers, in time, would be. Most of PCC's rich-bitch coeds weren't there to matriculate in the social sciences or in the humanities. They could have done that at Stanford, Bryn Mawr, or Vassar—where, after completing a year or so at PCC, they usually went anyway.

They were at PCC to matriculate in the college's two most popular noncredit courses: *Rose Queen I* and its corollary, *Rose Princess II*. Neither required a girl to crack so much as a book, though there were endless hours of homework—all of them spent before a boudoir mirror, primping. There was only one final exam—the annual contest for the selection of the Pasadena Tournament of Roses New Year's Day Rose Queen and her court of six princesses. Only Pasadena City College girls, at the time, were eligible to compete.

In Pasadena, the Rose Parade and Rose Bowl football classic were the events of the year; and the Coronation Ball, held between Christmas and New Year's in Pasadena's ornate Civic Auditorium, was a kind of mass debut. It was Hollywood, Palm Beach, Newport, and Bucks County rolled into one, and steeped in the tradition of conservatism to which Pasadenans clung, almost desperately now, as a relic out of their past.

Almost as conservative were PCC's coeds—in every fiber of their bodies. And everywhere but in bed. Once under covers, however, PCC's blonde, blue-eyed WASPs (White, Anglo-Saxon Protestants, and mostly high-church Episcopalians) were hot-handed revolutionaries. Maybe they hadn't read Karl Marx, but they'd read (and re-read) Albert Ellis. Long before most other campuses were talking about the "sexual revolution," PCC's coeds were making it. And making out like there'd be no tomorrow. Given even half a chance, they were willing and eager to overthrow the whole moral code—without so much as a blink of a mascaraed eye. Back in the early sixties, that was plenty radical, considering that "the Pill" hadn't yet wholly supplanted the toothbrush on nearly every coed's "first-thing-to-do-upon-rising" list.

A psychiatrist, I suppose, wouldn't have selected PCC as the most comfortable campus for a first-generation Italian-American. And especially one, as myself, who traced lineage to a grandfather who'd peddled vegetables from a pushcart in the Bronx; a father who worked as a restaurant chef in Manhattan (and still does); or to a mother who, wrung out after a day of seamstressing in New York City's grimy garment district, had, once she divorced my father in 1952, given up trying to play both mother and father. She'd done the best she could and all she could afford—shipped my brother and me off to two years of Catholic boarding school in Andover, Massachusetts. I'd just turned thirteen. My brother was eleven.

In one sense, that was the end of my home life. My next real home (after boarding school I'd joined my mother and her new husband in California, but fell out with my stepfather and moved back to New York) was a Bronx loft-apartment all my own. I was fifteen then. For nearly six months I bached it, doing damned well what I pleased.

In contrast to my two years at Catholic boarding school, where six days a week we'd risen at 6:30 A.M. only to get down on our knees for half an hour of prayers before breakfast, now I got up at 2 A.M. to be a milkman's helper. We'd start out about 2:30 in his route truck. He'd deliver milk on one side of the street; I'd take the other. By 5 A.M., I'd be back in bed—and up again by 8 or so to get off to Evander Childs High School in the Bronx, where I was a sophomore.

I played tackle at Evander Childs, but we had a lousy team. Even so, the team was better than its coach. Bad as both were, I managed—even as a lineman—to get a small write-up in the *New York Post*. One of its sports writers said I was a player to watch. He went on to say that "when Divale tackles them, they take a long time getting up."

My first experience with the "grade game"—and its demoralizing corruption—was at Evander Childs High. In an English literature class I neglected turning in a term paper and was headed for an in-

9

evitable—and deserved—"D" in the course. By the rules, anything less than "C" made me ineligible for football.

In the "grade game," rules like that are made to be broken if you play on the varsity. And it doesn't much matter whether you're first-string tackle, as I was, or first-string tiddly-wink. To my coach it was more important that I make my "C" (for "Childs") than play by the academic rules. He had a little chat with my teacher. She erased the "D," upping it to an acceptable "C" with the understanding that every week during football season I'd hand in a one-page written report.

Considering that it was a class in English literature, you might have expected my penalty reports to be on Chaucer, Keats, or the English bards. However, I was assigned to report weekly on one of the more obscure literary lights of seventeenth-century English literature—a fellow by the name of Prep Football. I was supposed to report weekly on the previous week's game. I made just one report and never bothered to turn in another. Not another word was ever said.

My milk-helper's job brought in about $30 a week. With the additional $75 to $100 a month I was receiving from home, I got along nicely. The apartment I rented on the fourth floor of a turn-of-the-century mansion on the upper Bronx's Boston Post Road cost me just $12.50 a week. The landlady thought I was eighteen or nineteen. If she hadn't, I doubt she'd have sent her teen-aged daughter and a flock of pretty nieces and cousins up to tidy my room. My pillows must have been the most fluffed-over in the Bronx.

Tough as that neighborhood was, I got along all right. Even then I was just too big—I stood 6 feet 2 inches and weighed two hundred pounds—to fool around with. Nobody bothered me except the girls. And most of them, like the majority of my friends, were eighteen or nineteen. As a kid, I'd grown up big and fast. I'd been twice around the block before most kids my age had even ventured off their own front stoops.

Looking back—at my age the look isn't all that distant—my childhood comes to mind in a flash of vignettes, warmer than most and happier than many, despite my parents' divorce and my own, from them, in my teens. The thing was, I grew up in one of those big, warm, and emotional Italian families—a family straddling two cultures—where, when we all got together, there seemed always enough of everything (though never more than enough) to go around, whether it was love or lasagna.

A TV director casting about for an emotional Italian chef—and a good one—to portray himself would pick my father every time.

Born on the island of Sardinia, he'd worked a ship's galley for passage to New York. He brought with him a great chefing talent and an even greater suspicion that every restaurant for which he worked (and even the cooks in those he sometimes owned) was secretly conniving to steal his prized recipes. With my father, the thing bordered on paranoia. Every six months or so he'd quit, but not before telling the boss where to stick his ravioli. Still, he was never wanting for work.

Once, when I was about twelve, he returned home triumphant after a kitchen tizzy which, to my father's great satisfaction, had cost him his job. At the time, I recall, he was working as a sauce chef at New York's famous Latin Quarter. One of the bosses had casually inquired about a recipe he was preparing. Instantly, my father suspected the worst. For a whole week, whenever he was batching that particular recipe, he'd shoo everybody out of the kitchen—cooks, subcooks, even the busboys. The blowup, when it came, must have been magnificent—and in the best kitchen tradition. My father couldn't have been happier.

"It was time to quit, anyway," he said with a look of inner serenity.

I haven't seen my father in twelve years. It has been nearly that long since we've written.

Our falling out of touch, while hardly typical, contains in it some of the realities of the alienation of the family—through divorce, separation, and migration—which have led many of America's young to reexamine the social order in which they find themselves. For in the breakup and dispersal of family life lie some of the seeds of the young's own alienation—from society, from their parents, from the day-to-day world around them.

As for my mother, she is a trim and intelligent woman and, even today, very pretty. Since she was the family's oldest, and learned

English first (today, hearing her speak, you'd never know she was born in Italy), she was the one who tended, in her teens, to the family things that had to be done.

Mother was the family's pioneer. She divorced—which was all but unheard of in old world cultures. She broke from the constrictions of the Bronx (where most of her sisters and their families still live) and came west. She made a new life for herself and a very good life at that. It could have been mine, as well, had I chosen to share it. That I did not was not my mother's fault.

To me, mother represents one view of the "new woman's" reach to stand on equal terms with their men—as equal as each woman may choose or wish to be. That is their choice. The important thing is that society gives them the right to make the choice, as a generation ago it did not, and does not fully today.

The boarding school I attended was located in what had once been the administration building of one of Andover's largest textile mills, which, like a lot of others around the town, had closed down. Their owners had moved south for cheaper labor.

About half of the school's Catholic brothers were from New England. Most of the rest came from eastern Canada. When the brothers spoke among themselves, it was usually in French.

There never was a minute's "free time"—not a moment of it the whole day to think or talk or even to plain do nothing. "The idle mind is the Devil's workshop," the brothers were fond of saying. And they weren't about to give the Devil his due. From the crack of dawn, when we got up to pray, until 10 P.M. when we went to bed, it was all a kind of regimented togetherness. We played together, studied together, prayed together, ate together, and went to school together. Psychologically, it was straight out of the Middle Ages.

At recreation time you *had* to play. And if you weren't playing, you at least had to walk. You couldn't, ever, just sit and talk. It was the same thing on the school's outdoor ice skating rink where the town kids—including its girls—skated, too. Every time you stopped skating, maybe to talk with a girl, or just because you were tired, a brother would skate past.

"Keep skating," he'd say, "keep skating."

It was like that every waking moment of the day—keep studying,

12

keep eating, keep playing, keep praying. I never had much religion when I went in—and none at all when I came out.

Not many of today's youth have sampled, firsthand, so parochial a regimen. Nonetheless, they are questioning the dogma of organized religion as seldom before. It is not that they no longer believe in God. It is the Establishment's God—the Lord of the social status quo (which Jesus himself, in His time, went to the cross to defy)—which youth is questioning. And especially, black youths. A hundred years of prayerful obedience did not appreciably change their status in society. Ten years of marches, sit-ins, and defiance did.

The symbol of status in my family was "a job." Any job. A man was expected to work. When my grandparents and cousins got together, and fell to talking about some member of the family—perhaps a grandson—they talked and thought in working-class terms. Either it was "he's working" or "he's not working." I can never remember them describing what he was working at as a "good job" or saying, "he's making a lot of money." Those things—the "how much" and "what at"—weren't important. The prime consideration was the fact that you worked and were working. It was part of the peasant psychology that my grandparents had brought with them in the 1920s, and which others had brought a hundred years sooner.

Oddly, it was this very "work psychosis" which, in creating today's affluent society, created the conditions that spawned the New Left. For the New Left's is a perspective as viewed from the economic top—by those who by themselves or by inheritance have reached it. And having experienced it, they have largely rejected it.

The "other world" of the underworld was ever-present in our neighborhood. It was as though, looking under a bed or suddenly opening a closet door, you'd find the Mafia.

I remember there was a florist shop not far from my grandfather's store. The man who seemed to own the place, but never seemed to busy himself with the flowers, was—my mother indicated on several occasions—something more than merely a florist.

One day—I couldn't have been more than five or six—my mother and I were passing the place when the man came out and spoke with my mother.

"I hear somebody took your baby carriage," he said, referring

13

to my brother's expensive perambulator which mother had left in the foyer of our apartment building. Somebody had stolen it.

"That's a shame about your carriage," the man repeated, rather ominously I thought. He told mother he had some "friends" who were "looking into the matter." But we never got it back.

While hardly an example of Mafia efficiency, it's an incident on which I've reflected since. And especially after my own view of the amazing and sometimes brutal efficiency of the FBI. How is it that the Bureau, once turned loose, can infiltrate whatever it really sets sights on infiltrating, yet has missed the biggest target of all: *organized crime*. Recently, as though speaking for the New Left itself, *Time* magazine explained why.

"Without a fix . . . its ability to corrupt civil officials," said the national news weekly, "Cosa Nostra would not last out the year."

Yet, though born in the Bronx (on February 18, 1942), and having grown up knowing some of life's harshnesses, I didn't feel out of place at Pasadena City College. I rather liked PCC. And eventually I found my niche. As it turned out, it was to be with the campus's few activists who, even then at the onset of the campus rebellion, lived by the words of C. Wright Mills and Sartre, while the campus's majority, I suppose, turned more to Buckley, Kirkpatrick, and Goldwater.

I joined a fraternity, was briefly its president and, in time, treasurer of the Inter-fraternity Council. I first joined the frat in the fall of 1960 when, after graduating from Temple City, California, high school (I'd moved back to California and was living with my mother and stepfather again), I took a first fling at college. But I wasn't ready to settle down to studying, either at Pasadena or anywhere else. I dropped out before I flunked out—about six weeks after the semester started. About the same time, I flunked out at home.

I can't blame my stepfather. He tried hard, in his way, to be a father to my brother and me. But I couldn't abide by his rules, or the household chores he expected of me. For the sake of harmony in the house, my mother and brother did as they were told. I wouldn't and didn't.

Laziness had nothing to do with it. When it came to earning my way, I'd always been a hustler. Even as a freshman in high school I had a business of my own and earned as much as $200, sometimes

14

$300 a month. Some heads of families then—in 1957—didn't earn a whole lot more.

I'd started my egg route by going door-to-door in our Temple City neighborhood. At first I got orders, I suppose, because I was a kid. But after a first dozen, people kept coming back for more. Every Saturday morning, early, I'd pedal my bike the twenty miles out to an egg ranch near Baldwin Park, and handpick those eggs practically from under the hens. Prices varied from week to week, but usually I bought them for 33 cents a dozen and sold them for 50 to 60 cents. Within a year I was delivering two hundred dozen a week, and sometimes more. Considering the time involved, I earned as much as $10 an hour. Later on I did almost as well—$50 a week, anyway—selling shoes at a Kinney's shoe store.

It was about that time that my stepfather drew up that list of chores he expected me to be doing around the house. I bought my independence with a simple proposition: I'd pay board and room—we started at $15 a week and worked up to $25 or so—and I'd be just a boarder. Within reason, I'd come and go as I pleased. Our falling out came over a difference in interpreting the "within reason" clause of our verbal agreement. He ruled that midnight would be my curfew hour.

My flunk-out at home came one Sunday morning about the time I dropped out of PCC. The frat had some doings or other, and I stayed out until 3 A.M. I was sleeping when my stepfather, up early and on his way to the golf course, leaned over my bed. I remember looking up, still half asleep, and seeing him there, a golf bag over his shoulder and a putter in one hand. I don't recall him reprimanding me for the late hour I'd gotten in. Our relationship by then had disintegrated beyond mere reproach. What he said ran to precisely one sentence.

"Well, I expect you'll be gone by the time I return."

"Okay," I replied, and went back to sleep. I plain didn't give a damn. About noon I got up, took what few things I had, said goodbye to my mother (she was crying), and moved out. I was eighteen and never moved back.

For more than a year I simply dropped out. During much of that time I lived at the frat, earning the $25 a month it cost to stay there at odd jobs, but really doing nothing very much at all.

15

Once, discussing that drop-out year with one of my FBI handlers, I said I'd been a "kind of early hippie." He was amused. I mean, at a hippie whose "pad" was a fraternity house.

PCC at the time—as most campuses—was all but oblivious to the "student movement" which, then in 1961, hadn't yet come north.

Student concern for the big issues, which in time would split the nation, radicalize the campus, and turn the student movement revolutionary—the war in Vietnam, the industrial-defense complex's growing control of the campuses through research funding, the moral fraud of a society that granted nearly a quarter of the nation (its black, its poor, its aged, and its de-privileged) their "freedom" to be poor, to be discriminated against, and to be miserable, and the crass materialism which even then was tarnishing the American Dream—all these were but rivulets of the ground swell, and eventually the tidal wave to come.

There, at the onset of the sixties, the campus's bright, con-cerned, but alienated youths had, really, only three ways to go.

They could abandon the society to which they'd been born for another of their own choosing and making—the subculture of beat-dom, whose enclaves were the slums of the cities.

They could forswear an America they despaired ever of changing to become migrants and missionaries of change— as Peace Corpsmen in lands crying for change.

They could stay and fight—heading south to do battle on America's own but alien soil.

The first required only abject resignation to life; the second, a pioneer's zeal; the third, guts beyond guts.

For civil rights was the single big issue. And the battle was being waged mainly in the South. South they went—kids who'd been too young for Korea and mere toddlers during World War II, kids who had never tasted battle, discrimination, or poverty (most were white and from upper-middle-class homes)—to lead, plead, and be bloodied.

A handful of them were with the Reverend Dr. Martin Luther King, Jr., on that day in December, 1956, when the 381-day Montgomery bus boycott vindicated King's nonviolent pledge of "We Shall Overcome"—and Jim Crow no longer rode the buses in the city of the Confederacy's birth.

16

Scarcely a month later, on January 10, 1957, they rode south again—this time on desegregated trains and interstate buses (no boycott, simply an edict by the powerful Interstate Commerce Commission had done it, but Montgomery's bus boycott had forced the ICC's hesitant hand). South again they rode in 1961 but this time to be met by violence—as CORE (Congress of Racial Equality) "freedom riders" to challenge segregation in interstate travel facilities.

They joined the first lunch counter sit-ins of 1960, were shock troops and brigadiers for SNCC (Student Nonviolent Coordinating Committee) in its massive voter registration drives, and felt the bigot's wrath (and the bite of his police dogs and fire hoses) in the showdown summer of 1963. They put their lives once again on the line during "Mississippi Freedom Summer," 1964—and marched the "long march," Selma-to-Montgomery, in March, 1965.

The way was marked by milestones (the first of them, the Supreme Court's 1954 *Brown* vs. *The Board of Education* school desegregation decision) and by gravestones—for Medgar Evers, the NAACP's slain Mississippi staffer; for student civil rights workers Jim Chaney, Mike Schwerner, and Andy Goodman (the latter two New Yorkers); for Mrs. Viola Liuzzo, shotgunned to death during the Selma-to-Montgomery march; and for many more who never made the headlines and sometimes not even a southern morgue.

Almost all of the Movement's future leaders were hardened to activism in the southern wars. Later, of the Movement's violent trend, one of them would say, "We didn't invent violence. We found it ready-made—in the South." Tom Hayden, of the University of Michigan, and Paul Potter, from Oberlin, both SDS founders, were veterans of the southern wars. So was Mario Savio, leader of Berkeley's Free Speech Movement. So was much of the Movement's future hard core leadership.

I'd sat out the southern wars as a full-time mechanical draftsman. Even had I not been working, I wouldn't have been down south doing battle. I scarcely knew there was a war going on. Politics wasn't my bag.

I got my first drafting job early in 1962 without much trying. In high school I'd always been good at drafting. For a job application, I whipped up a few samples of my work in less than a day's time. I showed them around and one of the places I tried—a truck body manufacturer—hired me. I stayed there twenty months, was the only full-time draftsman the plant had, and quit only to reenter Pasadena City College in the fall of 1963. All through PCC I worked part-time —drafting—for another company, a trailer manufacturer. Working, I took three years to get through PCC's usual two. But my grades were up near the top of the class. I'd become a serious, dedicated student. Mostly, it had been hard work and hard study—until Wayne Shaw had come knocking at my door.

During the next few weeks we met a number of times just to talk things out. After that first visit to the house, we arranged to meet somewhere else and just drive around. Wayne didn't want to risk coming a second time, perhaps running into my brother or some of his friends, and my having to explain who he was.

I hadn't yet committed myself to working under cover for the FBI nor had Wayne definitely committed the Bureau. First, we had a lot of sorting out to do—where I stood on politics (I told him I was a civil libertarian, which was as close as I could gauge what little politics I had); and where my thinking lay on government, democracy, economics, and labor (I said I supported trade unionism and even admitted, though I hadn't belonged to a union at the time, that I'd been involved in a minor labor dispute).

"Yes," he nodded, "I know." Wayne had obviously checked me out at the company where I'd first worked. They'd told him about my complaining to an inspector from the Department of Labor's Wage, Hour and Public Contracts Division, when he'd visited the plant, about management's miserly ways. The company, though engaged in government work, and thus ruled by federal labor requirements, simply didn't believe in paying overtime—to anybody. Clearly the law, as well as wage earner rights, was being violated. But nobody there— my fellow employees were all breadwinners with families to feed—had the guts to speak up when the Department of Labor took the trouble to send an inspector out to see how things were going.

"They're going lousy here for the average worker," I told him, speaking for every last man on the payroll.

Eventually, my complaint cost the company $10,000 in back

wages. Some of the shop men got back paychecks of $750 to $800. Management, after that, wasn't too fond of me. Legally, however, I couldn't be fired. But they were dead wrong on one point: I had not, as they believed, called that federal inspector in. I'd merely told him the facts once he'd got there.

During our drive-around conversations, Wayne briefed me on what I might expect should I work under cover for the Bureau.

Eventually, I'd have to sign a security clearance and an oath swearing not to divulge anything I might observe or report to anyone but the FBI, or government agencies the Bureau might approve. If I violated my oath, I'd be liable for prosecution and a maximum fine of $2,500. I was to be a "subcontractor," not an official FBI employee. Hire me and put my name on the payroll and I'd be an employee of public record. Subcontractors to the Bureau plain didn't exist on FBI records.

No paper bearing my real name—except some locked away in my code-named FBI file—would ever pass across even an agent's desk, except those few in direct, daily contact with me. No check would ever be issued to me. I would be paid in cash by my handler. As a non-listed, nonpayrolled, paid-in-cash, code-named nonstaff FBI subcontractor, I wouldn't exist—on the record, anyway.

Out of the anonymity of "William Divale" would rise the even more anonymous "Wayne Dixon."

My code name was Shaw's idea. He suggested it because its initials—"WD"—were the same as for my real name. So I'd always be initialing things (pay receipts, transcripts of my reports, photographs) with what, after all, were my true initials. Even if I forgot and used the "wrong" initials, I'd be using the "right" ones. I couldn't go wrong. Later, for a lot of reasons, the most apparent being that same-as-name initials can be too easily traced to an informant, the Bureau forbade any similarity between an informant's real and code names.

How I'd make my reports, should we agree to work together, was left up to me.

"Think of yourself as a light bulb in the ceiling," Wayne suggested. "You illuminate the whole room so you see the whole roomful of people . . . *yourself* included. You include them all in your report."

A few days later we drifted into an understanding. I would begin working under cover for the FBI. There was no handshake, nothing to sign just then, nothing dramatic.

"I've decided to be your light bulb in the ceiling," I told Wayne at the conclusion of one of our conversations.

"Fine," he said, "we were hoping you'd take a shine to the idea."

For the next five years I was to be one of the brightest lights in the student underground.

2. Commitment to Communism

MY first FBI assignment—to infiltrate the student W.E.B. DuBois clubs, just then gaining a campus foothold—came toward the third week in April, and scarcely two weeks after Wayne Shaw had knocked unannounced and uninvited at my door. That afternoon Shaw met me on the Pasadena City College campus. It was to be the first time and last we ever met openly and the only time on campus. We'd agreed to meet, following one of my classes, by a bench beside PCC's Mirror Pool whose water reflects a picture-perfect image of the college's administration building. Wayne was there when I arrived.

"Let's just sit here," he suggested, "and turn our backs on the campus."

He offered me a lozenge (Shaw was a Mormon and didn't smoke), and got directly to business.

"You've heard of the DuBois clubs?" he asked. I nodded and said I had. Insofar as I knew, there were two DuBois clubs in the Los Angeles area. One was newly activated at UCLA. Another operated on the California State College campus in east Los Angeles. Then less than a year old, the W.E.B. DuBois clubs had been organized in June, 1964.

"*Four* DB clubs are now going in the LA area," Wayne corrected, "the two college affiliates you mentioned and a couple of all-campus catchalls—one out in the Venice beach area and another in central Los Angeles. Our information links all of them directly to the Communist party, USA, though, of course, they deny it."

He paused. "I want you to get involved with the DuBois clubs," he said, handing me my first assignment, and explained why. "It's through its DuBois clubs that the Party does much of its student recruiting. That's what we want you to point for—membership in the Communist party."

As it happened, a demonstration—in support of Dr. Martin Luther King, Jr.'s, historic Selma-to-Montgomery march of the month before—was going on that very afternoon outside the U.S. Federal Courthouse in downtown Los Angeles.

"Might be a good idea to get down there right away," Wayne suggested. "See what's going on . . . meet any DuBoisers you can. Several are there, passing out leaflets, I'm told. Perhaps you can strike up an invitation to join one of the DuBois groups."

That's how it started—cold turkey, you might say, with a cold canvass.

Yet within two months I was to become the activist second-in-leadership of the aggressive Central Los Angeles W.E.B. DuBois club and, by October, its chairman; a trusted delegate on the eight-member DuBois Southern California Area Council; and a member of the Communist party, USA. That, and the Movement's most sympathetic spy.

But that afternoon, at the Selma march demonstration, my progress was hardly propitious. By the time—around 5 P.M.—I got to the Federal Courthouse, most of the demonstrators had left. If there were any DuBois clubbers around, I didn't see them.

That evening, however, I followed to the letter two other of Wayne's suggestions: I mailed a subscription to the Party's West Coast newspaper, *People's World*. I got off another letter to the DuBois clubs (Wayne had given me their post office box number), saying I was a student at PCC, was interested not only in joining but in starting a chapter on my own campus, and would they please send me some literature. Two months later, when I was second-in-command of the central LA club, then the most active in the whole Los Angeles area, and went to our postal box to get the mail, there was my letter—unopened. Nobody in the interim had bothered to pick up the mail.

That tells you how disorganized DuBois was in its first year of life. My quick ascendancy to leadership provides yet another insight: the fact that in the loosely organized structure of the student movement, the active and the activist rise quickly—sometimes meteorically —to the top.

Those final few days in April, 1965, were hectic—but no less so than the next four and a half years would be. "Get involved . . . go active," Wayne Shaw had encouraged.

During the next few weeks, despite approaching final exams and the part-time drafting job I was still holding down, I made it a point to attend a meeting or lecture almost every night. They weren't hard to find. A raft of "special event" notices crowded nearly every issue of *People's World:* lectures, get-togethers, somebody showing films or discussing an issue. Mostly, it was merely a matter of showing up— and, in my case, getting acquainted.

One of the first functions I attended, on a Sunday late in April, was a dinner-lecture. A "backyard dinner," it had been billed in *People's World.* The backyard—as modest as the home to which it was appended in a black area of east Los Angeles—belonged to Bill Taylor, a Party functionary. Taylor and his wife had just returned from the Soviet Union. With dinner over, Taylor gave an informal lecture on the trip, contrasting his impressions of the USSR in 1965 with the first time he'd been there, back in the thirties.

I was less interested in what Taylor said (although I dutifully reported his rambling travelogue to my handler) than in the thirty or so people who'd come to listen. While perhaps all of them weren't Party members, they were at the very least active sympathizers. And most were in their fifties or sixties. I was made downright conspicuous —too conspicuous for comfort, I thought—by my youth.

The group's advanced age—thinning hair or no hair at all seemed the pate of the day—was a graying documentation not only of the repressive age of McCarthyism, so recently passed, but of the Party's history of doctrinal flip-flops, back-steps, and about-faces, all made in pursuit of Moscow's line, which during World War II and afterward drove away more converts—notably the young—than it lured. What with most youth spurning the Party during the war years and the Party's own moratorium on recruitment when, during McCarthyism, it went underground and virtually ceased to function, Party member- ship by the sixties was bunched at opposite ends of the age spectrum.

At one extreme were the old. Most were diehard comrades who had joined back in the thirties and forties, and because the Party had become as much part of their personal as their political lives, stayed on as though the Party were some kind of social club. For many of the Party's aging, it had become precisely that.

At the other extreme were the youth—some from the campuses, but perhaps the majority the sons and daughters of old comrades or those from the more deprived of working class families. It was in an attempt to bridge this obvious, even embarrassing, age gap that the Party had founded the W.E.B. DuBois clubs which, so far unsuccessfully, I was attempting to infiltrate. The Taylors' get-together proved hardly the place to begin. Present was precisely one youth: me.

Still, it was a starkly revealing encounter. That evening the Party's "generation gap" was visibly showing. That it was (and remains to this day) explains why New Left youth scorn the Old as doctrinaire fogies who are politically as conservative as they are puritanical.

The Party's lack of youthfulness (and youth) was just as obvious at the Party's National Convention—the first it had held in seven years—which I attended as a delegate in June, 1966. For all the baldness present, it might have been a burlesque hall (rather than Webster Hall, in Greenwich Village). But it was Gus Hall, the Party's aging general secretary, who was on stage and at his verbose best. His thirty-thousand-word harangue, which sounded like an editorial clipped from a 1950 issue of *Pravda,* ran to just over three hours. I was one New Leftist he lost. I fell asleep.

When it was all over, I remember a studious looking youth among the handful there saying, with a shrug, "Man, that was just too much. He never did get with it."

As far as the New Left is concerned, the Party never has.

The Old Left's problem, of course, went far deeper. It was doctrinally bound to a different Marx—to Marxism with a capital "M." Likewise its was a Communism with a capital "C." The student movement's is a lowercase blend of "c's," "m's," and, depending on the issues and the moment, a goodly assortment of the rest of the alphabet, too.

Even the term "New Left" was coined in derision of the "Old." For America's ever-growing-more-politically-activist youth, however, "New Left"—as adopted by the earliest founders of the Students for a Democratic Society—was much more than an ideological slogan. "New Left" wasn't simply against something—the Old Left. It was for something: a radical, though then evolutionary, change in American life. "New Left" described the social democratic course which SDS's collegiate organizers envisaged and were charting for America. Nonetheless, the term "New Left" marked—at the time of its adoption in December, 1961, then nearly six months before SDS's official founding convention at Port Huron, Michigan—a declared doctrinal break with the "Old Left," and everything the latter stood for.

Not until February, 1965, when the U.S. began its bombing of North Vietnam, and the New Left, until then almost wholly concerned with civil rights, took up the cudgels against "U.S. Imperialism," would the mainstreams of "Old" and "New Left" ideology become tributaries to one another's thinking.

It was the civil rights movement, in which nearly all of SDS's founders had actively participated, that launched the New Left. Yet, though "New Left" as a doctrinal label grew out of the South and the civil rights movement, it had come by way of Britain (where the phrase was then in vogue) with a boost from New Left philosopher C. Wright Mills. Mills's "Letter to the New Left" and the philosophical journals *New Left Review* and *Studies on the Left* had suggested "New Left" as the generic label for those seeking a new prescription for America's chronic ills.

Though most SDSers in those earliest years were too busy making history to write it, "New Left" was a term around which they galvanized even before SDS's fledgling National Executive Committee, meeting in Ann Arbor in December, 1961, drafted Tom Hayden to write a charter for the new youth movement it was shaping for activist students in the North. Hayden's epic "Port Huron Statement"— adopted by SDS's founding convention in June, 1962—was the first definitive document to define the principles of the New Left.

In it, Hayden began with a critique of human values, the decline of the democratic processes in America, and the failure of both

25

"liberals" and the labor movement to alter the downward course of American society. The "Port Huron Statement" (PHS, as SDSers refer to it) called for sweeping reforms—*not* revolution. It suggested that these reforms could be made and America yet saved from itself by a realignment by youth of existing political parties. Specifically, Hayden meant the Democratic party. The charter closed with an appeal to the youth of the campuses—tomorrow's voters—to join together in a "New Left" to lead the transformation of America.

Much of what the "Port Huron Statement" said was antithetical to the Old Left. It wrote off both "liberals" and labor—the bastions of Old Left strength—as having shown themselves incapable of bringing about the changes SDS sought. It advocated change by political evolution rather than by revolution. And it demanded that America reshape itself in the image of libertarian democracy. There was precious little of the "Old Left" in what "New Left" youth were saying.

But the New Left is far from being a made-in-America phenomenon. The disenchantment of youth is worldwide. And so, almost everywhere that youth rises is the doctrinal difference—and defiance —of the "New" for the "Old."

Wherever youth protests the conditions of the society in which it finds itself—in Czechoslovakia, in Japan, in France, in Russia, in Red China, and the U.S.—it is the Old Left, frightened by what it mistakenly believes to be a creation of its own image, that allies itself against the young rebels.

In France, it was Old Left Communist-dominated labor and its unions who refused to follow radical students out on strike in May, 1968—thus breaking the back of the student revolution that threatened to overrun Paris and the whole of France.

The brutal suppression of the Czech student revolt and, with it, that country's last vestige of freedom, was engineered by the Czech and Soviet Old Left, backed by Red Army tanks and troops.

In Japan, Old Leftists are as frightened of the revolt in the universities—which, during the first six months of 1969, closed down seventy-seven of the country's 379 colleges and universities, and led to 5,120 student arrests—as is the Sato regime itself. Old Leftists were in the vanguard of supporters for Premier Sato's new, tough "dispute control" law, aimed at repressing Japan's disenchanted students.

In the United States, the Old Left pays only lip service to the liberation of women and black people, applauds the Soviet Union's crushing of the Czech students, and was so scathing of the Students for a Democratic Society that not until 1967—by then, far too late— did the Party even seek to influence (and, ironically, tone down) SDS's course.

This was the reason the FBI, in the spring of 1965, had aimed me for eventual Party membership by way of the W.E.B. DuBois clubs. As yet the Party played no role within SDS itself, and had even less influence. The recruiting arm of the Party was its DuBois clubs, not SDS. But during those first few weeks my aim had been embarrassingly off the mark.

I came away from that first function—the Taylors' backyard dinner—with a reasonably full stomach (which, considering that my bathroom scale was climbing close to the three-hundred-pound mark, I scarcely needed), but otherwise empty-handed. I hadn't met so much as a bona fide DuBoiser.

A few nights later I did. With that first contact came an unexpected surprise: Mario Savio.

Mario, leader of Berkeley's free speech movement (FSM) since the previous October, was, at twenty-three, the "father" of the student movement. A brilliant student—valedictorian of his Queens high school; one of forty national finalists in Westinghouse's 1960 science talent search; a straight "A" scholarship student in physics and mathematics at Manhattan College before migrating to California, and finally to the UC Berkeley campus in 1963, by way of the voter registration drives around McComb, Mississippi (where he'd been badly beaten by a white mob)—Savio had led the first major demonstration on an American campus: Berkeley's Sproul Hall sit-in of the previous December.

Now, on that evening in late April, Savio had arrived, unannounced and unheralded, to join his father and forty or so others, many of them Old Leftists. The occasion was a dinner and lecture sponsored by the Italian–American Cultural Society. Oddly enough,

27

it was held at the Hungarian Workmen's Home Society's hall, known locally as "Hungarian Hall," on South St. Andrews Place, in Los Angeles. The *People's World* announcement had made no mention of Mario.

Perhaps there, in the last few days of April, Mario should have felt compensated for the jail term he faced. For he was among the 780 Sproul sit-iners arrested on orders of then Democratic Governor Edmund "Pat" Brown. Eventually, he would serve 120 days in California's Santa Rita prison for his leadership in the Berkeley sit-ins. It was a price that Mario—a lean, frizzy-haired six-footer with a trace of a stutter, even when exhorting his campus rebels—had been prepared to pay. He had, in fact, paid it before. He'd gone to jail, previously, for his part in 1964's summer civil rights sit-in (some called it a "take over") of San Francisco's Sheraton-Palace Hotel.

Almost singlehandedly, Savio had moved the student movement from its social democratic stance as obedient petitioners to militant radicals.

At Berkeley, during the fall of 1964, he had challenged the growing authoritarianism of the campus's administration. He had faced up to the university's Regents for their meddling in what many considered a student right—the use, for debate and political solicitation, of a tiny, 26 by 60 foot patch of bricked-over ground just outside the university's principal entrance.

He had brought to the nation the concept of the "university factory"—and the need for political change to make real the American Dream for all citizens, not simply for the educated like himself, not only for the above-average wage earner or for the socially privileged. He had demanded on a campus then renowned for its academic freedom the most elemental of all freedoms: that of speech. More significantly, he had focused on the larger national issue: the quality of life itself in America.

Two-thirds of Berkeley's 27,000 students, a survey by the university's own sociology department showed, had supported him and the FSM in its goals. Fully one-third had supported even the FSM's sometimes violent tactics of protest—its demonstrations and sit-ins. More telling was a Regents-commissioned study of the Berkeley trouble, its findings then soon to be released. It would almost wholly vindicate Savio and the FSM—and place the blame almost equally on the Regents themselves and on UC's administration.

For their money ($75,000), the Regents obviously expected the study—conducted by Harvard attorney Jerome C. Byrne, partner in the respected and conservative Los Angeles law firm of Gibson, Dunn & Crutcher—to whitewash their own precipitous hand in UC affairs.

What the Regents got instead was a defense of Savio and the FSM—and a statement of the Movement's philosophy and fears—put more eloquently than even Savio himself.

"This generation of students," assessed the Byrne report, "acts from a dissatisfaction with the rate of change in American society. The opportunty to act in behalf of change is the essence of life itself."

The elemental tragedy, concluded the Byrne report, and it might have been the student movement speaking, "is the clear revelation of the deep mistrust of the young for their elders and the implicit denial of hope in one for the other."

For all these things, Mario might, that evening, have considered his martyrdom vindicated. But he did not. For by the spring of 1965, the FSM had disintegrated into the "Filthy Speech Movement."

Obscenities were not Mario Savio's bag. Neither were they Dr. Clark Kerr's, the quiet-spoken Quaker president of UC's nine campuses and then 72,000 students, who presided over the world's largest university. On March 10, Kerr had submitted his resignation, though he later retracted it. Eventually, however, he would leave the campus. So would Mario, but far sooner. Less than a week after his "surprise" appearance at the dinner I attended in Los Angeles, Savio would announce his departure from university life, from his activist role in campus affairs, and from the FSM, which dissolved with his parting.

In time, Mario would marry, father a son, serve his time in prison for his part in the UC sit-ins, run halfheartedly for state senator on the Peace and Freedom party ticket—and settle down in the Berkeley area where he now works in a bookstore. Only occasionally —as during 1969's People's Park demonstrations—would his voice be heard in public protest.

But that evening, Mario was served up as a kind of after-dinner treat. One of the diners rose, introduced himself as Joseph Savio, and said he had a surprise. His son, Mario, he announced, had just come down from Berkeley and, if nobody objected (none did—the applause was deafening), Mario would say a few words.

Mario's few words ran to precisely three hours and ten minutes. In them, in the most minute detail, Mario traced—meeting by meeting and confrontation by confrontation—the birth, zenith, and pending demise of the free speech movement. Few historians could have done better. But, then, Mario was no casual recorder of history. He had helped shape it.

Afterwards, I congratulated Mario.

"I hope you were taking notes," he said half in jest.

"I was," I told him in all seriousness. The next day I turned them over to Shaw.

Mario Savio wasn't the only surprise that evening. The other was the two couples I met, about my own age, and the only other youths who'd turned out for the affair. One of the girls was wearing a DuBois club pin.

"Oh," I said, and I suppose my excitement showed, "you're in the DuBois club!" We talked a while about the clubs, how I'd written them but had never gotten a reply and how I was interested in joining. She took my name and address and promised to let me know the next time there was a meeting.

I'd made my first DuBois club contact.

A day or so later I received a DuBois mailer. It announced a kind of "social"—a Friday evening showing of some slides of the Selma march—at the Hollywood hills home of a Los Angeles attorney whose daughter, it turned out, was a DuBoiser.

The house was one of those hideaway places. This time it was strictly a youth turnout, and a turn-on to Allen Zak, a Movement reporter-photographer who'd done some work for *People's World* and for the underground Los Angeles *Free Press,* and who had just returned from Selma.

Zak's slides—which captured marchers and hecklers alike, the faceless who'd gone south to march with Dr. Martin Luther King, and the famous, including folk-songstress-activist Joan Baez—held my

30

interest less than a girl I met there: Stephanie. She was the daughter of an old comrade who had once appeared before HUAC (the House Un-American Activities Committee). Stephanie was one of the few Movement girls I ever seriously dated. When, much later, I broke up with her (we are still friends), I vowed I would never—could never—become involved with a girl whose every kiss, literally, it was my obligation to report to the Bureau.

As an undercover informer, I could never have a really meaningful, totally honest relationship with any activist girl. For never could I throw open my whole life to her. Always there would be a silent secret that I would have to withhold—the admission that I was a spy.

In all those nearly five years I told only four people of my Bureau connection. One was a trusted friend. I told him one day shortly after I'd agreed to work with Shaw. I wanted someone to know, in case anything ever happened to me, what I'd been doing. Not for three years did he tell his own wife. On three other occasions—the only times over those years I felt I was deeply in love—I admitted my Bureau ties. But the girls, sworn to secrecy, kept my secret. None ever told.

The door to DuBois, until then seemingly closed, opened—first a crack, then all the way—after that hill-house social.

I was invited, in fact, to a DB May Day picnic being held the very next day—May 1, 1965—at Los Angeles' Griffith Park. There, seventy-five kids, the majority of them from the campuses, did their thing and participated in a way-out treasure hunt each of whose limerick clues was political. They jibed at Lyndon Johnson, protested the U.S.'s involvement in Vietnam—and the nation's failure, after more than one hundred years, to emancipate the black American. The rhymed clues spelled out not only the treasure's final position but, ultimately, the DB club's own, politically.

The rhyme-game's innovator was Mario Romo, a handsome Mexican-American youth in his early twenties, who chaired the Central LA DuBois club and was also a member of the Party. Over the next months I was to work closely with Mario as subchairman ("Action Chairman") of the Central club. I later succeeded him as leader.

Also at the picnic I met Jim Berland for the first time. Berland was a leader in the Young Democrats on the UCLA campus—the YD, not the DB, being his political area of "work." For he, too, was a Party member and later would head the Southern California Party's Youth Commission. There at the May Day get-together, Berland was being congratulated all around for having just gotten himself elected UCLA's 1965–66 delegate to the prestigious National Student Association (NSA). Few, if any, on the UCLA campus knew of Berland's Communist ties.

Officially, after the May Day picnic, I was in DuBois. Joining had proved considerably easier than I had anticipated. Membership came almost as a matter of course to those youths who expressed a genuine interest in the socialistic outlook for change. For in those days DuBois described itself simply as a "socialist youth organization."

Once I remember asking a DuBois club officer about the overtone of Party control I sensed, more than saw, in my own club chapter.

"Oh," he said, "I imagine there are Communists in the DuBois clubs. But it's certainly not a Communist organization."

Not until five months later when I joined the Party did I learn that my own Central DB club, like the DuBois organization nationwide, was wholly Communist controlled—and had been since its founding convention, June 17–19, 1964, in San Francisco.

I made the discovery at my very first Party "club" meeting. The Party group I'd been invited to join was the Jose Martin club, named for a famous Latin American revolutionary.

On this particular evening the club was meeting at the home of one of its members in the Echo Park district, in central Los Angeles. There were eleven people there that evening—and every one of them, save for one "older" member (who was about forty-five), was in the DuBois clubs, the majority of them members of my own Central DB club. And all of them, like myself, were Communists and Party members. "The Jose Martin club," I was told, "sponsors your Central Los Angeles DuBois club."

Never, at our DB meetings, had the slightest mention been made of a "sponsor," much less the existence of the Jose Martin club.

It was a bit eerie, I confess, sitting in on a meeting of a group which even I, although among the chapter's top leadership, hadn't known until that moment existed. And eerier yet to discover that they are your "sponsor" and, in fact, make the running of *your* DuBois club *their* entire business. It was precisely this kind of backstage business that doomed DuBois from its beginning.

On dozens of campuses New Left kids joined DuBois, hopefully to make it the instrument of the changes they sought for America. Soon enough they discovered that no matter what their suggestions from the floor or how diligently they might work in one direction, the club seemed—as though helmed by a phantom captain—to be steering a preset course of its own.

Many campus kids dropped out, disgusted. But many of those who remained, and others who joined to fill the ranks of the drop-outs, never once suspected the truth. Somewhere, behind every DuBois club, was an unseen, unmentioned "sponsor." The "sponsor's" policies, political actions, and even nominations for elective office were prefabricated and carried whole to the DuBois clubs, and only occasionally were the DuBois' rank and file so much as consulted.

We in the Jose Martin club, typically, would decide who would be nominated and elected. Always there were enough Party members in each DuBois chapter to assure the election of those "spontaneously nominated."

As a Marxist and New Leftist, I was to witness—in the space of but a handful of years—the "sponsored" destruction of two of the Movement's most promising vanguard organizations: the W.E.B. DuBois Clubs of America and the Students for a Democratic Society.

The DuBois clubs would fall victim to its Old Left—the Moscow-lined Communist party—"sponsor."

SDS would die at the hand of a similar "sponsor"—the Maoist-leaning Progressive Labor party.

As a New Leftist, I still mourn their shameless murders.

And so, literally over a weekend (that May 1 weekend), I found myself a DuBoiser.

Membership was—even then before upward spiraling inflation—a downright bargain. For something like $1 a year (which went on my Bureau expense account), I was a paid-in-full member. I received the DuBois monthly magazine, *Insurgent,* and its occasional theoretical journal, *Dimensions*—and also one of its billfold-sized bright red membership cards. What was significant wasn't its color, but rather the fact that four cards were imprinted for each new member. One was the member's copy, one each went to the regional and national offices, and the fourth stayed with the member's chapter. Later, when I was area chairman of the Los Angeles DuBois clubs, I managed to get hold of the entire file of regional membership cards. One day I handed them to a Bureau agent who had them Xeroxed and back in the DuBois files—their absence unnoticed—in scarcely more than an hour's time.

Campus activism, I soon enough discovered, has its penalties—an incessant round of meetings, actions, and activities. For me they began with my weekly DuBois club meeting, usually held in a member's home. The pace grew more hectic when, scarcely three weeks after I'd joined, I was elected action chairman of the Central Los Angeles chapter. (My nomination, I would later learn, had been suggested and sanctioned by our "sponsor," the Jose Martin club.)

"Your job," Mario Romo told me when he put my name up for voting, "will be simply that—to head up the club's action activities . . . demonstrations . . . picketing . . . leafleting, things of that sort."

At that time, the Central Club had about thirty "core" members. Core people could be counted on to show up rain or shine and even for dull business meetings.

Frankly, I didn't find them dull. I was learning about Left activities, organization, and activism. I was interested and I had risen quickly to leadership. Now, as one of our Central Club's two representatives (Mario Romo, its chairman, was the other), I sat on the DuBois Los Angeles Area Council. So my calendar—already Xed with a weekly DB club meeting and my action activities—got yet another X for the every-week Area Council conference. Somehow, I still found hours enough to hold down my part-time drafting job and to attend two full summer school sessions at Pasadena City College.

One of the brightest people in West Coast DuBois was John Haag, chairman of the Venice DB club, head of the Area Council, a Harvard graduate in English literature, and the congenial host and owner of the Venice West Coffee House—a hippie-and-bongo hangout which, eventually, Venice's do-gooders would close down as a public nuisance.

John Haag had joined DuBois because it was working for what John, himself, had worked for and believed in: An America at peace with itself and the world, and capable of stretching its supposed "freedom" to include every man: black or brown, iconoclast or hippie. I don't think John really ever knew that the DuBois clubs were the progeny of the Old Left—the Communist party itself. More and more, of course, he became aware of the Party's manipulation—sometimes devious, sometimes outright—of club programs and policies. When he'd had a stomachful, he quit.

It was at Haag's Venice West Coffee House that I wrote my first activist leaflet. The occasion was the Watts riots—those five days of black anger (August 12–17, 1965) that ignited Los Angeles' ghetto, galvanized the white community to fear, and revealed, as perhaps no racial conflagration up to its time, the depth of black America's despair.

The leaflet was, as I recall, John Haag's idea. Leaflets are the vanguard's communicative link with its peers and the public. While the public might not read a theoretical journal, a leaflet passed out at supermarkets, along lines of march, or on campus gets instant readership and response. The leaflet John had in mind had three aims—to reach, calm, and reassure Los Angeles' frightened whites (many of whom were crowding sporting goods stores as they sought to arm themselves), build sympathy for Watts's black rioters, and combat white backlash.

I was elected, along with Gil C., another DBer, to write, edit, and print the DuBois Watts leaflet, and to have it ready for next morning's protest demonstration in front of the Los Angeles Police Department's adminstration building. A coalition of New Left activists were going down there to march against the LAPD's brutality in the Watts riot.

It was about 10 P.M. when Gil and I began putting the leaflet together there in the Venice West Coffee House. But we'd scarcely

35

started when some old bag came up and invited Gil for a stroll on the beach. He left me—to do the whole job alone.

The leaflet I wrote explained why Watts was Watts, and why black Los Angeles was rioting. I told about the rats, the filth, the police harassment and brutality. It was a blunt declaration of the righteous reasons for what, at that moment, seemed so wrong to so much of the white community.

I wrote that leaflet right off the top of my head. I had never so much as set a foot in Watts (and still haven't), much less seen a rat or police brutality there.

I finished my leaflet writing at 2 A.M. An hour later, a fellow DuBoiser and I were grinding out one thousand copies on our club mimeograph machine. To do it—because the mimeo happened to be in one of the DB girls' apartments—we had to let ourselves in and do the printing without waking her. I finally dragged back to Temple City and into bed by 6 A.M. Two hours later the demonstrators in front of the Police building were passing out my leaflet.

Activist though I had turned, I was then yet a long step removed from the operational core of DuBois—Party membership, the goal toward which Wayne Shaw and the Bureau had pointed me from the outset. Nonetheless, the Bureau sent word it was elated with my progress. Still, the compensation Shaw passed to me on the fourteenth of every month—and always in cash—was trivial enough: $125, of which $50 was nontaxable reimbursement for expenses and the rest my salary for services.

Two events were to seal my commitment to communism—and win me a coveted invitation to join the Party.

The first was the once-a-week intensive ten-session course in Marxism–Leninism, taught by Marvin Treiger. Of all the people I was ever to meet, inside or outside the Movement, few had the brilliance or charisma of Treiger. A profoundly learned Marxist, a UCLA graduate in history (later, he would get his MA in history on the California State College campus), Marv had forgotten more Marx than most Party people remember. Yet, in time, he would quit the Party and become involved in the founding of the Revolutionary Union (RU)—one of the probable successors to SDS.

36

Treiger's Marxist course, which began sometime in August and would run nearly through October, had, though at the time I didn't realize it, a deeper purpose than merely an historical probing of the bulwarks of Marxist ideology—it was to sift out those whom the Party aimed to recruit. It wasn't, in fact, until after the course's final session that Treiger, over a cup of coffee, asked me if I'd be interested in joining the Party. By then, the Party not only had decided that I *should* join, but through one of its "deep cover" contacts had actually checked me out on the Pasadena City College campus. By then, too, Mario Romo had quit the Central Los Angeles DuBois club, and I had become its chairman.

The tip-off—and inevitability—of my Party membership was the hush-hush, week-long night course in Marxism I was asked to attend. None other than the Party's National Secretary for Education, Hy Lumer, flew out to the Coast to teach it, although there were just seven students.

The whole thing was cloak-and-dagger. Saturday, the class's first day, we were told to meet at a Party member's house. Once there, we were given the address where the class was being held. We were told to park a block or so from the house and walk the rest of the way, staggering our arrival. When we got there, we were locked in for the whole day. They served us lunch. Leaving—our departures at five-minute intervals so as not to arouse the neighbors—we were handed sealed envelopes with the address of the house where the next session would be held.

"Don't open your envelopes until you get home," one Party member warned, "then memorize the new address and burn it."

All the secrecy was silly. Three-quarters of what Lumer taught was standard textbook Marx, available on most library shelves.

The second milestone on my now seemingly relentless march to Party membership was the DuBois clubs' National Leadership Conference held in Chicago early in September—the first DB convention since the founding one of the previous year. Before my attendance as a convention delegate, I'd been viewed with something akin to aloof suspicion. I returned from Chicago to find myself suddenly and unexplainably "accepted"—and on my way up. The change,

37

I discovered, wasn't prompted so much by the fact that I had gone to the Chicago conference, but that, to get there, I had hitchhiked. Louder than words, my dedication had spoken through my thumb.

What I remember most vividly about that 2,166-mile hitchhike, Los Angeles to Chicago, was the Okie-type kids (two youths of about twenty and a girl) who picked me up outside of Albuquerque, New Mexico. I rode with them all the way to Springfield, Missouri.

They had been living in Los Angeles, down near the Watts area, and were going "home"—to Kansas. The trunk of their car was absolutely stuffed with liquor, expensive clothes—even a brand-new color TV set.

"It's all loot," one of those white kids boasted, "from the Watts riot. We just kinda helped ourselves to the fun."

Here they were, white racists I was sure, who'd been in there grabbing right along with the rest. But once back home, they'd be holier-than-thou-ing it to their racist kin about "them nigger looters" down in Watts.

On its surface, that W.E.B. DuBois Clubs of America National Leadership Conference wasn't noticeably different from many others I would later attend. But behind the scenes it was.

About two hundred delegates attended, all students and from all across the nation. The conference, which ran four days and was held in Chicago's Ukrainian Hall, spent the first few days in workshop sessions. The delegates broke up into discussion groups on "how to go about doing it" themes that ranged from how to build up local chapters to community, campus, and high school organizing. And all of it in terms of the gut issues of the time—civil rights, poverty, peace, and Vietnam.

DuBois and SDS, though poles apart ideologically then, held in common the Movement's self-dedicated purpose—to raise through protest, activism, and demonstration the social and moral conscience —and consciousness—of the nation.

A single street corner demonstration—in behalf of a local wrong —may seem wasteful, meaningless, and even a bit silly. It is not. It is one tiny nudge given to the national conscience. A myriad of tiny thrusts and people who once said "nigger" or "Negro," who once hawkishly supported the Vietnam War—these people, a trickle of them at first, then larger numbers, begin to change.

The Movement, with neither the capital nor Madison Avenue's creative tools, must work in its own piecemeal way. Yet, thrust by thrust, it has already achieved subtle, even significant, shifts toward change and self-criticism.

Americans are no longer as smug or complacent about themselves or their society. They are questioning and beginning to doubt. And doubt is the first prerequisite for social change. Doubting, Americans are beginning to look inward, to their own hearts. Many, recognizing in themselves some of the inbred prejudices—of race, color, and thought—which all along Movement youth have been telling them they would find if only they took the time to search their own souls, are beginning to change.

For example, millions now say "black" when they mean "Negro." Communities which, a decade ago, might have risen forcibly in arms to halt the first local bussing program now concede that bussing is "right" and even the "American way," though deep in their still-racist hearts it hurts them to admit it.

Vietnam's hawks have fallen prey to the doves—as did President Lyndon Johnson himself, and as Richard Nixon knows he, too, may unless he pulls American troops out of the rotten mistakes of Vietnam and Cambodia. The whole draft system has been revamped toward equality—where the black, the poor, and the noncollegian share equal risk with every draw of a draft number. General Hershey, the draft czar who sent millions of uneducated, underprivileged, and nonwhite American youths to their premature deaths on the battlefield, has been banished to forced retirement.

No single protest, no handful of demonstrations, no ten or even one hundred speeches did all these things. What accomplished them— small and faltering as they are on the road toward really significant social change in America—were those tiny thrusts.

But internal politics—more than the programming of strategy for national activities—consumed, and to a large extent split, the DuBois National Leadership Conference in Chicago.

Already in view were the divergent tugs and pulls which, in less than a year, would doom DuBois to fatal factionalism. At work—and visible—was the Party's heavy hand.

On one side was arrayed the New Left—those DuBois delegates from the campuses who looked to the campus and their student peers for their organizational strength.

Against them stood the Old Left and its delegates—those Du-Boisers who took their strength from and paid their first allegiance to the American working class.

It was an all but classic standoff: the New Left versus the Old Left.

New Left DuBois youth—who made up about 90 percent of the conference's delegates—demanded student and campus emphasis in everything DuBois. The Old Left, tied to the old tradition, insisted that the future of DuBois lay in the working class—and specifically, in working class, noncampus youth.

Never was the factionalism—New Left versus Old, collegian versus noncollegian—more evident than during the convention debate for the DuBois clubs' elective leadership.

Ed Vickery, representing the working class orientation of the Party, opened his campaign speech for the DuBois national chairmanship with a flat, almost prideful statement.

"I'm not a student," declared Vickery. "I'm a worker."

He was proud that he was *not* of the campus. It was in the image of the working class, he declared, that—if elected—he intended to build DuBois and its national program.

Opposing him was "K.O." Hallinan, the lawyer son of Vincent Hallinan, the well-known West Coast attorney active in leftist causes. It was "K.O." who would later defend the "Oakland 7" (the seven GIs who had demonstrated against brutality in the Army's Oakland, California, stockade).

Hallinan declared that the DuBois clubs were an instrument of the campus. On the campuses, he correctly pointed out, was where the action was. The campuses were moving, were actively supporting change. American workers, risen to the American middle class, were not only moving, they were sitting on their hands.

In the end, the issue was never clearly decided. Hugh Fowler, a

DB leader from the San Francisco bay area, and a middle-of-the-roader, was nominated as a compromise candidate. Fowler was elected, becoming the DuBois' 1965–66 national chairman. Hallinan was voted to the DuBois leadership's second-in-command. And the campus versus noncampus issue was temporarily laid to rest.

Right after the DuBois convention there was a Communist party youth conference in Chicago. It had been timed to coincide with the DB conference, many of whose delegates were Party youth. But I wasn't invited to attend. As yet, I was not a Party member.

Scarcely had I returned to Los Angeles, however, and plunged once more into Marv Treiger's Marxist course, than it became apparent that sooner rather than later I'd be asked to join the Party.

"They're going to check you out," Wayne Shaw warned me during one of our meetings. "They're going to test you on ideology . . . but just how or when is anybody's guess."

My "check-out" by the Party came scarcely a month later and where I'd least expected it—on the Pasadena City College campus. It was to be one of the most revealing experiences in all of my nearly five years under cover.

One day I'd gone to the Student Union for lunch and, afterward, to study. It was in the afternoon, as I recall. I'd gone through the cafeteria line, had eaten, and was taking my coffee cup back for a refill when, walking through the door that led to the coffee urns, I bumped into this fellow—a student, but nobody I knew.

"Excuse me," I said.

"That's all right," he replied, glancing up. And then, strangely, a look of recognition animated his face.

"Oh, hi!" he said. Then, out of the blue, he introduced himself. So I introduced myself, too.

At that moment, I didn't give it a second thought. I'd never seen him before. His name hadn't rung a bell.

Finished with my second cup of coffee, I went up to the Student Union lounge to study. Suddenly, from nowhere, Mr. What's-His-Name, the fellow I'd bumped, appeared. He came over, sat down right beside me, and said, "You know, I've seen you around campus . . . and I've been meaning to talk with you."

41

I became suspicious, though likely I wouldn't have had not my handler warned me of the all but inevitable Party "test" to come. With scarcely a moment of small talk, Mr. What's-His-Name began to sound out my politics. What, he wanted to know, did I think of Vietnam? What was my attitude on racism and imperialism?

I caught on fast to what, to the uninitiated, might have sounded like a bungling attempt to nail down my politics. Coming out point-blank like that, he figured that whatever I *really* thought might come unglued. Were I not really a Marxist, I might spill the beans.

Instead, I dished them right back at him. I gave him a straight Left line. In fact, I really out-Lefted him. He had expected me to say I was against the Vietnam War (which I was). I told him I was not only against the war but that the reasons I was against it went deeper than that. They went to the basic problems of American society, and deeper still to imperialism and capitalism. Then I led with an ideological uppercut. I tried talking him into joining the DuBois club.

He smiled a smile that told me I'd not only passed the test, but had gotten an A-plus.

After that, I began questioning him. He told me he was new to the Pasadena City College campus (which explained why neither his face nor name was familiar). He'd come out from Massachusetts with his family just that summer. He said he believed in all the things I believed in, but that openly practicing that kind of politics you might lose your ability to have a life in American society as it was presently constituted. He said he admired me for my political activism, but that he, personally, couldn't run the risk.

He mentioned that he had an uncle who was a professor at Cal-Tech (California Institute of Technology). Cal-Tech was only a few blocks from the PCC campus. Not only was it one of the Department of Defense's major brain centers, but it operated Pasadena's Jet Propulsion Laboratory, one of the basic research and hardware sources of the U.S. space program.

My new friend commented that he hadn't seen his uncle, the Cal-Tech professor, for years, until recently, which I took to mean since he and his folks had moved from Massachusetts to California. I asked him to repeat his own name, and I made sure I had it right in my mind. With that, he said goodbye, and I never saw him again.

A day or so later, when I met my handler, I recounted the incident.

"*That*," Wayne said with a grin, "was your Party test."

Wayne, however, was far more interested in the probable name of the youth's uncle, the Cal-Tech professor. There was half a chance my interrogator for the Party and his uncle might have the same names.

Right there in the FBI car, Wayne reached into a file he carried. Since he was agent-in-charge of the Pasadena office, he and his staff ran routine security checks on Cal-Tech's professors as well as on the people over at Jet Propulsion Laboratory. Quickly, Wayne found the current Cal-Tech catalog that listed the school's professorial staff. Sure enough, there was a high-placed professor listed on Cal-Tech's staff with the identical name as my Party interrogator's.

But what interested me were the almost invisible blue dots that Wayne had penciled opposite several names on the Cal-Tech staff list. One of the little blue dots stood opposite the name of the uncle of my interrogator.

I didn't ask Wayne about the blue dots, or why my chum's uncle had one beside his name. I *knew* why.

Each dot marked a Cal-Tech staffer whom the Bureau either had suspicions about or had under active surveillance. My contact's uncle was one of those "deep cover" people the Party has everywhere— people with no visible Party connections, people who would never attend a Party meeting, never subscribe to a Party paper, never get involved in demonstrations. They are "resource people." When the Party wants something done it calls upon its resource people.

In my case, the matter was routine. The Party wanted me, a Pasadena City College undergraduate, checked out. Cal-Tech was only a handful of blocks from the PCC campus. The Party might even have known that its "deep cover" professor had a nephew who was also attending PCC. So it simply suggested that he ask his nephew to look me up on campus and sound out my true politics. No one would be the wiser. The prof didn't risk his "deep cover" position. His nephew—like his uncle, far removed from the Party—risked nothing, either. It was all very efficient and logical.

But the next time Wayne and I met, things had changed. Partly

43

because of that check-out, but more probably because I'd become increasingly valuable to the Bureau, we tightened our security procedure. Previously, when we met, I'd simply parked on a residential street near school. At first, I used my motor bike, later a Party car. Wayne would drive past, park, and I'd get into his car. We'd drive around, talking. When he let me out, I'd leave behind my reports from the previous week. When I got the Party car, we used to joke that if the Party was tailing me, it'd really be tailing itself.

Security was something we quit joking about after my Party check-out. Now we picked a long residential block. Its length was crucial to the kind of security Wayne Shaw had in mind. So was the sharp right turn at the end of the block.

The way it worked was this. Wayne would arrive a little before me and park his car at the beginning of the block. I'd drive by. But instead of stopping a little way down the block, as I'd done previously, I'd keep right on driving, make a sharp right turn and go all the way around the block. Wayne would be watching. If anyone was tailing me, he'd be revealed by the way he took that fast right turn. He'd have to speed up to keep on my tail. Instantly, Wayne would know I was being followed. The second time I passed my handler's car, he'd either pay no attention to me (meaning "you're being tailed, the meeting's off") or he'd gesture a kind of subtle thumbs-up (meaning, "Okay—park"). Given the thumbs-up "clear" signal, I'd park, walk back to his car and we'd take off for an hour of talking.

Never, to my knowledge, was I tailed. But during my years under cover, I was on several occasions fingered—I later learned—as a possible FBI plant. And once I was accused point-blank of being a fink.

A few weeks after my Party check-out, Marv Treiger concluded his Marxist course. After class that last evening, he invited me for a chat and a cup of coffee. Afterward, driving me back to where I'd left my motor bike, Marv said, "I suppose you know by now that I'm in the Communist party?"

"Yeah," I told him, "I rather figured you were."

"Well," he went on, "some of the Party people have been discussing you, Bill. We thought maybe you'd like to join the Party. We'd like to offer you an invitation."

44

For a long moment I didn't say anything. I liked Marv. I liked the DuBois and Party people I'd met. But even for me—an undercover informer—joining the Party would be a big step, and not one to take lightly.

"I'll have to think about it, Marv," I replied. "It's a pretty important thing. And you know the legal ramifications." (It was October, 1965, and Party members were legally supposed to register as Communists with the federal government.)

That's how we left it.

A week or so later, at the Bureau's urging, I became a member of the Communist Party/USA. The date was November 9, 1965.

3. The Black Rose Queen

I F the Federal Bureau of Investigation knighted its campus finks, by the fall of 1965—as I started my final year at Pasadena City College —I'd have been on the Herald's List. And my FBI handlers might have been addressing me as "Sir William."

I had done yeoman duty. From a mere knave in the FBI student informer brigade only six months before, I'd risen to lead the charge. In fact, rather than simply being a chronicler of events, I was helping to shape them. I was chairman of the Central Los Angeles DuBois club, had just returned as a delegate from the first DuBois National Leadership Conference in Chicago, had graduated from Marxist school, and had been invited to join the Communist party. All the time I had been reporting to the Bureau not only on the Party, its DuBois clubs, and the student movement, but on *myself*.

"... *William Divale*," my now-voluminous reports to the Bureau would chronicle (I am reading as I write this from several of them from that period), "*suggested that DuBois members should participate actively in upcoming demonstrations in support of Cesar Chavez and his grape strikers.*"

"... *Club chairman Divale agreed with DuBois member Carol W. that just as soon as she can she should join the 'Los Angeles Committee to End the War in Vietnam.'*"

"... *The turning point in U.S. participation in Vietnam— enunciated by President Johnson in his speech of July 29, 1965, for the first time pledging the U.S. to an all but unlimited troop commitment—is bound to change the whole complexion of student protest, Divale told the meeting. Now a second great issue has been joined with that of Civil Rights—the war in Vietnam.*"

Four years later, when I took the witness stand before the Sub-

47

versive Activities Control Board as a star witness for the government, New York attorney John Abt, among the most renowned and perhaps the ablest lawyer in defense of Communist cases, would pull these self-assertions from my own reports (the Attorney General had made available to Abt those reports of mine directly concerning his clients) in a clever attempt to discredit my reliability both as a prosecution witness *and* as a defender of the New Left. It was probable that Abt had never faced a government witness quite like me. I can understand Abt's dilemma. Here was a prosecution witness, a product of the FBI underground who, though admitting a high personal regard for his youthful clients, was nonetheless publicly charging them with membership in the Communist party.

Falsely, Abt insinuated that I'd included myself in those reports as a piece of public relations to gain status in the eyes of the Bureau, and to turn each of my rungs up the student movement's ladder into a pay raise. Abt, of course, knew I'd hardly grown rich in J. Edgar's service—not on a starting salary of $125 a month, with $350 monthly the highest I ever earned, and nearly half of that not "pay," but reimbursement for expenses either advanced or as repayment for those I'd actually paid out of pocket. Abt was equally aware, from years of questioning other FBI informants, that by Bureau rules informers must include themselves in their own reports. It is a standard measure of security.

Abt's dilemma grew, rather than lessened, at every stage of the testimony. An unfriendly witness he could handle. But an unfriendly "friendly" witness was something else. He was boxed in, and it was never more apparent than when he began questioning me about the very first FBI payment that Wayne Shaw had passed to me.

> ABT: Now, when Shaw handed you this envelope with $35 in it, did you open the envelope in his presence?
> DIVALE: Yes, I believe so. Yes, because I had to sign the receipt.
> ABT: Did you make any comment to him about the amount of money in that envelope?
> DIVALE: No—well, just "Fine."
> ABT: Did you say is it going to be like this all the time or

am I going to get a raise?

DIVALE: No. At that time I was relatively new at the game.

ABT: You were new at the game and you just took whatever he gave you, right?

DIVALE: Right.

ABT: You had no twinges of conscience at that time?

DIVALE: No. At that time I didn't know the people.

ABT: Now you do know the people, right?

DIVALE: Yes.

ABT [referring again to my "twinges of conscience"]: For the money you took and the reports that you made?

DIVALE: No. Mainly, because they are human beings and I——

ABT: A lot of nice people?

DIVALE: Oh, I think they are excellent people.

Later, when I re-read *Witness,* in which the late Whittaker Chambers, a *Time* magazine senior editor and former Communist courier, exposed Alger Hiss, who had sat high in the councils of government, as a fellow operative in the Soviet apparatus, my testimony did not sound so contradictory.

"Mr. Hiss was certainly the best friend I ever had in the Communist party," Chambers had replied to a question put to him by then Senator Richard Milhous Nixon. And Chambers continued ". . . I have testified against him with remorse and pity."

What Abt could not know was that some of my reports bugged the Bureau almost as much as they bothered him, but for different reasons. The report the Bureau got the most uptight about, I suppose, was one I wrote early in October, 1965, just at the start of PCC's fall semester.

"A number of people at Pasadena City College," I dutifully reported, *"will attempt this semester to establish a chapter of the Students for a Democratic Society on the campus. One of SDS's sponsors is Divale."*

I should say, in all honesty, that the Bureau never meddled in my affairs, never really seemed to object to what I was doing and, in fact, my handler and I often joked when, you might say, the Bureau caught me red-handed.

49

Regularly now I was showing up in FBI photographs. Often, after one demonstration or another, Wayne—during of our clandestine meetings—would hand me a stack of photos. I'd go through them, identifying people. Usually, he'd hold out till the last the photos the Bureau had snapped of me.

"And do you happen to know this bearded fellow?" he'd grin, handing over the holdouts. I'd scribble "Divale" on the back of each photo and tell Wayne this was one New Leftist the Bureau really ought to keep under closer surveillance.

Casual as may be the relationship between FBI handlers and their student informers, it has polarized against student protestors. But so, as the student movement evolved from social democracy, through radicalism and on to revolution, have the forces abroad in the land.

Outward casualness, when it exists, may mask the FBI agent's true prejudices, which are often deep, even frightening. I saw them surface during those Subversive Activities Control Board hearings of 1969, when I testified against Cliff Fried, the activist SDSer whom the SACB, based largely on my testimony, had fingered as a Party member and leader.

Most Bureau agents at the hearing hated Fried. And as much, I would judge, for his politics as for his personality. Behind the scenes, there in the courtroom antechamber where I waited to testify, J. Edgar's hired hands sounded off like red-neck southerners gathered for a lynching.

My own relationship with most of my handlers ranged the scale from close (in one case, a nearly father-son relationship) to casually friendly—and even right up to the end when my own views, maturing, had swung at nearly 180-degrees variance with most of theirs. If my handlers harbored any deep resentment of me, they never showed it.

Wayne Shaw's only comment, after I'd reported myself as one of SDS's prospective founders on the Pasadena campus, amounted to little more than a verbal chastisement.

"Listen, Bill," he said with some concern, "it's okay to get involved in all these things. You've got to do what everybody else does to be effective. But *you* [he meant *"us"*—the Bureau]'t can't be in the position of creating things. What's going to happen ten years from

50

now if this gets out? People are going to say, *'That guy'*—and they're going to mean *the Bureau*—'was behind all the trouble.' "

I said, "Yeah . . . yeah, Wayne, I guess you're right about that" and kept right on with my activities.

What I was doing that fall of 1965 on the Pasadena campus, which was still hanging tense following the Watts riots of the past August, was working to establish SDS, participating in lie-downs at Los Angeles' central produce market to stop trucks from unloading grapes from the strike-torn upstate Delano area, and helping to mount major student protest, on campus and off, on the Black Rose Queen issue.

The hatching place of certainly some of PCC's confrontations that fall, I readily admit, was the $60-a-month ramshackle house that Doug Layfield and I had rented on El Sereno Street, not far from the campus, in Pasadena's black ghetto. Doug, twenty-three, was a year younger than I. Like me, he was in his second and final year at PCC. We were both general social science majors and getting close to top marks.

But our level of social awareness, though perhaps higher than that of most others on so typical a suburban campus, would have earned us—had anybody been grading—no more than a C. For effort, however, we both deserved A's.

Philosophically, ours was a left liberal—and pacifistic—humanism, salted with Marxism, and influenced by the existentialism of Sartre ("There can be no other truth than this, *'I think, therefore I am,'* " Sartre had said); by Dostoevski, whom most sociologists remember less for his *Crime and Punishment* than for his *Notes from Underground;* and Mills, who out of them all wove the concept of twentieth-century man's alienation from the society in which he lives.

Like youth all across the nation, we were beginning to question: the Establishment (as Pasadena's School Board, which had moved scarcely an inch toward desegregation and wouldn't until, in January, 1970, it was ordered to do so by U.S. District Judge Manuel L. Real); basic American values which had created the ghetto we lived in and branded as "Communists" Cesar Chavez's itinerant grape-pickers because they were trying to rise from stoop-labor slavery and a wage seldom exceeding $2,000 a year; and a social conscience so insensitive

51

that it had molded the Pasadena Rose Parade into an annual white racist pageant which, in all its years, had never picked any but a lily-white queen and a lily-white cortege of princesses.

Of our house on El Sereno Street, Doug and I used to joke that it was a hotbed of roaches and activism. It also had a roof that leaked buckets whenever it rained. As for the roaches, they were simply un-believable. I mean, it was a regular confrontation between them and us as to who would win dominance over the place. It got so bad that when we went into the kitchen we'd rattle pots to scare them off. We tried poisons and everything we could think of. But they just wouldn't quit. Six months later, in the spring of 1966, I moved out, to get away from the buggers.

As for the activist part of it, there were—back in the fall of 1964 and through spring, 1965—a half dozen or so activists on the PCC campus. Most were influenced by C. Wright Mills, one of the patron saints of student activists in those days. They halfway supported the Cuban revolution and a few even looked up to Che.

Four of the group—Tom Good, a small, neat, brilliant guy; Walter Crowe, who later joined and still later quit the Party; Bill Shelby, who went out to UCLA with Walter; and Doug Layfield—had grown up and gone all through school together in Pasadena. That first year at PCC I was an appendage, rather than an intimate, of the group.

Another on-again, off-again member of the group—back when they'd all been in Pasadena schools together—was Sirhan Sirhan. Walt Crowe and Sirhan Sirhan were close friends during most of their early school years. Sirhan had even autographed Walt's high school yearbook.

"To Walter," Sirhan had scribbled, "the best socialist I know."

Although Sirhan was attending Pasadena City College during most of the time I was there, I never met him. He never dropped over to the house when Doug Layfield and I lived there. And he never took any part—other than in radical Arab affairs—in campus politics. Somehow, during his first year or so at PCC, he'd changed. "Kind of cracked up," Walter had diagnosed on several occasions. Walter was troubled to see what was happening to Sirhan because they'd grown up together and at one time had been so close. Now Walt seldom saw Sirhan. However, the fact that one of their rare get-togethers had occurred just two weeks before Robert Kennedy's assassination actually got to the ears of the FBI (I was the one who informed the Bureau). For a while, Walt was in all kinds of trouble. The Bureau and the Los Angeles Police had it all nicely put together. Since Walter was a campus activist and a Marxist, and since he'd once been a pal of Sirhan's, who had flirted with some of the same philosophies, though never really seriously nor very deeply, then it logically followed that Walter had somehow been tied with Sirhan in a plot to murder Robert Kennedy. The deduction, empirically, may have seemed logical enough, but it simply happened not to be true.

By the fall of 1965, only Layfield was still at PCC. The others had moved on. So Doug and I moved in together (my brother, Robert, had drifted off to the Monterey peninsula for the hippyish life he preferred). We made the house on El Sereno Street into something we could reasonably call home. We were joined in spirit, though not in residence, by Ed Navarro, a black student who was largely to spark the Black Rose Queen issue on the PCC campus, and by Bill Chandler, whose particular thing was the grape-picker's strike (Bill would later drop out of school to join Cesar Chavez's staff full-time in Delano).

The four of us, that semester, made up the leadership nucleus of what could only be tagged as a kind of "gentle" activism. Yet it was more activism than conservative PCC had, in its whole history, seen up to then. It wasn't that PCC's eight thousand full-time students (another five thousand were night-schoolers) weren't already raising their level of social awareness. Like collegians the nation over, they were. What they lacked was a marshalling force. The four of us—in quite informal chats—decided to supply the spark that might turn PCC's complacency into conflagration.

By June, we were to stage PCC's first "teach-in" (which pitted a Communist anti-Vietnamer in debate against one of Rand Corporation's think-factory pro-Vietniks); lead PCCers on almost weekly forays against truck-haulers and supermarkets who were trying to break Cesar Chavez's grape strike; nudge the Pasadena Tournament of Roses Association toward selection of a non-Caucasian Rose Princess (the closest it had ever come to breaking the color line was a Mexican-American princess back in the early forties); and make SDS one of the campus's most bandied-about words.

Significant in the big picture of the Movement was not that we did these things, but that they were being done on small college campuses all over the nation in much the same way as we were doing them. From just such fits and starts, from failure and frustration to move first the campus, then America, would grow the student movement of the seventies.

Moratorium Day '69 . . . Richard Nixon's pained withdrawal from Vietnam . . . the radical change of American public opinion against further, deep U.S. military involvements . . . the rising dissension within the U.S. armed forces . . . the courts' crackdown on dawdling school integrators . . . the galvanizing in the public mind of the stoop-labor slavery of America's migrant farm workers and Chavez's vindication, in March, 1970, as he signed the first union contract with grape-growers . . . the exposure, by HEW and the FDA, of one big-business consumer fraud after another (from cheating packaging to overpriced drugs) . . . the Power Structure's decision (out of fear, not forthrightness) to deal more Americans, including black and brown Americans, into control of their own lives and well-being . . . lily-white labor's yielding to black demands for union cards . . . the rising protest within its own parishes against the stratified conservatism of the Roman Catholic hierarchy (led by its own priests: the DuBays, the Groppis, and Berrigans) . . . the first moves to restructure higher education to relevancy—these things did not "just happen," nor did they happen overnight. They began on campuses no more significant than PCC's. For the revolt of the seventies has its roots in that 1965 period about which I am talking.

The first grape-pickers (actually, they were "grape-thinners") walked out of the fields in the spring of 1965. The "thinners" (who weeded between the vine rows) weren't Mexicans, but rather Filipinos. And the fields they struck were in California's desert-flanked Coachella Valley, not Chavez's San Joaquin Valley. But the strike quickly spread north to the Delano area where Chavez's fledgling National Farm Workers' Association (now, United Farm Workers Organizing Committee, AFL-CIO) was just taking root. The strike and boycott, which became nationally known as the Delano grape-pickers' strike, wasn't called to a vote until September 16, 1965, which happened also to be Mexican Independence Day.

54

Scarcely a month after it had begun, Bill Chandler was taking carloads of PCC kids up to Delano every weekend to man the picket lines. But so were activists from every campus in California.

At PCC, though, our big thing was the Los Angeles Central Produce Market and the "lie-ins" we staged there. Every night dozens of trucks bearing Delano grapes rolled into the Central Market. When we prevented them from unloading, their drivers often turned right around and hauled their grapes of wrath back the 150 miles to Delano, literally dumping them at the big corporate growers' feet.

Our house on El Sereno Street was the staging area for Central Market pickets. Kids would begin gathering there around 10 P.M. By midnight, we'd be down at the market awaiting the first trucks, some of which didn't pull in until 4 or 5 A.M.

Doug captained things. "Lip-in or lie-in," he'd tell those kids, meaning to try first talking drivers into turning back. But, failing that, to throw themselves under the wheels. It was plenty scary.

One rainy night six trucks were due in and we had four market entrances to watch—and block. There were about twenty of us, a dozen PCC kids and the rest Mexican youths sent to join us by Chavez's people. The first couple of drivers listened to reason. They didn't unload. But the third and fourth trucks, both arriving at about the same time but at different market entrances, were set to run our human blockade. They came at us, headlights blinding, their air horns blasting, but not as loud as we were yelling.

"Stop them!" Doug bellowed. And a girl and a guy flung themselves right in front of that first mammoth truck.

"Commie bastards!" the driver, a burly tough, shouted from his cab. Then, like a maniac, he hurtled from behind the wheel. He was going to move those kids, tear them limb from limb if necessary. He was a step away from doing just that when somebody caught him full in the face with a rotten head of cabbage.

He was clawing the stinking mess from his face when one of PCC's most demure little coeds, her blond hair all frazzled in the rain, walked right up to him and said sweetly, "You're a lousy scab. Go screw yourself."

The guy was so shocked he just turned around, climbed back into his truck and got the hell out of there.

55

The fourth driver didn't shock as easily. He came on fast through the pouring rain, his thirty-ton monster's horn screaming. What stopped him momentarily was Doug. He simply lay down fifty feet in front of that truck. The guy slammed on his air brakes fast. He'd scarcely got stopped when a dozen kids put their shoulders against the truck's huge bumper and started pushing! Those kids, who together didn't add up to twenty manpower, were figuring to push back that monster rig and its three hundred horsepower diesel engine.

"Stand clear!" the driver shouted, as he ground into gear and started forward.

That's how it went for a full two minutes—the truck moving relentlessly forward, those kids pushing, but giving ground, and being backed gradually into the brick wall of a warehouse. A split second before the truck's bumper whammed into the wall, the kids jumped out of the way. We stood there in the dark, cursing the guy and pelting his truck with vegetables enough to fill a supermarket counter. But he'd gotten through.

It went on like that, night after night. They'd come rolling in from Delano. We'd turn as many back as we could. Next morning, all through PCC's classrooms, you could spot the "produce pickets" —they were bedraggled and blurry-eyed but triumphant.

Still, too many got through. That, or the big supermarket chains, wising up, ordered grapes delivered directly to their stores. Picketing a couple hundred supermarkets was something we simply couldn't hack. We did, however, picket those markets in Pasadena which continued to handle and sell Delano grapes. There was hardly a Saturday that we didn't station pickets out in front of those places, handing out leaflets and trying to persuade housewives not to buy what, all across the country, was going by a new generic name: "forbidden fruit."

The national attention which thousands of Movement youth helped to focus on Chavez and his pickers paid off. For the first time the nation east of the Mississippi began to realize the dismal plight not just of the migrant Mexican, but of his city brother. Raised for all to see was the "Chicano" cause, and with it a new vocabulary in pathos: *la causa* (the "cause," both Chavez's and the Mexican-Americans'); *la raza* (the "race," the rallying cry for Mexican-American equality); and *la huelga* (the "strike"—Chavez's strike).

56

In our El Sereno Street pad, about that time, we had a problem that had nothing to do with Cesar Chavez and his grape-pickers.

Our problem was in swaddling clothes: Doug's baby. How he'd come by the child wasn't as vexing (to me, certainly) as was the habit of its mother, Doug's longtime girl friend, of popping in at odd hours and handing the baby over to us for safekeeping. Most weekends we wound up baby-sitting and diaper-changing.

"For Christ's sake," I joked one day, "here we are, trying to 'make a revolution,' and what we're mostly making is baby formula."

In my own workbook, nothing counted for more that school year than our revitalizing of the Black Rose Queen issue. Here was a made-in-America injustice so blatant as to mock the Constitution's Fifteenth Amendment.

At Pasadena City College, from whose coeds the Pasadena Tournament of Roses Association annually picked the Rose Parade's queen and her court, "beauty"—by a kind of gentleman's agreement —had come to be defined as "white." And, just as often, as white, Anglo-Saxon, Protestant. Never in the sixty years since 1906, when a queen and her court first became part of the annual Rose event, had a black girl reigned as queen or princess. Yet, by that fall of 1965, a goodly number of PCC's coeds were black, brown, yellow, or in between. The Tournament of Roses Association was colorblind. It could see only white.

To the millions who each New Year's Day watched the Rose Parade and Rose Bowl football classic on TV, the queen and her float had come to symbolize purity and patriotism. Radiant on her floral throne sat PCC's "loveliest" coed. Reposed around her was her court of six nearly as lovely princesses.

What no viewer saw was the annual pageant of humiliation that preceded the selection of the Rose Queen and princesses on the PCC campus. Only PCC coeds, in those days, were eligible to compete for the queen and her court. Competition was all but mandatory and had been since 1932 when PCC became the official progenitor of the Rose Tournament's queens. Every PCC coed (providing she had a C average, was single, and was carrying at least eleven units of college work) was expected to "go out for queen." Like it or not, she was supposed to show up for the preliminary judging and elimination.

While PCC's blonde and blue-eyed WASPs were home primping, PCC's non-Caucasian girls were apt to be doing almost anything else. For them, even showing up was much more than simply a farce. It was an annual insult. Yet, with all the inbred cruelty (and crudity) of their racism, the white power structure commanded their appearance, if only for the privilege of rejecting them out of hand. White to Tournament of Roses judges was beautiful. Any other color was dirty.

The issue had first been raised the previous year by the National Association for the Advancement of Colored People. The NAACP's Pasadena chapter charged the Tournament of Roses Association with a history of bias that not only excluded blacks but even "Caucasians of poor circumstances."

Plainly and simply, said the NAACP, the queen and her court were invariably Establishment girls who measured up in pulchritude and pedigree.

The issue was typical of those that foment confrontation on the nation's campuses. From the perspective of the white Caucasian there was no issue at all. From the black perspective, the issue went to the roots of black being.

Doug Layfield, Ed Navarro, and I organized a number of demonstrations—pegged to a petition we circulated on the PCC campus—in which hundreds of PCCers added their signatures to our stand against the tournament's blatant (and privately admitted) racism.

At the Queen's Ball, held as I recall at Pasadena's Civic Auditorium late in November, we paraded a hundred campus kids, all carrying signs. One sign, I remember, read, "Why *NOT* a Black Rose Queen?"

I'll admit it. We were naïve. Or, rather, the level of our social awareness was simply not yet sufficiently matured to understand that, insofar as the black community was concerned, we'd approached the whole issue of racism in Pasadena from the top down. What Pasadena's blacks really wanted were jobs and economic opportunity, not a black girl sitting up there on a Rose float. Economic equality—not social equality—was their first and most urgent need.

Top down though our approach had been, it got results. Two years later the tournament people quit their WASPish ways, broadening their queen-and-court selection. They threw the judging open to any high school or college girl in the whole area. That same year two of the Rose Parade's princesses were minority girls—Sylvia Peebles, the first black girl ever to be chosen princess; and Janice Lowe, a Japanese-American. Again, on New Year's Day, 1970, two minority coeds—Rebecca Patricia Gonzales, a Mexican-American, and Vicki Lynn Tsujimoto, from a Japanese-American background, rode down Colorado Boulevard as princesses.

The Vietnam teach-in of February, 1966, was something else again. It was a one-day affair, held in a Methodist church near the PCC campus (because at the very last moment PCC's conservative administration refused us permission to hold it on campus), and showed both sides of the issue.

Doug Layfield and I spent weeks lining up speakers. Finding vocal keynoters against U.S. participation in the Vietnam War wasn't our problem. Our problem was caging some hawks. While there were plenty of pro-Vietniks in those days (as any Gallup poll in 1965–66 plainly showed), few seemed eager to stand up before what figured to be a multitude of students and come out foursquare for war.

As teach-in day dawned, I somehow knew that no matter what our speakers might say, pro or con, we were going to shake up a sizable hunk of the PCC campus. And we did. During the teach-in's run of eleven hours, a crowd of upwards of six hundred people—all but about 150 of them students—jammed the place.

With a single effort we'd achieved singular results. We had reached and raised the political and moral awareness of fully 10 percent of PCC's entire student body.

Considerably greater effort went into our attempt to establish a chapter of the Students for a Democratic Society on the PCC campus.

At the outset, Doug and I toyed with the idea of starting a Du-Bois chapter on campus. But even in 1965, DuBois was far too radical, we concluded, for PCC's conservative majority. SDS, on the other hand, was still in those days pretty much—at least on its surface —what it had started out to be—a social democratic society of left- minded youth.

In fact, however, SDS had already turned the corner toward radicalism. The turning point had come during the 1965–66 school year when what amounted to a new generation of students (those just entering college midway through the decade) began to join SDS in droves. Completely missing was SDS's former clean-shaven look. Now it was the bearded look.

Internally, the change within SDS was even greater. Early the previous February, just after the U.S. began bombing North Vietnam cities, SDS had begun organizing for its first big-scale student march on the nation's capital. The march was scheduled for April, 1965. And for the first time SDS openly invited any and all who shared its anti-Vietnam views to join the march—including Communists.

LID (the League for Industrial Democracy), the socialist but democratic labor league from which SDS had sprung, blew its lid. Communists were not LID's bag. And, in particular, not Old Left Communists. What piqued SDS's LID sponsors was the obvious: philosophically, SDS was flying LID's coop. Politically, SDS had a leftist mind of its own, and it wasn't to LID's liking.

The League for Industrial Democracy's disenchantment with SDS was perhaps understandable. Ever since SDS's founding, LID had been the money behind the fledgling student organization. When SDS ran into a financial bind, LID paid the bills. From the beginning it had even paid the salary of SDS's elected national secretary. Moreover, it gave SDS rent-free space in its own New York City quarters.

For such favors, LID quite naturally expected some political respect from its offspring. But SDS, as alienated from LID as its members were from their own parents, told LID where it could go.

SDS's April, 1965, March on Washington drew 25,000 student marchers. But along the line SDS lost LID.

In truth, the Students for a Democratic Society no longer needed LID's financial support. Once anemic SDS had grown to more than 125 chapters on as many campuses. Its national membership roster stood at four thousand (but thousands more, who never paid dues, remained staunchly behind its banner). It had an annual budget of $60,000 from dues, advertising, literature sales, and contributions. SDS also had a new national office, newly removed to Chicago, with a dozen full-time staffers.

At SDS's national convention that June, delegates demonstrated their new independence. They voted to remove the long-ignored (but long-standing) Communist-exclusion clause from SDS's constitution.

The swing from social democracy to radicalism, and SDS's anti-imperialist bent, had begun.

All this, however, was scarcely visible either to the public or to the average campusite. Had you asked which one—DuBois or SDS—was then the more "radical," the vote would have gone almost unanimously to DuBois.

Yet the fact was that there was still no organized effort by the Old Left to make SDS its own. The Maoist-lined Progressive Labor party was already preparing to move into SDS, but not the Communist party/USA. The Party's leadership still scorned SDSers as a bunch of *bourgeois* radical kids.

Still, DuBoisers and SDSers often acted in concert—as on one spooky dead-of-night "sniping" (wall-sloganeering) expedition I joined. Three of us—myself, Ron Ridenour, a Party youth and later SDS leader at Cal State College, and a girl named Karan Koonan—set out, armed with aerosol sprays, to slogan the town red.

Aimlessly, we drove around most of the night. We scooted through alleys, circled blocks to make sure the coast was clear, and darted out of the car to spray giant slogans—"Peace and Jobs" and "End the Draft"—on building walls.

The U.S. Federal Courthouse, in downtown LA, was Ron's idea. It and the LA County Sheriff's headquarters, right across the street, were the heart of the Establishment. That's where Ron vowed to carry the "word" of the Movement.

"That's crazy. The place is crawling with cops," I balked. But Ron was driving and that's where we ended up—in front of the Fed building.

Ron parked, doused the lights, and we sat there in the dark, Karan on "lookout" in one direction, me watching the other. Suddenly, Ron was gone. When he got back all he said was, "Wait until tomorrow."

Next day's papers were splashed with Ron's slogans. The FBI was furious. The Establishment had been "attacked" and "taken" with paint guns. Furious, too, was the sheriff's department. Somehow, they'd got our license number. But to prosecute Ron would have blown my cover.

Even so, SDS was strictly hang-loose. Any group of five students

61

could simply apply to an SDS regional office (or direct to the national office in Chicago) for a charter. With a charter in hand the fun—and try for "affiliation"—started. To gain affiliation status on most campuses you've got to fight what amounts to "City Hall," which is, usually, the administration-dominated student government. Whether they call themselves the student council or the associated students or something else, they look into and approve or reject applications for campus affiliation.

The advantages of affiliation are many, not the least of them being an organization's privilege to use campus facilities—auditoriums, the cafeteria, or the student union—for meetings or functions. Unaffiliated, you end up an off-campus "orphan," an organization with no "kitchen," or even meeting privileges on campus.

One afternoon Doug and I went over to the regional SDS office, then located near the campus of the University of Southern California. When we said we wanted a charter to organize at PCC, the SDS staffer there gave us one of those "lots of luck" looks. Making the affiliation grade at PCC for a left-minded student society like SDS was the same as trying to raffle a case of Scotch at a meeting of the WCTU.

The short of it was we got the administrative runaround.

First, we made our case for SDS before the governing board that checked into campus clubs. They nixed us. Then we went over their heads to the executive board of Student Government. Here, we met some familiar faces. Many of the same students who had vetoed our club credentials also sat on the executive board of Student Government. So they ping-ponged us back to the club board. PCC's administration got into the act, too.

When we tried to bypass Student Government, and take SDS's case directly to the college's administration, everybody from president to deans had a pat answer.

"Well," we were told, "if the students don't want SDS on campus, we can't interfere."

Undaunted, we carried the fight for SDS directly to PCC's students through the campus's weekly newspaper, the *PCC Courier*.

By that time, SDS itself was almost a secondary issue. Primary was the basic right of any student organization that complies with the campus's organizational rules to be on campus.

I recall telling one of the Student Government stooges after he'd led a "no" vote against our SDS petition, that I didn't object so much to his voting "no" as to his reasons for doing so.

Bluntly I told him, "You voted 'no' simply because you don't agree with SDS policy, not because we don't have a perfect right to be on campus. We do. And you know it."

SDS just never made it on the PCC campus.

Although we hadn't been able to establish a chapter, I joined SDS then as a "national member." As a dues-paying ($5 a year) though unaffiliated member of SDS I had equal status with chapterites. I received SDS's official weekly newspaper, *New Left Notes,* and could attend its quarterly National Council and annual convention meetings.

In the spring of 1967 when the Southern California District of the Party ordered DuBoisers to infiltrate SDS I was, to my knowledge, the only Party member in the district who had only to look within himself to find SDS. I'd been an SDSer since 1965.

4. Eyewitness to Genocide

IN many ways, the second national convention of the W.E.B. Du-
Bois Clubs of America, convened in Chicago June 17–19, 1966—
which I attended both as a DuBois delegate (I still chaired the central Los Angeles club and sat on the governing Area Council) and as a
Party member (I was a member of the Party's Southern California
Youth Commission and would soon lead its Education Commission)
—mirrored the Movement as it was then and presaged what it would
become by the early seventies.

Slowly, but perceptibly, the tenor of protest, on campus and
off, had begun to change in the direction of radicalism and militancy.

The war in Vietnam was, perhaps, the paramount factor. By the
end of 1966. there would be nearly 400,000 American troops in southeast Asia. More than half of the U.S. budget—$58.3 billion—was
going to war. So were many more American youths. An average
30,000 young men were being drafted every month, with October's
46,200 call-up the highest for any month since Korea.

At Harvard, Defense Secretary Robert McNamara was jeered
(in part because the U.S. had begun bombing North Vietnamese
cities, in part because of the universities' now common practice of
supplying local draft boards with details of student academic standings
—making the universities an arm of the Selective Service System).

Inflation was spiraling. All across the nation housewives, fighting a
losing budgetary battle of their own, picketed supermarkets. War
costs and inflation had bogged down Lyndon Johnson's "Great Society"—which, as any freshman (high school or college) could see,
wasn't all that great.

Nearly one-fifth of the nation—more than thirty-four million

Americans, according to the government's own poverty index—was piss poor. In the South, one family in three was either "poor" or "near-poor," by the government's reckoning. Poor, too, was the progress in civil rights. What little advance had been made in the South toward school desegregation in the twelve years since the Supreme Court's 1954 ruling was more than offset by growing de facto segregation in the North. Johnson's 1966 Civil Rights bill died—due mostly to its open housing section and because, as a Gallup poll reported, 52 percent of Americans thought even integration's snail's pace too fast.

The forces of moderation, both inside and outside the student movement, were falling back before SNCC's angry demand for "Black Power" and the campuses' increasingly vehement cry of "Stop the War in Vietnam." Perceptibly, the militants were on the march.

I say "perceptibly" as one who witnessed the change from the inside—from not only inside the Movement but from inside its leadership.

If the average follower of the daily headlines was unaware of the Movement's changing stance, it was understandable. Most Movement members themselves were scarcely more aware of the new course on which the Movement was embarking.

The Movement, then as now, appeared to the casual observer as a bewildering proliferation of activism. Seemingly, the voices of change and protest had run through most of the alphabet, and might soon be plain out of letters, if not out of causes.

There was SNCC, CORE, RAM, PL, SDS, the RNA, MDS, MFDP, ERAP, MAC, the BPSD, US, the BSU, SWP, SPU, the BSA (definitely no relation to the Boy Scouts of America), the WRL, NSA, YSA, ISU—and no less than a hundred more.

Sorting them out (see "Who's Who in Campus Activism") was but a tiny first step toward understanding the reach, the scope, the contradictions, and the cohesion (or lack of it) which characterized the Movement. It was like two major rivers, flowing parallel, fed by an abundance of divergent tributaries, yet both moving toward a common goal—a basic social change in the American system.

One of these great mainstreams was predominantly black. It viewed social change in terms of racism, equal opportunities, and social justice for the black man in America. Its headwaters lay not only on the campus but in the black community as well.

The Movement's other great mainstream was predominantly white. Or, at least, non-black. While it agreed that all the evils of racism must be swept away before black America—thus America itself—could be truly free, its perspective was fundamentally non-black. It viewed social change in terms of the hypocrisy in the American social, economic, and political system. Its strength, and headwaters, lay primarily on the campus.

In so simplistic a first sorting out of the Movement, the alphabet of activism falls obviously—if not a bit uneasily—into place.

Within the black mainstream of the Movement are CORE (Congress of Racial Equality), SNCC (Student Nonviolent Coordinating Committee), the BSU (Black Student Union), the Black Panther party, the Urban League, the NAACP (National Association for the Advancement of Colored People), US (United Slaves), the MFDP (Mississippi Freedom Democratic Party), the BUS (Black United Students), BSA (Black Student Alliance), SAAS (Students Afro-American Society), and many more.

Within the Movement's non-black mainstream are arrayed most of the others—among them SDS, YSA (Young Socialist Alliance), NSA (National Student Association), the Yippies (Youth International Party), DCA (W.E.B. DuBois Clubs of America), SPU (Student Peace Union), the NEW MOBE (National Mobilization Committee to End the War in Vietnam), PLP (Progressive Labor Party), VDC (Vietnam Day Committee), SSOC (Southern Student Organizing Committee), and more.

Yet so gross a sorting of the Movement's mainstreams of activism tells you very little about the true composition and complexity of what most people caught up in the Movement have come to call "the struggle."

A second sorting, while likewise gross, differentiates activist organizations by the spectral breadth of their activism—whether *single or multi-issue* groups.

• The Vietnam Moratorium Committee (VMC), which organized and largely led the first nationwide Moratorium March of

67

October 15, 1969, and was staffed by youths formerly active in the ill-fated campaigns of Senator Eugene McCarthy and the late Robert Kennedy, had a single purpose—to call up Vietnam protesters, of whatever age, as the Movement's first public show of national strength.

• MDM—Movement for a Democratic Military—was founded by antiwar and antimilitarist U.S. Marines and sailors in 1969. It, too, had a single purpose—to protest the Vietnam War and the undemocratic structure of the U.S. military. Strictly military-oriented, MDM staged the first open demonstration by U.S. military personnel. It took the shape of a protest march, on December 14, 1969, to the gates of the Camp Pendleton Marine Base, one of the nation's largest Marine training and embarkation facilities, near Oceanside, California.

• Women's Liberation (WL), grown to ten thousand angry Movement feminists in the past few years, literally rose up to protest the "prone position" of women not only in the Movement, but in American society. "Sex is just a commodity," declared Roxanne Dunbar, of Boston, one of WL's leaders. In San Francisco, a group of angry WLers held an enterprising youth who was embarking on a quick-buck pornographic publishing venture for twelve hours while "indoctrinating" him in pornography's degradation of women.

In its first nationwide strike, called for August 26, 1970, Women's Lib mustered millions of feminist supporters demanding equal pay for equal work; the end of job discrimination; free, government-sponsored child-care centers (to free women from domestic servitude); and abortions, at no cost and whenever a woman decides she should have one.

• Catolicos por la Raza (Catholics for the People) likewise formed around a single issue—the Los Angeles Roman Catholic archdiocese's alleged unresponsiveness to the needs of the large Mexican-American sector of its faithful. Led by Oscar Acosta, a Mexican-American attorney, Catolicos por la Raza first pressed its demand for Church liberalization in "Chicano" (Mexican-American) affairs on Christmas Eve, 1969.

That night its mostly Catholic demonstrators interrupted the midnight mass at St. Basil's Catholic Church in Los Angeles, where James Francis Cardinal McIntyre, then head of the archdiocese, was presiding. It is significant that shortly after the demonstration, the Vatican retired Cardinal McIntyre and replaced him with a younger, more moderate prelate.

Characteristic of many single-issue protest organizations, these and others aspire to regional or nationwide activism and membership. All are organized around a single, focal issue. That is their beginning and end. They are single-issue and single-minded.

Hundreds of other single-issue groups are, if anything, even more limited in scope. They are tied not only to a solitary issue but to a single locale. They mushroom into being overnight, press their point, then disband or die.

Typically, the Student-Faculty Coalition Against Racism, at Brooklyn College, New York, sprang into existence with a single purpose, and one confined solely to the Brooklyn College campus—to force admission of more black and Puerto Rican students and the hiring of more minority faculty.

Berkeley's People's Park demonstrations, while they got national attention, were confined to the use, by "street people," of a small parcel of land belonging to the UC/Berkeley campus.

Many single-campus, single-issue groups begin—and end—as an "ad hoc committee"—a committee formed to deal with a specific on-campus grievance.

Thus, in March, 1970, the five black medical students among the UCLA School of Medicine's 448 "doctor-undergraduates," speaking in behalf of themselves and four other blacks in the school's premedical program, and backed by UCLA's Black Faculty and Staff Association, organized as a committee of nine. They demanded that the medical school admit more minority medical students, abolish a premedical program which the students insisted "brings minority students to the school as less than regularly enrolled students," and step up financial aid to those admitted.

Off campus, a local single-issue group may latch onto the auspices of a national single-issue organization to press a particular local issue.

In December, 1969, five Fort Dix, New Jersey, stockade GIs (who also were members of the American Servicemen's Union, an activist single-issue national organization working within the military services) filed suit in behalf of themselves and other Fort Dix stockade prisoners, demanding that the Army either abolish the stockade and its alleged abuses or make the reforms the GIs were seeking.

Multi-issue national organizations, by contrast, are "umbrella groups": They can and do concern themselves with any and all problems affecting youth, the campus, and the nation.

Among the largest of the multi-issue groups is SDS. Another, in its heyday, was the Southern Student Organizing Committee—the "SDS of the South" (see "Who's Who in Campus Activism"). The National Student Association (NSA) is another multi-issue organization. It addresses itself across the whole spectrum of student, national, and even international affairs.

Yet within so expansive and all-embracing an alphabet of activism, differences run wide and deep.

The BSU (Black Student Union), with Black Panther backing, trends toward hard militancy on black campus issues. SNCC (Student Nonviolent Coordinating Committee), by contrast, is less militant and is busier off campus than on. In sharper contrast are the Urban League, the NAACP, and SCLC (Southern Christian Leadership Conference, organized by the late Dr. Martin Luther King), which decry militancy, champion moderation, and have long pressed their demands through the courts or by nonviolent demonstrations. Typical was SCLC's Poor People's March on Washington in 1968.

Campus activists may, from time to time (and often simultaneously), work in three or four single-issue groups while holding membership and primary interest in a mass-action organization.

In all of Los Angeles, during late 1965 and early 1966, our DuBois clubs had, by actual count, only seventy-five hard-core members. Precisely thirty-four of them were also Party members. We could count on another two hundred activists, most of whom were not Party members. Still, with each of the seventy-five hard-core individuals involved at any one time in perhaps two, three, or more "actions" (most, in behalf of single-issue groups), those seventy-five activists looked to outsiders like a battalion when, in fact, they were scarcely a company.

Consider my own case. During the 1966–67 school year, I

marched on Washington, D.C., with the W.E.B. DuBois clubs, joined the anti-Dow sit-iners on the UCLA campus, backed the BSU in its campus demands, participated with the VDC (Vietnam Day Committee) on its Berkeley, California, antidraft march, worked with the PAC (Peace Action Council), and organized a weekend Marxist retreat for Party youth.

Only a deep insider—one who sits in the inner councils of leadership—can possibly piece together a true perspective of any particular group in the Movement—where it has been, where it is going, and how and by what routes it arrived where it is. Not even most members or even most convention delegates have this kind of insight.

Suppose that in June, 1966, you had arrived with me at Chicago's Coliseum (where, in 1969, SDS would hold its last convention as a viable entity). Let's say that here, at the DuBois clubs' second annual convention, you've stepped into my shoes. You are a voting delegate. As such, presumably you are in the "know." Soon enough, however, you discover that you are a virtual know-nothing.

So, like most delegates, you circulate around the convention floor, meeting old friends and making new ones. Immediately you notice a change in this year's delegates contrasted to those of a year earlier at the DB National Leadership Conference. The whole complexion of DuBois, you might say, has changed. Many more of 1966's delegates are black or brown. During conferences even the most casual conversation reveals a second difference. Many of these DB kids are high school drop-outs or, at the least, have gone—and expect to go—no further than high school. Within a single year the nearly lily-white, collegian composition of DuBois has changed markedly. Of the convention's one thousand delegates from across the nation, about two hundred are black. And fully 60 percent of the delegates are "working-class" kids.

The DuBois clubs, you might tell yourself, are *democratizing,* reaching out to youth of all economic, social, and racial strata.

Like the Chicago reporter who came to the very same conclusion in print, you'd have been less than half right.

DuBois had not "democratized." To the contrary, it had turned rigidly bureaucratic.

71

What that reporter and most delegates missed was the significance of three *visible* changes that had taken place.

First, a few weeks prior to the convention, DuBois club national headquarters had been moved from its founding city, San Francisco, to Chicago.

Secondly, the clubs' new stance on the Vietnam issue was a call for "negotiations now."

Finally, club membership and the editorial direction of DB publications—*Insurgent,* its monthly news magazine, and *Dimensions,* its theoretical journal, published occasionally—had shifted from their former emphasis on campus affairs to those more attuned to working-class youth.

A fundamental redirection had occurred inside the then dying DuBois clubs (for on March 2, 1966, U.S. Attorney General Nicholas Katzenbach had petitioned to have the W.E.B. DuBois clubs declared a Communist-front organization). Yet few convention delegates were even aware of DuBois' organizational about-face.

Neither were most delegates privy to the bloody doctrinal in-fighting which had wrought the changes. Had they been, they'd have known that the DB clubs had wholly capitulated to Communist party control.

The in-fighting between DuBois' campus-oriented leaders and those of the Party, prone to noncampus working-class youth, centered around two phrases descriptive of what DuBois' stand should be on the Vietnam War, and, ultimately, reflecting the whole future organizational outlook of DuBois itself.

DuBois' pro-collegian militants argued that DuBois' stance ought to be one advocating the immediate withdrawal—lock, stock, and missiles—of all U.S. troops from Vietnam. In 1966, that was militantly radical, even revolutionary. *It was the New Left outlook.*

The Party's pro-working-class perspective (in effect, its anti-campus, anti-intellectual persuasion) was far less militant. And for a number of reasons. Certainly one among them was the obvious: working-class youth were being employed in U.S. defense industries nourished by the Vietnam War. So the Party advocated a policy of "negotiations now!"—meaning that U.S. troops might remain in Vietnam (and, presumably, the Party's working-class youth at their war-factory workbenches) while negotiations went on. *"Negotiations now" was the Old Left outlook.*

The difference between immediate *withdrawal* (the campuses' stand) and *negotiations* (the Party's working-youth stand) might, to the uninitiated, seem merely a matter of semantics. In fact it was as night and day. One said "get out"; the other, "stay—and talk."

The issue split DuBois' leadership, though very few DuBois members even knew there was a debate going on, much less one that inevitably would change the whole course of the organization.

Reflecting the Party's view, DuBois president Hugh Fowler, and Mike Myerson, DB's international secretary, championed the Old Left's "negotiations now" line. Against them were arrayed the top collegiate leadership, including K. O. Hallinan, lawyer son of San Francisco's left-leaning attorney Vincent Hallinan.

Mike Myerson's siding with the Old Left pro-negotiation people was enough to baffle even an insider, and only proves a point: Among radical leftists, 2 plus 2 does not necessarily add up to 4. More likely, they add up to something like 3½.

Consider youthful, twenty-five-year-old Mike Myerson's unchar-acteristic Old Left position and his activist background:

A native of Washington, D.C., Myerson had grown up immersed in activism. He'd been a member of SLATE, the UC/Berkeley cam-pus's radical youth organization from which the free speech movement had taken some of its impetus. Myerson had organized against ROTC and led demonstrations against the House Un-American Activities Committee. In 1962, he'd headed the U.S. delegation to the Com-munist-dominated World Youth Festival at Helsinki. As a leader of the Ad Hoc Committee to End Discrimination, he had stage-managed the San Francisco Sheraton-Palace Hotel sit-in of March, 1964. At the time, Myerson charged that of the hotel's 550 employees, only thirty-three were black, and most of these held menial jobs. Myerson was also a founder of the DuBois clubs.

Then, in 1965, Mike Myerson had set out to become a kind of self-appointed ambassador to North Vietnam. In July, that year, at the Communist World Peace Conference, again in Helsinki, Mike made contact with North Vietnam delegates and arranged to visit Hanoi. And he did, in September, 1965, becoming one of the first Americans to do so.

Myerson returned to the U.S. in triumph. Ho Chi Minh himself had named Mike an "honorary nephew," and had given him some trinkets of his special affection—a Viet Cong cap (which Myerson habitually wore), a Viet Cong flag (carried by Mike in a number of demonstrations), and a ring purported to have been cast from metal melted from a U.S. fighter plane shot down over North Vietnam.

For all his close affection for Ho, you'd have thought Mike would champion the "withdrawal now" position. But Mike Myerson was first and last a Party man (and shortly would join the staff of the Party's International Publishers in New York). So Myerson, with hardly a blink, lined up with the Party's "negotiations now" position.

The schism in DB's top echelon grew so wide that Gus Hall himself flew out from New York for a secret meeting to settle things. The meeting, held in San Francisco at the DuBois national office, was a command performance. The Party's Southern California chairman, Dorothy Healey, was on hand. So were Paul Rosenstein, then head of the Southern District's youth, and Bob Duggan, chairman of UCLA's DuBois chapter and, by June, 1966, an elected member of the Party's National Committee.

Gus Hall not only settled things his way (in favor of the worker-youth "negotiation now" policy) but, having once set DuBois policy, decided to make it a habit. He spirited the national office back to Chicago to get it away from the "radical influence" of Berkeley, and to lodge it near the "working-class heart" of America. Overnight, DuBois publications and recruiting turned away from the campuses and toward working-class youth.

I had been an eyewitness to genocide. Bludgeoned by the Party's own bureaucratic hand, the DuBois clubs had been dealt a fatal blow, one from which they would never recover.

So DuBois' outward "democratization" at its Chicago national convention was wholly illusionary. It had, in fact, been "'de-mocra-tized" by the Party. Few, if any, delegates knew the real "inside" story, nor why so extraordinary a working-class orientation had come over DuBois. Even fewer Party youths on the West Coast knew of Gus

74

Hall's showdown flight to San Francisco. Dorothy Healey, Bob Duggan, and Paul Rosenstein knew. I knew. And so did the FBI.

At Chicago, husky, six-foot Franklin Alexander, twenty-five, became DuBois' new national chairman, and the first black youth elected to DB's top job.

Alexander was fated never to serve out his year-long term. In March and again in April, 1967, he was to find himself on the all-black campus of Texas Southern University, in Houston, during the months of unrest that preceded the TSU riot of May 16–17, 1967. Arrested for allegedly helping to fuel the flames, Alexander shortly found himself in jail—and, paradoxically, in trouble not only with Houston's police but with the Party's national New York leadership who had engineered his election to the DuBois chairmanship.

I knew the Alexanders—Franklin and vivacious Kendra, who would become his wife—from Party and DuBois work on the West Coast. Both were from Los Angeles. Later that same summer of 1966, Kendra and I were among seven top Southern California Party youths selected, by the national leadership, for two weeks of Marxist indoctrination at the Party's Lake Ellis, New York, summer camp.

I was always particularly fond of Kendra. Unlike some Party girls I'd met, she had made one unflinchable commitment with life: She knew she was a girl. About some of the others, I had my doubts. That was because so many Party girls had doubts about themselves.

The thing is, the typical Communist female runs to aggressiveness, in every confrontation save those with guys. Hand a Commie coed a packet of leaflets and assign her a place to pass them out, and she's the warmest thing under the noonday sun. But hand her a line under a full moon, and she's likely to turn coolly inactive. What's wrong isn't necessarily her guy, but what's going on deep down there inside the gal—a pitched battle with her own repressed femininity. Some Commie coeds aren't sure they are—or even want to be—girls. Eventually, they've got to come to grips with themselves and make a fundamental choice.

If you're of an analytical turn of mind, you tell yourself—as you size up one of the "undecideds"—that come the day she makes her big decision, you hope you'll be around to see how it comes out.

So, for a couple of months, you sort of stand off, watching her.

She looks female, dresses female, but she's all up-tight with inner aggressions and with the outward kind, too. If you watch carefully, and are attuned to this kind of thing, you can all but see her feminine and masculine chromosomes flailing away at one another.

Suddenly one day it happens. She shows up at a meeting with clipped, shorn hair. Somewhere, on a beauty shop's floor or in her own boudoir, she's left behind a couple of feet of locks—and also, her femininity. She's made her choice. Unspoken, though plainly announced, is her decision: From here on out she'll pursue an ever more masculine Party role.

That goes for some Party girls, but happily not for all. A year or so later, in Montreal, a Party girl and I slept out most of a week-long conference. I can't recall a word of ideology passing between us the whole time.

New Left women are of a different stripe. They're "liberated." What they've liberated themselves from are their mother's apron strings and also their mother's moral hypocrisy. They don't lie abed dreaming up confrontations. That's where they have them—as often, as long, and with whom they please.

But that summer of 1966 I put a lot more miles than women under me. I spent the whole time yo-yoing between Chicago, New York, Washington, and Los Angeles. Oddly, the string I was on was manipulated both by the Party and the Bureau (which, to encourage my conferencing and conventioneering, began then, as afterwards, paying $15 per diem while, officially, I was on Bureau business).

Early in the summer it was *Chicago* (and the DuBois national convention); then on to *New York City* (for the Party's eighteenth national convention—the first "open" convention it had held in seven years); then back to *Los Angeles* (where, as a member of the District's Youth Commission, I organized that Marxist study weekend down near the Mission San Juan Capistrano); on then to *Washington, D.C.* (for DuBois' "National Assembly of Youth for Jobs," which met on the grounds of the Washington Monument); up to *New York*'s Lake Ellis and the Party's two-week Marxist summer school; and, finally, the 2nd Socialist Scholars Conference, convened at the Hotel Commodore, in *New York City*.

Things were so breathless that summer I scarcely found time, in each city I visited, to check in briefly with the local Bureau agent.

My seemingly endless crisscrossing of the nation was neither as willy-nilly as it appeared, nor as nonchalant. I was seeing the inside of the Party and the Movement in action—and so I suppose, in part through me, was the Bureau. I was also getting a rare insight into the Bureau's penchant for playing the role of spoiler or participant rather than merely being the calculating observer.

The Bureau played spoiler in the summer of 1966 in the case of the "Dorothy Report." The "Dorothy" was Dorothy Healey, chairman of our Southern California District. The "Report" was a highly critical analysis of the failures of the Party and its top leadership—a critique Dorothy had delivered before the Southern California District convention, held just prior to June's national Party convention in New York.

Sounding more like a New Leftist than an Old, Dorothy had bluntly taken aim at the national leadership and blasted them as a bunch of old mossbacks "who follow every move of Soviet policy without criticism." Her put-down of the Party's floundering youth policy was even more critical—because, if anything, the problem was more critical. DuBois was going down the drain. Dorothy blamed the Party's leadership—meaning Gus Hall, and his heavy-handed control over the DuBois clubs.

Our convention's delegates liked the report, had it mimeographed and sent three hundred copies on to New York, suggesting that it be distributed to the national convention delegates. But when the Los Angeles delegation arrived for the convention—and I was one of them —the national office people took us aside and squashed the "Dorothy Report." Distributing it, we were told, would jeopardize Party unity. Reluctantly, Dorothy agreed that probably it would.

But unity within the Party has never been one of the FBI's aims. So the Bureau decided to do a little jeopardizing. Mainly, I suppose, the Bureau thought it a downright shame that Dorothy's best efforts weren't going to get the reading in Party circles they rightly deserved.

The Bureau ran off a couple of hundred copies, contrived a nice letter over Dorothy's faked signature—a letter informing the Party's leading lights that here was a report she'd made which she thought everybody might like to read—and mailed them to the Party's leadership across the country.

The Bureau's handiwork stirred a regular caldron of disunity within the leadership ranks. It also put Dorothy in a spot. Indignantly, she claimed it was all an FBI trick. Not many really believed her, except, of course, me.

The Party's by-invitation-only secret Marxist school that summer —to which about 180 of the Party's youths had been summoned— was the first of three intensive schools of its kind, each more selective, that I was to attend. (At the last—one of the Party's rare, three-month High Party Schools—there were just eighteen of us brought into New York from all over the country.) Popularity had nothing to do with the Party picking an individual. What did was the youth's potential for future Party leadership and his grasp of the more profound principles of Marxism.

We all met at the Party's Jefferson Bookstore, right off Union Square, in New York City, and went by chartered bus to the Party's summer camp on Lake Ellis, about two hours' ride north from the city.

It was a beautiful place consisting of approximately six hundred to eight hundred wooded acres, with a boat dock (but no boats) and a dozen buildings and cabins that had seen better days. The Party, I suppose, was putting its money into future leaders, not into past luxuries. To bring those 180 youths to camp—all but forty of them from such distant places as California, Texas, and Oregon—and to feed them could have cost the Party no less than $20,000.

The camp's teaching staff, which read like a roster of the Party hierarchy, measured up to its investment. One instructor was Hy Lumer, the Party's Educational Director, who also taught at the other national schools I was to attend. Lumer's specialty was the historical and philosophical approach to Marxism. Another was Betty Gannett, managing editor of the Party's theoretical journal, *Political Affairs,* who also taught theory. Danny Rubin, the Party's Organizational Secretary, taught, you might say, the "practical" side of communism: How to organize and agitate.

Of the school's 180 kids, about half were under twenty, and the rest ranged in age upwards to about twenty-six. Sixty were black or Puerto Rican kids, most from New York City, and few if any of them were either Party members or serious students. They had come expecting a couple of free fun weeks, not a nine-to-five discipline of study. By the second week most of them packed up and went home. I remember one New York kid complaining, "Hell, they've got a whole lake full of water here and not even a canoe."

What remained was what the Party should have limited the school to in the first place: forty to fifty hard-core New Left campus kids, most of them DuBoisers. After that we got down to serious study.

And that's when the fun really started. It began around noon one day, with the drumbeat of a helicopter's rotors.

"On the dock!" somebody yelled.

A helicopter had landed on our dock. What stepped out of the chopper was a reporter from one of the big New York daily papers and a photographer. But not for long. Although by that time our secret was already out, we still weren't welcoming the press.

All fifty of us beelined, yelling, for the dock. The reporter and his cameraman hopped back into their 'copter and roared off moments before we reached the dock. Had they not, we'd have pushed that 'copter right into Lake Ellis.

It wasn't our first "invasion." A photographer—from the New York *Daily News,* I think it was—had sneaked in through the woods a few days earlier. Somebody spotted him taking pictures and the whole camp just took out after the guy, chasing him through the woods like whooping Indians. We caught him, but didn't take his scalp—just his film. A day or so later the *Daily News* splashed its scoop—*SECRET COMMIE CAMP MEETING*—all over its front page. The Party's secret school was no longer secret.

After the 'copter incident, and especially following that *Daily News* story, the Party brought up walkie-talkies from the city and we formed a security guard. We assigned security shifts and guarded the place twenty-four hours a day. The biggest kick was "night patrol" when a guy and gal would team up for six hours alone in the woods.

The security patrol wasn't so much to guard against the press as against right-wing types who, on other occasions, had penetrated similar Party campouts and broken things up. And that's what all the security business ended up doing: breaking up any more serious study. Marx's "Negation of the Negation" theory isn't something you can comprehend blurry-eyed after a night of guard duty.

Right after camp I dropped in on the 2nd Socialist Scholars Conference, at New York's Commodore Hotel. Nearly two thousand of the nation's top socialist scholars, most of them university professors, were there. I counted only a handful of Party people, including Bettina Aptheker, her father (who was one of the speakers and heads the Party-sponsored American Institute of Marxist Study), and a couple of others. If anything, the conference was anti-Communist in the sense that many of the scholars looked down upon Communists as intellectually unsophisticated. The keynote speaker was Isaac Deutscher, a scholar and biographer of Trotsky who, with his white goatee, looked like the masquerade of the Old Bolshevik himself.

The biggest surprise was the arrival, uninvited, of a big contingent of New Left SDS kids. They took almost immediate exception to some of the scholars' scholarship, even telling some to their faces that the papers they had delivered were more praiseworthy for rhetoric than for research. In some instances the kids were more right than wrong. Those SDSers managed to turn the conference's final day into a miniature campus confrontation: New Left students versus their Old professors. It was as if those kids just couldn't wait for the opening of fall classes to begin stirring up the intellectual jungle.

On the plane back, I sat next to a kindly old lady who was making a flying pilgrimage to her grandchildren on the West Coast.

We fell to talking and I mentioned I'd been to a camp back east. Since I really didn't know how to phrase it—obviously, I was a bit old to be a junior camper—I said I'd been a camp instructor.

"One of those nice Boy Scout camps?" she inquired.

"Not exactly," I replied, and let it go at that.

5. The Demarcation

FALL, 1966, in many ways, was a clear-cut demarcation in my student and activist life. I graduated, so to speak, to the upper division in college, in politics, and under cover for the FBI.

That fall—shortly after my return from New York where I'd attended the Party's Lake Ellis Marxist school and also its eighteenth national convention—I transferred from Pasadena City College to the University of California's Los Angeles campus. Transferred, too, was my DuBois chairmanship.

I handed over leadership of the Central LA club and assumed leadership of UCLA's DuBois club, which I headed that fall. New, too, was my pad. Walter Crowe and Bill Shelby, who'd preceded me by a year to UCLA, suggested I join them. The three of us became roommates. We found an apartment on South Barrington Street in west Los Angeles, not far from the UCLA campus. I switched Party clubs, too, moving my membership to UCLA's Student Club which met off campus in various members' homes or apartments, including my own. At least our UCLA Party club didn't trifle with titles. It called itself a "student" club, which it was.

With the other Party clubs to which I belonged, we were always reorganizing, if only to change names. The Jose Martin Club had become the Eastside Club and then, facetiously (Party youth savor a pinch of humor with their Marx), we'd renamed it the "Workers and Peasants Club." In its entire membership there wasn't an honest-to-toiling worker, much less a peasant.

I also acquired a new FBI handler—Richard Bloiser. Fortyish but already balding, Dick had graduated from Ohio State and was one of the Bureau's photography specialists. He was also something of a

81

gun nut. While most agents contented themselves with carrying one gun, Dick packed two—his "extra" being a mean-looking .38 magnum.

It was Bloiser, as I recall, who, after scanning the first of my written reports to pass into his hands, said firmly, "We'll have no more of this."

What Bloiser objected to was my handwriting. Its legibility, however, wasn't what worried Dick. He was concerned about the security risk it represented, and especially my rising security status within the Movement and the Party. Ever-present was the danger that somehow one of my written reports might fall into the Party's hands.

"Should that happen," Dick said cryptically, "you wouldn't be long with us."

At the time I didn't know whether he meant I'd be fired from the Bureau for a breach of security or, more ominously, that he might be alluding to the possibility of foul play.

Bloiser meant neither. His justifiable concern was that if the Party acquired one of my handwritten reports, it might pass it to Soviet handwriting experts, in the Soviet's Washington Embassy or in Moscow itself. The USSR's crack handwriting experts would have scant trouble, given anything else I'd ever signed (my DuBois membership application, perhaps), in fingering me as an informer. Exposed, I'd be booted from membership. In the old Stalinist days it would have been worse.

"From now on, everything goes on tape," Bloiser ruled, and told me to go out, find a good but moderately priced tape recorder, and put the works on my Bureau expense account.

In time that tape recorder was to lead to one of the Bureau's more embarrassing foul-ups, and to the exposure, at the Bureau's own hand, of one of its longtime undercover operatives.

One day about a year after I'd started taping my reports, Ted A'Hern, who was my handler then, returned some of my tapes which the Bureau's clerical people had transcribed. One of the reels, I noticed, wasn't mine. I chucked the "orphan" into a drawer.

A few months later, when I got around to using that reel, and had run through a foot or so of its tape before beginning to record, I suddenly heard a woman's voice. That "orphan" tape, from *another* Bureau operative, had been returned to me unerased. Somewhere, I knew, I'd heard that voice before—but where?

Even though the lady operative hadn't signed off with her code name—as I always did with my "Wayne Dixon"—it wasn't difficult to narrow things down to three possible names. The three were the only ones mentioned in *each* of the tape's four reports. And by the Bureau's rules, an informant's own real name appears in each of his reports. Since her voice was familiar anyway, I knew exactly who she was.

If she'd been Mrs. Gus Hall herself I couldn't have been more shocked. I mean, she was that high up, that active, in Party affairs.

Next time I saw Ted I told him that the Bureau had a "problem" —that the Party's top people suspected someone of being an FBI fink. When he demanded to know who the person was, I named her. At first he played it cool. But the more I went on, telling how one Party leader after another had come to me, saying they suspected this particular gal, the more Ted sweated. I kept him on the stick like that a couple of weeks. I really hated to, because Ted was an all-right guy, but the game was just too much fun to quit.

Finally, I couldn't stand tormenting him any longer. At our next meeting in his car I took out the orphan tape, put it on my machine, and turned up the volume.

"You bastard," Ted exploded. If he'd been anyone but a real cool FBI number, he'd probably have told me where I could shove that tape. Instead, he took it with him. One thing you could say. The gal's cover had slipped, but lucky for her at the time only the Bureau and I had been watching.

My own cover, there in the fall of 1966, likewise needed some quick mending. The problem was my Bureau salary. While the $300 a month I was earning hardly made me a capitalist, it was more than most collegians earned. How could I explain it?

Between my weekly stint of half a dozen activist meetings—my Party club, UCLA's DuBois and SDS chapters, the DuBois Area Council, and the Party's Youth Commission in addition to participating in anti-Dow, Vietnam, and anti-ROTC demonstrations on campus;

the weekly meeting with my FBI handler, plus a full load of college work—I scarcely had time to breathe, let alone work.

But how could I explain my income? Outsiders, of course, wouldn't be apt to ask. But Walt and Bill, with whom I was splitting our apartment's $135 monthly rental, were sure to grow curious. A pat explanation like, "Oh, my folks are helping out," wouldn't work with them. Both knew my parents weren't. The "cover" I devised was logical enough. I said I was receiving a student loan.

Even so, money was always a problem. But of the three of us, Walt Crowe was the worst off financially. Parking cars on weekends, he earned barely $115 a month. It was all he had to live on.

One afternoon just after the semester started Walt came back to the apartment in a kind of a Marxist's seventh heaven.

"I found it!" he exclaimed, simply elated. "A twenty-nine-cent hamburger."

What Walt had actually found—in a little co-op grocery not far from our apartment—was "chopped meat," and at only twenty-nine cents a pound. Since we each came and went at odd hours, we usually provided and cooked our own lunches and dinners. For months after that Walt's diet consisted of nothing else but his bargain chopped meat, beans, eggs, and tortillas.

One day I happened to be in the co-op grocery and, for the first time, I noticed the twenty-nine-cent chopped meat Walt had been living on. I also noticed something he'd apparently missed: a little sign atop that bargain meat counter that read, "Dog Food."

For a whole week I didn't have the heart to tell him he was eating dog food. Besides, he was actually beginning to like the stuff. When, finally, I did tell him, he all but barked, but kept right on eating it, anyway. It was all he could afford.

For my part, I was growing no leaner despite my steady diet of politics. But I was becoming a bit more savvy. Better than any primer on "How to Play Politics" was the Poor People's Convention held in late September, 1966, at East Los Angeles Junior College.

What made the Poor People's Convention so instructive was the way it started and ended. It began as one thing—a formative new political force around which the minority poor could organize and gain political strength—and ended up as quite another—as both the birthplace of the Peace and Freedom party, and the first effort to bring all the factions of California's New Left together in political unity.

A year later, at Chicago's Palmer House, the Movement would attempt the same thing on a national scale at its tumultuous National Conference for New Politics.

Of that 1967 Labor Day weekend New Politics convention in Chicago, *Esquire* magazine's political editor, Dwight MacDonald, would later write, "It was the most futile, depressing and wackiest left-wing gathering I have attended, and my experience has been extensive. . . ."

Our Poor People's Convention might easily have fitted the same description.

What the New Left was attempting during 1966–67—but has still failed to accomplish by the early seventies—was to join the whole of the radical Left into a single force in national politics. The idea was to create a "third party." But by 1968's national election it had, in practice, become the "fourth party." This was because of the unexpected intrusion of George Wallace's American Independent party.

Whatever its position in the pecking order of American politics, the result was the Peace and Freedom party (PFP). Thus far, the PFP has come closest to doing what both our Poor People's Convention of 1966 and the 1967 National Conference for New Politics (NCNP) set about doing, but without either notable or lasting success.

All this, of course, occurred in what SDS refers to—with increasing derision—as its "participatory democracy" days. This was an era (roughly, 1960 until the Democratic National Convention of August, 1968) during which SDS, and even the then more radical elements of the New Left, still believed they could accomplish the changes they wanted in the American system through the ballot.

After Chicago, after Mayor Daley, after the machine politics of the Democratic party "establishment," the Movement as a whole no longer believed it could make its way through the democratic electoral process. "Participatory democracy"—SDS's creed whose very name suggested participation within the framework of the Establishment—was finally and for all times discarded. Dead was the New Left philosophy born of the early sixties. Far from participating in Establishment politics, or even trying to organize a regular political party of its own, the New Left (which even then was turning more and more Old Left) simply sat out the 1968 presidential election.

On campuses all across the country that election fall, the consensus was voiced with a single slogan: "The Young make love; the Old make obscene elections."

The Movement, in fact, threw its energies into active nonparticipation. It staged "Don't Get Out the Vote" campaigns, urging the electorate to forsake their franchise as a silent protest against Establishment power politics. The Movement's mounting activism had, on the record, forced Lyndon Johnson to take himself out of the race. There was simply nowhere in all America, except perhaps Spring Lick, Kentucky, where the President could speak without violent demonstrations and hecklers who threatened to drown out his Texas drawl. Nor did the President take lightly his Secret Service's concern that it was growing every day more difficult to provide for his physical security.

It was not without reason that the 1968–69 school year was—before spring, 1970's Cambodia/Kent State University uprising—the campuses' most violent, involving more than three hundred demonstrations and sit-ins, and upwards of forty-five hundred arrests.

From 1960's "Freedom Now!" the cry by 1966 had yielded to "Power Now!" By 1968—and especially after the fall political conventions—it was "Revolution Now!"

Columbia University went to the barricades on April 23, 1968, the same month that one thousand Oberlin College students struck (and dug a mass grave for the senior class on the administration building's front lawn). On May 19, Ohio University exploded. On election eve students staged a twenty-four-hour strike at North Texas State University, protesting police "harassment" of their "antielectioneering." Election results were still coming in when sit-ins struck City College of New York and the University of Wisconsin. On November 11, Kent State University—long a hotbed of SDS activity—began ten days of confrontation and violence.

What had come out of Chicago—in the Movement's view—wasn't new politics but no discernible change: a Hubert Humphrey versus a Dick Nixon. The candidates of America's youth—Gene McCarthy and Bob Kennedy—were dead, the one eliminated by backroom skullduggery, the other by a ballroom bullet. The Movement simply chose to deal itself out.

It dealt itself in only in those few states where either the Peace and Freedom, Freedom and Peace, or New Parties (all advocates of the "new politics") had managed to get on the ballot.

But even when it voted, the Movement didn't expect its particular "new politics" party to win, or even to come close. Rather, it worked to prevent it from losing too badly, and to make use of PFP in the struggle to raise the American social conscience.

Before the Chicago Democratic Convention, the Movement's rallying cry had been "Fight City Hall!" Afterwards, it was "Burn It Down!"

Understand the Movement's alienated evolution from electoral radicalism to no-vote revolution and you understand the eerie significance of the Poor People's Convention of September, 1966, and that of the National Conference for New Politics, one year later.

The former was the New Left's *first* attempt to play at Establishment politics. The latter was its *last* effort to do so.

Yet, paradoxically, the begetting of a political party hadn't even been on the agenda of our Poor People's Convention. It just happened that way. And here is how it evolved:

For a year or so various people in the New and Old Left, on campus and off, had been talking, often independently, about the New Politics and how they all ought to come together and form some kind of continuing body with cohesive political force. It was at the Poor People's Convention that they all finally got together. From that gathering emerged a steering committee and, eventually, the Peace and Freedom party.

The Poor People's Convention, as I've said, was actually held for an entirely different purpose: to bind the minority poor into a political force dedicated to minority and poor-people problems—jobs, better schools, a better break from society and for their draft-age kids who, without college deferments, were being cattle-boated off to the warfronts in droves.

It was the kind of thing both the Old Left and the New felt they had to participate in, and just about everybody did.

One of the convention's co-chairmen was Jim Berland, who

headed up the Party's youth, had until recently been UCLA's delegate to the important National Student Association (NSA) and was a big-man-on-campus where he was known as a Young Democrat, not as a young Communist. I'd first met Berland at that DuBois May Day picnic where we'd followed a trail of Left limericks to fun and prizes. Berland's genius was organizing. When you needed something organized, you needed Jim Berland.

His talent was never more in evidence than the following spring when the Peace and Freedom party was a going thing and Dr. Benjamin Spock was invited out to UCLA to speak at one of those huge campus convocations. Eight thousand students turned out to hear him.

But it was Jim who turned out at Los Angeles International Airport in a university-owned car to meet Spock. While Spock was in Los Angeles, Berland more or less had charge of him. I suppose the good doctor was appreciative for being assigned so congenial a keeper. I doubt he knew that Jim was a Party member or that the several cocktail parties Jim had arranged in his honor weren't in-gatherings of university people, but of Party and Peace and Freedomers.

The idea was to talk Dr. Spock into tossing his stethoscope into the political arena as candidate for President on the Peace and Freedom ticket. The Party backed Spock for President (although seldom loud enough for him to overhear), reasoning that the average voter who was against the Vietnam War would be more inclined to vote for Spock than for some way-out radical (such as Eldridge Cleaver, who eventually headed PFP's ticket). Spock declined his courtiers, but Berland, true to his word, had delivered his man within courting reach.

So when the Poor People's Convention was organized, Berland was asked to help put it together. Also playing a leading role was the Californians for Liberal Representation (CLR). The Party had a firm foothold there, too, because it was into the CLR and similar ultra-liberal democratic groups that Party members went during and after the McCarthy era. They still attended their weekly Party meetings, but they considered themselves "surface Democrats."

The Party itself participated because the convention fitted its concept of an "antimonopoly coalition"—the Party's belief that in the struggle for socialism you had first to start with a coalition of small capitalists, middle- and working-class people, and the poor. These people, united into some kind of third party or front, could be counted upon to struggle against the main enemy, monopoly capital or big business.

The Maoist-liners attended, too. Where the Party and the Maoists differed (other than the former siding with the Soviets and the latter with Mao) was in procedure. The Maoists—whether they were members of the Progressive Labor party or simply independent radicals—refused pointblank to work within capitalistic or electoral politics. To the Maoists, the future lay in the streets. The Party— adhering to the "gradual stage" theory of revolution through evolution —believed it lay at the polls. Philosophically, you might say, this put the Party and the Maoists poles apart. Still, no single group dominated the Poor People's Convention. SDS was there. So was SNCC. So were representatives from a dozen other New Left campus groups.

Right there was the trouble—the same kind of trouble which was to turn the National Conference for New Politics, a year later, into what even a Left-leaning national magazine called "The Freak-Out . . . at Chicago."

In the squabble for control of the convention the poor people plain didn't have a chance.

The convention was held over a long weekend. Friday's first session was jam-packed, and mostly by Mexican-Americans, blacks, and the honest-from-hunger poor who had come in the hopes of organizing to better their condition of life. There must have been three thousand people present. By Sunday, attendance had dwindled to six hundred, and few of them were the poor. In all the in-fighting among the convention's vocal Left organizers, the poor were simply left out of things. Disgusted, most of them gave up even trying—or attending —after the first couple of sessions.

I remember saying to myself, "I'm a New Leftist, but this sure as hell isn't what the New Left is supposed to be all about."

A few months later I was to see the New Left as, then in its days of political innocence, it was supposed to be. The place was the UC/ Berkeley campus. The setting: SDS's quarterly National Council (NC) Meeting, December 28–31, 1966.

It was my first National Council meeting, and I shook some of those SDS delegates to the depths of their youthful New Left souls.

I showed up as a declared, "open" Communist—and worse, as *the* representative of the Southern California District of the Communist party.

If I'd been a Russian bear, with a hammer in one paw and a sickle in the other, I couldn't have surprised some of those kids more.

"You've gotta be kidding," a dozen of them told me.

Some never did believe that I wasn't kidding. SDSers weren't buying communism then, or Communists, and certainly not the Old Left brand. Why, if I'd ever gotten up before a meeting of UCLA's (or any college's) SDS in those days, and spieled Party jargon such as "people's liberation," "U.S. imperialism," or "monopoly capitalism," I'd have been hooted (and probably booted) out the door.

Even the Party wasn't in favor of my going brazenly badged like that.

"Really, Bill," said Dorothy Healey, then the Party's district chairman. "I'm not sure that's a very good idea."

Correctly, Dorothy pointed out that the Party, as a matter of policy, wasn't buying any part of SDS. The Party thought some SDSers even then too radical and discouraged its youth from SDS involvements or ties because it was pushing its own youth organization —the DuBois clubs. Reluctantly, the Youth Commission elected me its convention representative. And mostly, I suppose, because it was buying representation at a bargain price of $15, which the Party voted me for expenses. With the FBI chipping in $100 or so more, I was off for Berkeley and one of the last NC meetings SDS could call its very own.

How I got there (by air), found a place to stay (SDS put conventioneers up in members' or sympathizers' homes), and how I rattled them a bit with my "double-badged" presence, wasn't as important as the profound insight I got into SDS and its haphazard structure which, in its own way, was even then a kind of organized anarchy.

There were three hundred delegates from perhaps two hundred campuses, and making the whole scene were only three Party youths, which demonstrates how "un-infiltrated" SDS was in those days. And of the three, only one—a coed from Washington State—was a voting delegate from her campus. The other Party member, besides myself, was Carl Bloice, the black reporter for *People's World* who, at the time, was also the DuBois clubs' National Education Director. Both were concealing their Party affiliations behind their badges: the Washington State coed behind her delegate's badge and Bloice, behind his press pass. I was the one and only "open" Communist. There were also about ten or twelve Maoist-leaning Progressive Labor party SDSers scattered throughout the delegates. But as yet they'd hardly made their presence felt within SDS.

The overriding presence—as I reported to the Bureau—was what I called "negative anarchy." The Bureau was hard put to understand what I meant at the time, just as it had, then, a hard time understanding SDS and the student movement.

SDS drove the Bureau crazy.

"Who is a member and who isn't?" my handlers were forever asking. "Who is a leader?"

"That," I used to tell them, "depends on how far the leaders press their leadership and how far their followers follow."

SDS's anarchy was plain "to hell with it, up your ass" anti-authoritarianism. The campuses' alienated hadn't rejected parental and campus authority simply to vote authoritarian leaders—or even organizational structure—over themselves. Just as they had rejected the structured society, they rejected structure within SDS. "Organized" was a dirty word to most SDSers. That it was revealed the strong anarchical trend which, from the beginning, made SDS not only loose as a goose but as unpredictable as clip-winged coot.

The attitude of many SDSers was, "If you've got something to say, and if I feel like listening, I will. And if I don't, I won't. But you're free to talk until your tongue falls out."

That was SDS's brand of anarchy. And once it was organized, which by 1968 it would be, it would become as antisocial as in 1966 it was unsocial.

To show you what I mean, sit in with me on one of that National Council meeting's big debates staged in UC/Berkeley's Student Union. But get the picture first. Here are three hundred SDS delegates, representatives from their campus chapters, arguing since 2 P.M. about what SDS's national policy ought to be on the draft. Now it's 8 P.M., six hours later, and the policy fight is still on. For one thing,

91

nobody is willing to give the chairman the authority to shut off debate. Besides, nobody really wants to vote on the issue because that might end the matter, and who wants to end it. And everybody knows that even if the vote should go against their point of view, they damned well don't have to abide by the vote—and probably won't.

On one side of the draft argument are the more anarchical of the lot who say, "Abolish the draft for all times—who needs it?" Opposing them are the less anarchical who say, "Abolish the draft now, but not necessarily for all times. Maybe in the future, say to fight fascism, as during World War II, the U.S. will need to draft men."

So the only big issue is over that head-of-a-pin phrase: "for all times."

Now the clock shows 8:15 P.M. and the chairman moves to the microphone.

"Ed Keating," he says, referring to the founder and publisher of *Ramparts* magazine, one of the resounding radical voices of the time, "has been in the audience since seven thirty, the time he was scheduled to address us. We invited him here and he was kind enough to come. I suggest we suspend debate on the draft issue and let Ed Keating speak."

From the far corner of the auditorium half a dozen SDSers chorus, "Screw Keating . . . screw the chairman!" From the opposite corner come further cries: "Debate it . . . debate it!"

Now Keating has risen from his seat and is walking up the aisle to the podium, speech in hand. But with "Screw Keating" and "Debate it" chorusing all over the place, he retreats to his seat.

And now the debate is on. No, not on the draft issue, which has been almost forgotten, but on whether to let Keating speak now, forty-five minutes late, or wait longer.

The debate over whether or not to let Keating speak goes on for twenty long minutes. It is hardly less heated than the draft issue itself. Somebody takes the microphone to say Keating has no damned right to break up an NC policy debate. Someone else blames the chairman for inviting Keating to speak at seven thirty when he should have known the draft issue would run far into the night. Somebody else says there ought to be more speakers and less debate. He is contradicted by another delegate who's for more debating and fewer speakers.

It is all but anticlimactic when, at last, Keating speaks. Had he been speaking on anarchy (he wasn't), he could well have pointed to that auditorium full of SDS delegates as an almost clinical example of organized chaos and abject rudeness.

When I reported this show of anarchy in detail, one of my baffled handlers asked, "I take it some of the delegates didn't like Mr. Keating?"

"Hell, no," I retorted. "They thought he was an all-right guy. A lot of them read *Ramparts,* which is more radical than even their own thinking, and swear by it. But they weren't about to submit to structure—the chairman or anybody else cutting off debate. If Keating took it as an insult, that was just tough."

Ironically, less than two months after the Keating debate, Ed Keating and his *Ramparts* magazine came close to getting me fired from the FBI.

What did it was a *Ramparts* story that shook U.S. internal security to its fragile roots. In its March, 1967, issue, *Ramparts* revealed that for fifteen years the U.S. Central Intelligence Agency had been secretly financing the nation's top student organization—the U.S. National Student Association (NSA).

And the CIA admitted it. The CIA claimed, however, that all it had really been doing (while picking up as much as 80 percent of NSA's annual $800,000 budget) was to aid NSA's participation in world youth conferences, most of which had previously been Communist-dominated. With CIA funds, NSA had been able to organize free-world youth conferences, free of Communist control. The CIA, through dummy foundations and some real live ones (including the Billy Graham Spanish-American crusade and the John Hay Whitney Trust for Charitable Purposes), had channeled its "contributions" not only to NSA but to other student organizations. One suspicion, later confirmed, involved the possibility that some U.S. student delegates attending international student conferences had been spying for the CIA.

But *Ramparts'* basic beef was that a government agency—particularly a cloak-and-dagger outfit—should intrude into campus affairs,

93

the weight of its money (up to $650,000 annually to NSA alone) enough to control policy of what, on its face, was a national, student-run and independent policy body. NSA (see "Who's Who in Campus Activism") sponsored hundreds of foreign trips, conducted a massive student exchange program, represented the U.S. campuses at international student meetings and annually held a National Student Congress. Some three hundred American colleges and universities were affiliated with NSA and elected campus representatives to help set NSA policy.

Ramparts' exposé came close to killing off the FBI's campus undercover operation and me along with it.

I remember meeting with Ted A'Hern, my FBI handler, in late February, 1967, just after the *Ramparts* story broke. We met at a little seventh floor hideaway restaurant in a bank building on Los Angeles' Wilshire Boulevard, and Ted immediately put it to me straight.

"I've got bad news," he said. "Johnson [meaning President Johnson] is raising all kinds of hell. The Bureau's been told to drop its student agents."

Ted said the Bureau would fight the decision right up to the White House and beyond—to the Congress, if necessary—rather than destroy its campus undercover network. At the very least the Bureau wanted to retain a few of its most valuable informers. My name was on the "retention" list.

Two years later I'd have said, "Cross my name off—I've been wanting out, anyway." But in early 1967, I hadn't yet reached that frame of mind. I didn't want out, and I told Ted so.

As Ted painted it, the picture was bleak. Lyndon Johnson was furious that the CIA had been caught meddling on the campuses. He had ruled that henceforth no CIA or FBI agent was to set foot on a campus except on routine business. Ted, for example, might still peruse UCLA's administrative files while running routine security checks. But he couldn't come on campus to see me (which he almost never did, anyway). In fact, the Bureau was to sever all connections with student informers.

The thing hung in the balance for a couple of weeks and then blew over. But almost until he left office, the "Johnson Rule" (as it was called in the underground) prevailed. The Bureau no longer permitted its agents to come on campus or to infiltrate student groups. Now, more than ever, the FBI's student undercover informers had to do what the Bureau itself could not.

If, before, I'd been one of the Bureau's eyes on campus and within the Movement, now I had to be both its eyes and ears.

6. Secret War for SDS

T HE worst-kept secret in the campus Movement was rooted in the spring of 1967.

It was then that the more progressive districts of the Communist party—notably those in New England, Wisconsin, Oregon, and Southern California—decided to infiltrate the Students for a Democratic Society.

Everybody—the FBI, Progressive Labor (which nearly a year earlier had begun to adopt SDS as its own), and certainly SDS's top leadership—knew about it. Most SDS members didn't. The majority of them still aren't aware of it today, now more than three years after the fact.

The decision, brewing for nearly a year in our Southern California District, came to a head one Saturday at a meeting of the Youth Commission on which I served as education chairman, as well as being a newly elected member of the Party's ruling forty-member District Committee.

Quietly, throughout that spring and summer, word was passed to Party youth in our district—many of them DuBoisers—to get interested in—and into—the SDS chapters on their campuses.

The "secret" order was—"get with it . . . get with SDS."

Was ours some kind of diabolical plot, the kind right-wingers are forever seeing beneath every bed and behind every closet door? Hardly. We weren't trying to outfox the FBI (I'd reported the decision to the Bureau within hours). We weren't even attempting to deceive SDS, even though it would be months before more than a handful of SDSers knew how or why or precisely when the CP had come onto their scene.

We were trying to keep the secret—with no great success as it soon became evident—from the Party's own mossback national New York hierarchy and, in particular, from Gus Hall, the Party's general secretary. Up to then and even afterwards Hall and his New York people would have no truck with SDS. They simply didn't trust the aims or already considerable achievements of the "new youth." Basically, moreover, Hall and his people were anti-intellectual. And, if nothing more, the Movement's youthful leaders were bright, intelligent, and very often the best students on their campuses.

Intellectualism had run like a current through the Movement from its beginning. Almost all of its moving voices—among them Carl Davidson (Penn State), Tom Hayden (Michigan), Greg Calvert and Carl Oglesby (both from Swarthmore), all top SDSers and most of them former SDS presidents—were, unashamedly and without apology to the Establishment, the Movement "elite."

While Old Guard adults—whether far-right Republicans or left-of-left Communists—were wont to chastise the "arrogant elite-ism" of the student vanguard's leadership, certainly the Establishment, from its own glass house, could ill afford to throw stones. Its own "elite" were plain to see: Bill Buckley, Ayn Rand, Sidney Hook, David Lawrence—and, in time, even Al Capp.

The Party's leaders were suspicious of intellectuals and intellectualism. Moreover, they vastly misjudged—because they could not comprehend it—the different youth grown up in the sixties.

These youths were simply not definable by any previous standard. It was as though they had skipped, in one jump, from puberty to manhood and womanhood, from childhood to adulthood.

This was precisely what Eric Hoffer, America's "muscular humanist," a best-selling author (*The True Believer, The Tempest of Our Time*) and a member of the National Commission on the Causes and Prevention of Violence, was to tell the McClellan Committee, then trying to unravel the student movement, in 1969.

"Senators," Hoffer declared, "I remember that the first thing that hit me . . . when I was there [during 1964's Berkeley demonstrations, which launched the Movement] . . . was that there are no more children in this world . . . no more children, no more childhood.

"You have men now. There was [another] time in history [as

today, on the campus] when there were no children. They didn't have children in the Middle Ages. They didn't know how to paint children. They painted dwarfs. Anybody in the Middle Ages who could walk and talk put on an apron and went to work. It was bad medicine to ask a man's age in the Middle Ages. Madame de Sévigné tells us that in Louis XIV's army the officers were fifteen years old. There wasn't one soldier older than eighteen in the whole army.

"Now," Hoffer concluded, "you have men [on your campuses] . . . shrewd people, intelligent people, and they want action."

Hall and the New York people still played SDSers off as a bunch of bourgeois radicals, kids toying with revolution. The Party's national leadership was correct on the first score, but dead wrong on the other.

Bourgeois most of SDS's members were, for sure. Most were from middle- to upper-middle-class backgrounds, and many came from wealthy homes. SDS had not pulled itself up out of the ghettos or grown from working-class neighborhoods. A surprising number of SDSers were the "privileged" protesting the very inequality of their own "privilege" which from birth, and in the name of "democratic equality," had handed them a silver, it not a golden, spoon.

But the Party's national leadership couldn't have been more wrong about the radical propensities of SDS's admittedly bourgeois youth.

SDS in the spring and summer of 1967 simply wasn't all that radical. It wouldn't trend toward radicalism for another six months. Not until SDS's traumatic National Council meeting at Indiana University the following December, to which I was a delegate, would its radical bent be obvious. By then, in late December, 1967, Progressive Labor's Maoist revolutionaries had been working within SDS for nearly a year and a half. And the Party by then, too, was fully, though belatedly, committed to shaping SDS to its own image as well.

But there in early 1967 most SDSers were as yet neither fully polarized against the system and its Establishment, nor had they fully lost faith in America. Most SDSers in 1967 would still have subscribed—as they would not by 1969—to SDS's founding precepts, laid down in 1962 as the preamble (italics are theirs) to SDS's constitution:

I LIVED INSIDE THE CAMPUS REVOLUTION

Students for a Democratic Society is an association of young people of the left. It seeks to create a sustained community of educational and political concern; one bringing together liberals and radicals, activists and scholars, students and faculty. It maintains a *vision* of a democratic society, where at all levels the people have control of the decisions which affect them and the resources on which they are dependent. It seeks a *relevance* through the continual focus on realities and on the programs necessary to effect change at the most basic levels of economic, political, and social organization. It feels the *urgency* to put forth a radical, democratic program whose methods embody the democratic vision.

Then, too, up to 1967, the Movement still believed that it would be what it called the "new working class"—even then being mass-produced on high school and college campuses—which eventually would bring about the changes it foresaw.

But the Party Old Guard, having grown out of the "old working class," could not buy SDS's concept of a new working class composed not of blue-collar types, but rather of the highly trained technicians, engineers, teachers, and managers being turned out on the universities' educational production lines to meet the needs of the "new capitalism" for an ever-higher level of college-trained "worker."

Both of these New Left precepts (though shortly they would be abandoned)—"participatory democracy," which decreed a kind of self-determination by each individual over those matters most directly affecting his life and happiness; and the "new working class," a university-trained new class of white-collar, even executive-type revolutionary, tutored to activism through high school and university— rejected the Old Left's very structure and power base.

The Old Left's structure was largely disciplined by "democratic centralism"—a doctrine which said that once a policy was established, all members were bound to abide by it. As for the Old Left's power base, it remained where traditionally it had always been: in the dwindling ranks of America's workers and toilers, few of whom had come within spitting distance of a campus, much less set foot in a college classroom.

To the Old Left, everything espoused by the New Left was alien

100

socialism. What SDS had devised in its faltering way was a made-in-America philosophy fashioned to meet a made-in-America problem: the deep-rooted alienation that great masses of American youth—most of them without any political motivation whatsoever—were feeling toward the society and the life style to which they'd been reared. Those who felt this alienation strongest, and were most articulate in explaining why they felt as they did, were the campuses' SDSers.

The turn off of the national Party's leadership to SDS was due partly to the generation gap (adults, notably the aging, led and dictated Party policy), partly to SDS's strictly on-campus habitat ("smart aleck" collegians weren't the Old Left's bag), partly to SDS's New Left philosophy (its very name being a slap at the Old Left), but mostly because SDSers were an economic and intellectual world removed from the sons and daughters of the working class to whom Hall and much of the national leadership were attuned.

Yet by the spring of 1967 the New York leadership's cherished DuBois clubs had fallen victim to a fatal malady: an overdose of Old Left top-down dogmatism. All the decisions were being made at the top, by the Party. The patient would rally enough, however, to be present at its own wake in the fall of 1967—the DuBois Club National Convention at Columbia University. Thereafter, no DuBois organization existed anywhere outside of New York City. And even these few clubs were politically as toothless as toads, and not even within jumping distance of the mainstream of campus politics.

One of the unholy ironies of the student movement was the death of the DuBois clubs by the Party's own hand in 1967.

That spring I helped administer Marxism's last rites in Southern California to the DuBois clubs I'd helped lead and shape. The same September I attended the DuBois' national funeral in New York City.

Well before that, however, DuBoisers in those more progressive Party areas I mentioned previously had been told to "get with SDS."

Our mission was urgent. The hang-loose Students for a Democratic Society, though it didn't realize it at the time, was about to get itself organized.

The organizer, who had moved quietly but persuasively into SDS's scene as early as 1966, was the Progressive Labor party, or

PL, as it has come to be called. PL was strictly from Mao. As such, it was extremist, aggressively militant, and unabashedly revolutionary. These were and remain the three planks of its activism, and PL is the very first to admit it.

The Party went into SDS hesitantly in a futile, belated attempt to save SDS from PL and from itself. We failed.

There's scarcely a scanner of headlines who isn't familiar with SDS. It's just as safe a bet that fewer than one in a thousand ever heard of PL.

Yet, by the time of SDS's June, 1969, National Convention in Chicago, SDS for most practical purposes *was* PL. What had done in SDS was Progressive Labor. Divided into more parts than Caesar's Gaul, SDS still squirmed enough at the "Chicago 7" trial and during the Moratorium Day demonstrations to look alive. But insiders knew what even SDS's own philosophical doctors hesitated to tell it: SDS was dying. At best, it had a year, at tops two, to live. SDS had been as mortally stricken by PL as the DuBois clubs had been by the Party.

What is PL?

Progressive Labor (launched as the Progressive Labor Movement, PLM, but after 1965 calling itself the Progressive Labor party, PLP) came into being only in 1961, and at about the same time that SDS itself was founded. PL's organizers were aggressive pro-Maoist revolutionaries who'd been expelled from the Communist Party/USA a year earlier—in 1960—for their "Albanian heresy." They had sided loudly and vociferously with pro-Peking Albania in its dispute with Moscow.

What PL had going for it was youth and revolutionary extremism.

As for youth, the oldest of its top leadership—among them Milton Rosen, William Epton, Fred Jerome, and the better known Mortimer Scheer—was forty. PL's average membership age was twenty-five.

As for its extremism, PL wasn't one to hide that, either. It didn't say that its brand of Marxism was "democratic socialism" or simply a bit "radical." It proclaimed not only its revolutionary fervor but also its revolutionary heroes: Mao, Che, Castro, and Ho. And roughly in that order.

102

Plainly and simply, PL was a home-grown brand of Chinese communism. This was not to say that PL was—or is—the errand boy of Peking. Rather, what PL brought to the radical Left were the *words* of Mao, the *guerrilla tactics* of Che, and the *national liberation* and *anti-imperialism* fervor of Castro and Ho.

If PL had been content to confine its revolutionary ardor to its own club meetings, its few thousand (some said less than seven hundred) hard-core members of 1966 would hardly have stirred a ripple in American society. Instead, PL took its brand of Marxist extremism to the campuses by way of the Students for a Democratic Society.

PL did so because as late as 1966 it still lacked what every Marxist party (and non-Marxist, too) must have: an official youth group. The Democratic party has its Young Democrats (YDs). The Republicans have their YRs (Young Republicans). PL, of course, wasn't casting its eyes in either of those directions, but rather to its leftist peers. Looking around, PL discovered that the CP had the DuBois clubs (established just one year before PL became, officially, the Progressive Labor party). The Trotskyite Socialist Workers party had its Young Socialist Alliance (YSA). Both of these leftist youth arms of their respective parties were on campus. But, as yet, PL wasn't. PL simply and straightforwardly decided that rather than go to all the bother of organizing a youth arm of its own it would adopt one already notably established: SDS.

Had you been reading *Commonweal* magazine in early 1966, you might have guessed that PL would, sooner rather than later, do just that. In a remarkably perceptive article in the magazine's February 4 issue that year, David McReynolds, field secretary of the War Resisters' League and an associate editor of the magazine *Liberation*, one of whose founders was Bayard Rustin, pondered PL's problem. McReynolds noted that PL's leadership was young, aggressive, and coldly disciplined in organizational technique.

In his article, McReynolds speculated on PL's obvious lack of kith or kin.

"PL," he wrote, a bit incredulously, "does not have an official youth group."

Nonetheless, he reported that if not an official relationship,

103

PL at least had friendly relations with the May 2nd Movement (M2M), a radical student group that had taken its name from the first anti-Vietnam rally it had sponsored—on May 2, 1964. But the fledgling M2M, as McReynolds hinted and as most readers between the lines may have surmised, was hardly the kind of campus connection the ambitious PLers ultimately had in mind.

A few months later PL did the predictable. It decided that the campus connection it *really* wanted was the Students for a Democratic Society. That summer of 1966, PLers began to "merge" into SDS. While it would be three years before they would remake SDS into their own Maoist image, Progressive Labor within a single year did irreparable damage: Effectively, it put an end to New Left philosophy.

Shortly after PL's decision that SDS would be *its* youth organization, the New Left philosophical well seemingly ran dry. SDS's bright young minds, which had conceived "participatory democracy" and the "new working class," simply abandoned their creativity—at least, in the New Left tradition (interestingly, SDS would say in 1967 that it had never officially adopted the "new working class" concept). For all practical and philosophical purpose, New Leftism no longer existed within a year after PL's merger into SDS.

In this book I will continue to talk about the New Left as though, as a philosophy, it still existed, if only to differentiate it from the others. But the poignant truth is that much that was New Left ceased being "New" and became increasingly "Old" and stringently Old Left Maoist with the coming of PL.

Gone was the Movement's purity and much of its idealistic innocence.

What developed after that, on the nation's campuses, was an all-out, chapter-to-chapter fight between Party-aligned SDSers and PL-aligned SDSers for control of the Students for a Democratic Society. For control lay not in SDS's Chicago national office, but on the campus—in SDS's then 140 chapters. Win the campus chapters, and you controlled SDS's thrice-yearly national council meetings and annual convention. Control them, and eventually you would control SDS's national office itself.

Thus, in SDS chapters coast-to-coast, the battle was on: PL

104

versus the Party. It was the Sino–Soviet war of ideology transplanted for the first time, though in miniature, to the American campus.

It was quite a spectacle. Yet the majority of SDSers of those days were not even aware that a battle was going on.

I suppose the most interested sideliner of all was the Bureau. Every now and then—although my Bureau reports summed up into a kind of play-by-play playback—Dick Bloiser, my handler, would ask, "And how goes the battle?"

The battle, as Dick knew, wasn't going well for SDS.

In New England, New York, Wisconsin, and other areas where the Party's youth had joined SDS's on-campus fight, the square-off was between tactical equals: Marxists fighting Marxists. But elsewhere, and particularly through the Midwest, the standoff usually developed between SDS's New Leftists and PL's Maoists. In direct, in-chapter confrontations like that the average SDSer, no matter how canny, didn't stand much of a chance.

It wasn't that SDS's entrenched PLers openly admitted they were fighting Progressive Labor's battle against what was really their own piece of the Movement, SDS. PL kids no more admitted their Progressive Labor membership than most Party youth within SDS admitted theirs. The thing was, the campus' SDSers were looking for answers—a way to achieve Student Power and eventually national power. SDSers, bluntly, were desperate for answers. They wanted fundamental changes in the society in which they lived but nothing they'd tried up to then had brought—or seemed soon to bring—the rightful and needful changes they demanded.

PL had the answers, by the bagful. PLers came to campus SDS meetings with everything figured out. And much of what they said made sense and won friends within SDS. The average chapter SDSer, a vocal champion of New Left philosophy, was understandably impressed when anybody had the self-confidence and certitude to stand up and say, "This is the way we ought to go. This is the way that gets results." Results were what the whole Movement was demanding, SDS the loudest of all.

What the average SDSer didn't realize was that the fellow who sounded so sure of himself was merely repeating policy statements he had been instructed to promulgate in a PL meeting the night before.

For, just as my Party club made policy and carried it nearly whole into the DuBois club I chaired, so did PLers—in their often secret campus meetings—formulate SDS policy and carry it just as ready-made into their SDS meetings. And if that didn't work, PL had other ways to wrest control of an SDS chapter. The wonder of it was that PLers never amounted, in all, to more than a handful of SDSers. Even on many campuses today, if you ask the average SDSer about PL, he's likely to shrug, "PL? It doesn't count for much in our chapter." Actually, insofar as policy, philosophy, and leadership go, PL nowadays counts for just about everything in SDS.

Let me show you how the unseen battle—Party SDSers versus PL SDSers—was waged on my own campus, UCLA. It was typical of what was happening all across the country.

In the fall of 1967, then almost a year and a half after PL's entry into SDS but only six months or so since Party youth had left the DuBois clubs in our areas to join SDS, things came to a head in UCLA's SDS chapter over the seemingly simple matter of "structure." The chapter didn't have any. Organizationally, it was as loose as a goose. That's how many SDSers wanted it. From SDS's outset, its New Leftists had fought against structure even within their own structure—SDS. They were antiauthoritarian at home, on campus, and even within the Movement. "Ad hoc" was their thing, which means more or less off the cuff and just going along. But every organization needs some structure, if only to call meetings to order. So, reluctantly, most UCLA SDSers agreed they'd have to get to structuring themselves.

But the chapter's PL faction, meeting in secret caucus, had already organized the chapter. PLers came to the meeting with this big, ready-made structure. If the PLers had had their way (and had not I and a few other Party people spoken up), they'd have won the chapter right then, in the third week of October, 1967, rather than when they eventually did in the spring of 1968.

PL's organization plan would, in effect, have structured PL into control of the chapter. It cleverly made the PL minority into a working majority. Of the chapter's thirty-five or so members, perhaps six were PLers, and another four or five, those who sided with PL. There

106

were four Party people, including myself, and I suppose another three or four who supported us. So, when you got down to a nose count, SDS independents numbered about fifteen, PL and its sympathizers perhaps ten or eleven, and the Party, eight or nine. Nose-for-nose, the PLers were a distinct minority. And the more so because we Party people sided with the independent majority, giving us what amounted to an approximate twenty-five to ten advantage.

PL's ready-made structure turned this statistical table upside down. Its plan was to break the chapter into four or five small committees, each of which would be virtually autonomous to make and proclaim policy in its own field of work. Now, at general chapter meetings, PL's strength was seldom more than one-third of the membership. But by segmenting SDS into bits and pieces, and in naming each piece's chairman—who inevitably would have been either a PLer or one of its sympathizers—PL almost certainly would have controlled the pieces and, in effect, the whole.

On such occasions, or when PL advanced its own particular brand of Marxism as the philosophical or tactical road for the chapter to follow, one of us among the Party people would rise in an attempt to explain to the chapter's independents what was really going on.

I'd never come right out and accuse a PLer of being a member of the Progressive Labor party. I'd simply say something like, "Well, the position that Jeff Jones is suggesting . . . which is also the Progressive Labor approach . . . simply isn't the right approach for SDS on the UCLA campus."

Afterward, a few SDS independents might come up and say, "I didn't know that was PL's line . . . or even that Jeff was a PLer."

It was like that, meeting after meeting, that whole fall and winter. Hep to politics as most SDSers were by 1968, many of them didn't recognize what was going on right under their noses and in their very own chapters between PL and the Party. So you could excuse them for missing the bigger, national picture, too. SDS's national brass, of course, knew the "big picture"—and, somber as it was, it might have been painted by Albert Pinkham Ryder. Greg Calvert, one of the New Left's most resonant voices, tried to purge Progressive Labor from SDS at the National Interim Committee meeting of October 15, 1968. By then, it was too late.

The stark truth was that nothing quite like Progressive Labor and its disciplined, tightly knit cadres of often bright, always ruthless collegians had ever shown up on campus before. That they hadn't was easily explained. There weren't any Maoist-Communist youths much before 1965, when PL reorganized and really got going.

Besides, PLers didn't look, feel, or breathe differently from any other radical youths on campus. They weren't little green monsters. Their hair-style was what everybody else was wearing. If anything, PL kids were cleaner-cut, smoked less pot (and often no pot at all), fooled around less, and didn't sleep around much at all. Compared to New Left kids, PLers were downright prudish. That was because Progressive Labor itself was Maoist Old Left prudish. When then seventy-two-year-old Chairman Mao swam those purported nine miles down the Yangtze in July, 1966, he was modestly attired in a swim suit (the typical New Leftist would have made that river swim bare ass).

To Chairman Mao that swim wasn't for fun but to prove his revolutionary fitness, even in old age. It was much the same with PL's campus kids. Revolution was their thing, and often the only thing in their lives.

I used to tell the Bureau that while the average SDSer was scheming how to take over a campus building, PLers were scheming how to take over the chapter. That was the difference.

But there was another sizable difference. Many PLers' "major" on campus was politics. Not, you understand, formal political study as taught by professors (PLers weren't figuring to join the ranks of Establishment politicians), but the pragmatic kind of politics taught in confrontation. SDS was, so to speak, their classroom.

Typically, they'd take just a couple of courses—enough to keep them on campus and in campus politics, but not enough to graduate any time soon.

By contrast, most SDSers, including its Party kids, were serious students who hoped, in time, to get a degree and to work within the system. To live under capitalism, they studied hard to prepare themselves for careers and professions.

PLers, on the other hand, didn't want nor expect to live under capitalism. They wanted nothing whatever to do with the system, least of all its employment opportunities. They wanted to overthrow it.

This helped to explain why PLers within a typical SDS chapter were its hardest workers. SDS was their major. Revolution was their future lifework. When things needed doing—say during finals—most SDSers begged off. Study came first. PLers, who generally weren't taking many courses, anyway, and for whom revolutionary politics always came first, were the ones who usually ended up doing the work. And those who work in an organization are those who lead.

Even so, SDS might have saved itself. Certainly UCLA's SDSers might have if they'd been aware they were dealing with a new breed of super-revolutionaries, and had the foresight to run the whole chapter through one of those quick-response tests the psychologists are forever giving. The PLers would have been unmasked instantly. Their reflex answers would have been straight from Mao.

Say "business" to a PL kid, and he'll snap back "exploitation"; say "black Americans," and he'll say, "a colony of black colonials within the American capitalistic system"; say "United States of America," and he'll retort, "world imperialist"; hit him with the word "radical" (the New Left kind) and he'll growl, "a phony right-winger"; say "revolutionary," and he'll say "liberator."

The most indoctrinated of PLers are like vending machines. Ask the right questions and you get back the same answers, every time. The thing is, your average vending machine doesn't believe in what it's vending. PLers did—and do.

That these words and phrases have become standard vocabulary among SDSers and the campuses' extremist leadership tells you how top-to-bottom has been PL's influence and indoctrination. For behind its catchwords lie Maoism's all-pervading revolutionary philosophy. By 1970 the philosophy of Maoism, as well as its vocabulary, would be the Movement's, too.

Not without reason did Red China and its Maoists let it be known as far back as 1967 that they recognized Progressive Labor as the only doctrinally correct Communist cadre in the United States. In fact, PL had become an extension of Peking—the first Maoism to grow up on U.S. soil. There is equal likelihood that Progressive Labor is as well financed from Peking as the Communist Party/USA is from Moscow (and it was hardly a secret in our Party club that, one way or another, Moscow was footing part of the Party's operating expenses).

Now, PLers didn't just march into our SDS chapter and take over. They moved in quietly, persuasively, often by ones and twos. How then, by 1968, were they able to control UCLA's chapter, and many like it all across the country?

One answer was stratagem. PLers never expected to be the majority, nor need they be, to control. They could split an SDS chapter into little pieces, and control the pieces. More often, they simply built allies on campus, both inside and outside of SDS. Inside, they were the consummate planners whose programs and confrontations generally worked. And success makes friends. Outside, they had close ties then with the more radical of BSUers—who preferred Marxism from non-Caucasian Peking rather than from lily-white Moscow. PLers were even able to convince Jewish SDSers that PL's pro-Arab, anti-Zionist, anti-Israel line was really anti-Establishment, not anti-Semitic. PL professed to be pro-Jewish "people" but anti-Israel "nation" (a government it saw as just another example of oppressive capitalism).

So to control an SDS chapter, PLers themselves never needed numerically to add up to a majority. It was enough if their influence, their alliances, their coalitions, and sympathizers did. That was PL's secret weapon in its secret war on SDS.

PL's take-over of UCLA's SDS chapter was typical of how it went, chapter by chapter, across the nation.

By the fall quarter, 1967, the chapter's PLers, in coalition with independents, were able to elect as chapter chairman an independent who was pro-PL.

The next quarter—winter, 1968—PL for the very first time managed to boost one of its own PL members to the chapter chairmanship. Thereafter, and right up to today, UCLA's SDS chapter was wholly PL controlled.

From early 1968 on the Party had virtually no influence within SDS. Party youths simply didn't have the "right politics." In SDS, the right politics were about as far to the left as the political spectrum went.

110

Beginning then, almost everything within SDS was Mao or Maoism.

Unlike many Party youths, I didn't quit the UCLA chapter. While, in effect, I'd been bound and gagged, I stayed mainly because the Bureau wanted me to remain an SDSer. Then, too, I knew my way around. Politically, I'd already demonstrated more than a little resiliency. Even though I had the "wrong politics," I managed—despite PL's growing influence—to get myself named the chapter's only voting delegate to SDS's National Council meeting at Indiana University, in late 1967.

In truth, PLers didn't attempt, even after they controlled the chapter, to drive out opponents. They needed all the warm bodies they could muster. But my effectiveness within the chapter gradually went into eclipse.

PL, of course, didn't invent this kind of power grabbing. It is plain power politics. All I'm saying is that SDS, the vanguard of the student movement, had never before had to deal with an internal political force as shrewd, as organized, and as ruthless as Progressive Labor. PL knew the ropes and pretty soon that's where it had SDS—on them.

I'd been on them myself during most of the previous summer, but PL wasn't to blame. The Party was. It'd gotten to where, come "vacation time," I usually found myself shuttling back and forth across the country to attend one conference, school, or convention after another. One summer I think I did the cross-country bit three times. For my trouble, I came closest to blowing my cover as an FBI informant.

One evening, after a DuBois Area Council meeting, four or five of us dropped by a west Los Angeles pie place for the usual: a second helping of politics. The conversation turned to finks. Suddenly, one of the girls said point-blank, "You know, Bill, someone was saying you might be a fink."

I gasped, inaudibly I hoped, and fought hard to get hold of myself.

"Really?" I asked. "And who said that?"

"Someone," she replied, mysteriously. "It's just, well, you know, you don't really work but you've got money. And you're always flying off to someplace or other."

111

"Listen," I rasped, turning mean and belligerent as the Bureau had said an informant must to save himself, "why doesn't the lying bastard confront me to my face?"

Then Walt Crowe, who was along, put in: "Yeah, Bill, I heard the same thing about you once when we were on the Pasadena campus."

Stunned, I sat there as Walt told of an SDS kid who'd reported seeing me park my motorbike on an Altadena side street, hop off and get into what the kid had described as "a blue, government-looking car."

That SDSer had had me dead to rights. He'd eyewitnessed one of my meetings with Wayne Shaw.

"That," I pooh-poohed, "was my step-dad's car. His old blue Chevy. He's an insurance salesman. I remember the place. I think he had an appointment near PCC one afternoon and just phoned, asking me to meet him. That's all there was to it."

And that's all there was to the encounter. It just blew over. I'd explained things to Walt's satisfaction. Having cleared that one, the other—the suspicion the gal had brought up—cleared itself.

But the incident explained why the Bureau, once it'd hiked my monthly pay to $225 plus $125 expenses, $350 in all, never went higher, though my handlers kept saying the Bureau really wanted to, providing I got a job to "cover" a pay raise. The Bureau wouldn't risk my security—paying more and my having to explain where the money came from. From Washington, the Bureau was forever needling my handlers, asking "when is Divale going to get himself a cover job?" But I never did. I had enough on which to live and get through school. And with the Bureau picking up the travel tabs, to keep criss-crossing the country as I was doing now like a filmland commuter. That "shuttle" summer of 1967 was no exception.

Right after school, in mid-June, I found myself one of a handful of Party youth from across the nation asked by the national Party leadership to come back to New York for its cram summer course. The school ran three weeks and it was held the same place as the summer before, on Lake Ellis, a hundred miles north of New York City. There were thirty-five people there this time, twenty-five of us students, with our average age about twenty-three. Altogether, we

112

represented a couple dozen colleges and universities, among them Harvard, Penn State, Wayne State, CCNY, Brooklyn College, Berkeley, and UCLA.

I think it was there that I came closest to being a Marxist emotionally and intellectually. But I also saw more clearly where my disagreements lay.

Things were different that summer. Security was tighter. Danny Rubin, the Party's organizational secretary, and Helen Winter, wife of Carl Winter, the editor of the Party's *Daily World,* were running things and they wanted to avoid the problems we'd had with the press the previous summer. Once there, we were told we couldn't leave.

I suppose, being always wary of finks, they figured somebody might sneak out and tip the FBI. What also was different was the plumbing; that year it wasn't working. Every day a couple of us would go into town for water and to do everybody's washing at a coin laundry.

One time or another just about everybody who was anybody in the national office, including Gus Hall himself, came up either to look in or lecture. Mike Zagarell, head of Party youth, and himself hardly more than a kid, was there. So was Henry Winston, the black national chairman of the Party; Claude Lightfoot, another top brass, and, of course, Hy Lumer, the Party's educational director and former editor of *Political Affairs,* the CP's theoretical journal.

With it all, things got off to a good old prudish Marxist bad start. I mean, Lightfoot got up and said there wasn't going to be any boozing this year, as he hinted there had been the previous summer. He said smoking was bad, too.

"When we get socialism," he promised, "we're going to pass laws forbidding people to smoke."

I just sat there and thought . . . crud. Here he's supposed to be a lawless revolutionary and he can't wait to get in so he can make some more laws.

Next up was Henry Winston and his thing was pot. Here he was saying that "drugs are the way capitalism corrupts youth." On the "outside" (outside the Party), I'd always been lectured just the opposite: that that's how Communists corrupt youth.

Then Mike Zagarell said his piece, which concerned guns and

113

how anybody who had brought one was obligated to turn it in at once. Nobody turned any in because nobody had brought weapons.

Finally, it was Danny Rubin's turn. His special pitch dealt with our mail and how we were either to write postcards or hand him our letters unsealed. He had appointed himself chief censor.

In the old days, Party youths wouldn't have stirred at malarkey like that. We damned near revolted. Before it was over we got back our beer rights and most of the other things, too.

I got back to Los Angeles in mid-July, but stayed only long enough to change my residence from the apartment to UCLA's co-op before heading back east again. The DuBois clubs' national convention (the last I would attend) was being held at Columbia University. En route Bill Shelby and I planned to stop off in Chicago for the National Conference for New Politics—that first great ingathering of the New Left. But we didn't make it. The drive-away car—a 1964 Nash Rambler—I was supposed to deliver to Rock Island, Illinois, gave up forty-five miles outside of Tees Nos Pas, a Navajo and Ute trading post in northeastern Arizona. We were way off the beaten path when the car just ran out of life.

"Well," I remember Bill grinning, as he tried to keep his cool in all that heat, "we're stuck smack-dab in what you came to see."

We were *there*, all right—way out in the middle of nowhere. However, for me, a future anthropologist, it was better than the archives of the Smithsonian. We'd taken that route to Chicago so we could stop off to poke around some Indian ruins near Mesa Verde National Park, which was about where we were. I'd gone the same way on a number of other cross-country occasions, combining Indians with ideology, and all in a single excursional package. But while there were plenty of ruins within driving distance, there was none within walking reach.

For a whole week, while a garageman flew in one part after another from Denver and the drive-away firm in Los Angeles took its time telegraphing money to bail us out of our mechanical jam, the only place we did much poking around was Cortez, which falls short of being the garden spot of Colorado. By the time we got to Chicago, the New Politics Conference had run its course.

So, too, as I was shortly to discover, had the DuBois clubs.

114

I'd no more than arrived at Columbia than I knew things were going to be different. Going into the convention hall, I ran into Danny Rubin, the Party's organizational secretary. In the audience that evening was the whole national hierarchy, even including Jim Jackson, the Party's international secretary.

The Party's adult top brass—having moved DuBois national headquarters again, this time from Chicago back to New York City —were finally doing openly what they'd been doing all along anyway: running the show.

I estimate there were three hundred delegates. They mirrored the astounding change that had come over DuBois since the Chicago convention of the previous year. There, it had already begun to look more like a conference of high schoolers and drop-outs than a meeting of campus youth. At Columbia, the transformation was complete.

Fewer than seventy-five of the three hundred delegates were students. About 150 were minority youths, perhaps fifty of these Puerto Ricans, the rest black kids. I don't think I heard the words "student" or "campus"—or really any ideas worth talking about—the whole time I was there. These were slum kids interested in the gut issues of the streets.

I was all for DuBois' keeping one foot in the community. But by that fall DuBois, nationally, had both feet in the community and not even a toehold on the campuses. It had completely lost its student base.

There wasn't even a fight over the elective offices. The Party had already picked who was going to win. A couple of people were nominated from the floor but they quickly rose to decline. *They* knew, even if the naïve delegate nominating them *didn't,* that the offices were already filled.

Right in the middle of the ordeal, one of the New York student delegates turned to me in plain disgust.

"What is this?" he asked. "What's everybody declining for? Either we have elections or we don't."

"We don't," I said dryly, and got the hell out of there.

DuBois was dead. The Party's hierarchy had been both its midwife and undertaker. But I was glad I'd returned for the funeral. An old friend had passed.

115

7. The Politics of Confrontation

O NE word in the lexicon of campus activism captured the manner and mood of the Movement in the fall of 1967. The word was "confrontation."

One Saturday in late October, thirty-five thousand marched on the Pentagon, burst through a cordon of troops and U.S. marshals, and briefly occupied a portion of the GHQ of U.S. military might. During that same "Stop the Draft Week," five thousand stormed the Oakland, California, Induction Center. And on Boston Common, scores burnt their draft cards to the cheers of four thousand youthful protesters. Three weeks later they hit New York's Hilton Hotel to disrupt a dinner of the Foreign Policy Association and its principal speaker, Secretary of State Dean Rusk.

Of the Pentagon protest, in which more than four hundred were arrested—among them author Norman Mailer—and scores injured, one of the Movement's best-read "underground" newspapers declared:

> It was a demonstration considered by many [in the Movement] to be an almost perfect example of the principle of active confrontation. . . .

Just as revealing was an incident in Oakland, California. There, as two thousand cops, outnumbered better than 2 to 1, flailed against waves of screaming protesters, a youthful leader of the confrontation took himself momentarily out of the action. Blood streaming from a billy-club gash in his forehead, he steadied himself in dazed euphoria. Blinking back blood, he scanned the scene triumphantly.

"Beautiful!" he exulted. "Simply beautiful!"

In the chemistry of confrontation, blood was an analeptic, sheer numbers a molecular bond, and those flailing cops the essential catalyst for success.

Much of the same kind of "beauty" on the campuses that fall was strictly from Dow.

Dow Chemical Company, compounder of nearly all the napalm "instant fire" used by U.S. forces in Vietnam, had become the campuses' Target No. 1. In a way, it was ironic. For, some of the very same students who so vehemently scourged Dow's napalm for its wanton taking of life used another of the company's products, Saran Wrap, for amorously preventing it. In lieu of the Pill or higher-priced prophylactics, the wrap worked almost as well.

At Harvard, Dow's visiting lab director, Dr. Frederick Leavitt, was held captive seven hours in a conference room by three hundred angry Harvardites.

At the University of Wisconsin, sixty-five students were injured and nine packed off to jail as police and twenty-five hundred campus protesters clashed over Dow's right to recruit for jobs on campus.

Everywhere, Dow was on the run—literally. Dow recruiters were chased off a dozen campuses, barricaded in recruiting centers, spat upon, and burned in effigy. The Movement converged on Dow's small Torrance, California, plant where most of the napalm was made, struck out at trucking firms that hauled the stuff from plant to embarkation ports, and lay siege to local Dow offices.

As Dow president Herbert D. Doan was to assess in November that year, ". . . it's a stinking, lousy, goddamn mess."

It was all that and much more. For the Dow demonstrations, wild-firing campus to campus, demonstrated the strategy and strength of the Movement. Until Dow, the Movement, testing its newly found radicalism, had fought with what one SDS national officer dryly called "words and phrases": "peace," "academic freedom," and the "multi-university."

Dow was something else. Dow was tangible. It had form and substance. As an outpost of the Establishment, Dow was vulnerable to isolation, to siege and attack. And Dow was here and now. Unlike remote Washington, distant Saigon, or the elusive CIA, Dow was not only visible but on campus. Its recruiters regularly visited the campuses, as did recruiters from other major corporations, to pick

118

likely graduates for future careers in Dow. So Dow was also flesh and blood.

Wrapped up in one package labeled "Dow" was a three-letter target that easily sloganized ("Dow—How?" "Dow—Now," "Dow —POW!") and readily symbolized both the military-industrial complex's influence and its dependence on the campus. And Dow made napalm whose grotesquely burnt victims, photographed in their last agony, were in themselves horrors of war.

Moreover, unlike ROTC, Dow had no campus connection. It was a mere visitor. Attack ROTC, and you were attacking fellow students who were ROTC members (and who, as was to happen by 1970, might even strike back). Attack Dow and you ran no such risks.

Dow became the Movement's first major tangible target. Almost overnight confrontation was significantly escalated from its era of mere "words and phrases."

Now campus militants could point to a Dow recruiter and say, "There goes Dow!" The conference room used by Dow recruiters for campus interviews became, by extension, "the Dow office." The cars of Dow recruiters were "the Dow fleet."

"Peace" couldn't be run off campus. Dow recruiters were. The "multi-university" doesn't deflate. The tires of the Dow fleet did. "Academic freedom" couldn't be barricaded and besieged. Dow offices were.

Paradoxically, the Dow demonstrations for the first time turned vocal the suspicions that long had troubled the mind of adult America. And well they might. For behind the anti-Dow demonstrations, indeed, lurked answers to many of the questions millions of Americans then —as now—were asking.

Were student confrontations part of a larger "plot" of university and national disruption? Was there a link between widely spread, seemingly spontaneous flare-ups, whether against Dow or other less tangible targets? Did confrontations "just happen"? Or were they planned, provoked, and manipulated? If so, who were the cunning manipulators?

I was one of the manipulators—and had been long before Dow. Nearly every march of protest and demonstration on the Pasadena City College campus during 1965–66 had a common hatching place: the house Doug Layfield and I shared on El Sereno Street. As DuBois club chairman at UCLA, and later as an SDS activist, I was among the planners of protest on the UCLA campus. Confrontation and its strategy were high on the agendas of nearly every national conference and convention I ever attended. Most of those conventions held workshops whose main business was "confrontation" and how to make it work.

No confrontation in which I ever participated was "spontaneous." None ever "just happened." Some were more intricately planned than others. And some were scarcely planned at all. But every one of them was planned.

Many were cunningly, even brutally contrived to shock, intimidate, and revile.

When two hundred revolutionaries seized five of Columbia University's buildings and occupied President Grayson Kirk's private office, even their wanton vandalism and desecrations were planned beforehand. Several SDSers had been assigned as "pissers." In brazen, premeditated contempt for Kirk, they dutifully did their duty: urinated in the president's wastebasket.

The strategy of confrontation, obviously, is no simple thing. Neither is confrontation any one thing. As a step above *petition* and nonviolent *protest,* confrontation's militant goals are seldom its visible targets and almost never what the headlines proclaim them to be.

I recall the first meeting on the Pasadena campus which, before it was over, laid the groundwork for our confrontations (mild as they were in those days) on the Black Rose Queen and Delano grape-strikers issues.

I'd opened that informal gathering, attended by no more than half a dozen of the campus's militants, with a question—"How can we get the PCC campus moving toward activism . . . toward a re-examination of its own life values?"

The obvious answer was to find issues around which to organize protests and demonstrations—issues calculated to prick the social conscience and eventually raise the social awareness of PCC's phlegmatic student body.

Eventually we found the issues: the Black Rose Queen, the draft,

120

and the grape-pickers' struggle. We felt deeply about these issues. But we might have felt as deeply about a dozen others we never raised or attacked—the campus bookstore's sky-high pricing in deference to off-campus book merchants, the curfew for coeds, or the catering service's rancid cafeteria fare.

Why the Black Rose Queen and not the price-gouging bookstore? Complex though our reasoning was, it came down to fundamentals. Wrapped in a single issue—the Black Rose Queen—were all the big issues of the Movement at the time: black equality, civil rights, women's liberation, and even the relevancy of PCC's educational priorities. "Making Queen" was more rewarding than making the academic Honors List. Then, too, it was an issue which, through its intimate ties with the annual Pasadena Tournament of Roses, had national attraction and was almost sure to get nationwide publicity.

Still, any issue might have done almost as well. The issue itself was never our target. The target was PCC's campus and its eight thousand socially unaware and politically lethargic undergraduates.

But confrontation's objectives go deeper.

Recently, in its special staff report, "The Politics of Protest," the Commission on the Causes and Prevention of Violence, after extensive interviews with Movement leaders, summed up the tactical reasons those who most often make confrontations gave for making them. Laid bare were confrontation's ultimate objectives:

1. *Confrontation arouses moderates to militancy.* Creating turmoil and disorder stimulates the otherwise quiescent to take more forceful action in their own behalf. Liberals may thus be persuaded to support radical demands even while opposing radical action. Extreme tactics also shock moderates to self-reexamination.

2. *Confrontation educates the public.* Direct action isn't intended to win particular reforms or to influence decision-makers. Rather, its purpose is to provoke a *repressive* response from authorities—a response rarely otherwise seen by most Americans. When confrontation evokes violent official response (as the slaying in May, 1970, of four Kent State University students by National Guardsmen), the uncommitted can see for themselves the true nature of the "system."

3. *Confrontation "liberates" and conditions radical youths for future and larger confrontations.* Confrontation is the radical recruit's

121

basic training. Much like the military recruit, he comes to the service of campus radicalism bringing with him all of his "civilian" and often middle-class mores. Like most middle-class youths, he is shocked by aggressive or violent behavior. His cultural fear of violence is psychologically damaging and, from the Movement's viewpoint, politically inhibiting. Confrontation provides the physical experience of opposing institutional power and "liberates" the recruit from his abhorrence of violence.

4. *Confrontation prepares young radicals for repression.* If and when the Movement seriously threatens the power structure, repression—by police-state measures—is inevitable. Development of the young radical's resistant attitudes toward police and authority is a necessary preparation for more serious resistance (revolution) in the future. Or, as one maker of confrontations summed it up, "Fascism is a real possibility in America. We don't intend to be either 'Jews' or 'good Germans.' "

Never once, you'll notice, was an "issue" even mentioned. Issues are not the serious stuff of confrontation.

Yet, while the confrontations I helped plan and participated in never "just happened," none could have happened at all had not the campus's mood and the level of its conscience been ready to accept and support them. Once the campus's ready-state was raised to the ignition point, *always* there was an "igniter"—something that made the confrontation take place.

How do confrontations happen? To see how, participate with me as an eyewitness in a classic among confrontations. The occasion is the second day of UCLA's anti-Dow demonstrations in the fall of 1967. The confrontation which "just happened" on November 14 that year is a textbook example of "what makes them go." For sheer drama it has few equals. Nor have any, I suspect, been more ingeniously or more "spontaneously" ignited.

We are among a crowd of angry, chanting students who, for an hour now, have milled outside UCLA's Job Placement Center.

Had you stood in this same crowd only yesterday you would be struck with the change of mood that twenty-four hours have made. Yesterday's protest was almost frivolous. One student had toted a sign asking, "Have You Tried Mint-Flavored Napalm Yet?" Another, a Pill-minded protester, had humorously tied napalm to the birth control issue. "Stop the Population Explosion—Stop Dow," his sign proclaimed.

But that was yesterday—Monday. Today it is Tuesday and the mood has visibly and audibly changed.

Now five hundred frenzied students, like hounds toying with their quarry, circle the university's Placement Center. They pick up the chant, "Dow Come Out."

Inside, a shaken Dow recruiter is holed up. He has locked himself in the job office's closet-sized coffee room. And he isn't about to come out.

"Dow COME OUT!" the crowd roars. "COME OUT!"

Repetitive, naked as a fist, the chant's anger and fury mounts. And so, too, the angry mood of the chanters.

A major confrontation is in the making. Still, the crowd hesitates. Heady though it is at the sound of its own power, it is at the same time unsure—though between its sound and fury and the quarry stands a puny restraint: only a door and a handful of campus police.

Missing to make it move, to unleash its hesitancy, is a single necessary ingredient: the spark to ignite it.

Suddenly, not simply a spark but a human torch arrives.

A student—bearded and in shirt sleeves—thrusts himself before the crowd. Slowly, matter-of-factly, he moves to the microphone that has been hastily set up.

The crowd thunders.

Ever so slowly the student begins to roll up his left sleeve.

"DOW COME OUT!" the crowd roars.

He takes from somewhere a grayish dab of stuff. He plants it on his bare arm and leans toward the microphone.

"I WANT YOU PEOPLE . . ." he shouts. And suddenly the chant dies in five hundred throats. It is as if each knows what is about to happen, yet in fact none but a handful really know.

"I want you people," the student with the dab of stuff on his bare arm bellows, "I want you to know, to smell how flesh smells when it's burned by Dow's napalm."

A gasp goes up here and there in the crowd.

Nonchalantly, the student strikes a match and ignites the dab of homemade napalm plastered to his arm. It flames up. A foot-high flame jets from his naked arm. He thrusts the arm, burning, toward the crowd so they can see it burning . . . so they can feel in themselves what he feels. The sick-sweet stench of seared human flesh wafts over the crowd. The student grimaces in pain, then smothers the flame.

"DOW OUT!" But now it is no longer a chant. It is a roar of unleashed anger. Suddenly, as one, thirty students bolt for the Placement Center door.

The confrontation is made.

Dramatic as that confrontation was, it was only one of a dozen major SDS-led "Dow Days" staged, almost simultaneously, on the nation's campuses during a single four-week period in October and November, 1967.

On October 26 alone, Dow "actions" flared on three major campuses: at the University of Illinois, where three hundred students, led by SDSers, staged a sit-in at the chemistry building; at the University of Minnesota, where fifteen students began a two-day anti-Dow fast; and at Harvard, where Dow's lab director was held captive those nine hours.

Was it all a "plot," intricately masterminded and centrally directed from SDS's Chicago national office?

If by "centrally directed" you mean on direct orders from SDS's national office or, in fact, on anybody's "order," the answer is "definitely no."

If by "masterminded" you mean the stage had been carefully set on SDS's national level for a contagion of "spontaneous" local confrontations with Dow, the answer is "most assuredly, yes."

The contradiction is easily explained by a contradiction: To its very dissolution, SDS was the most coordinated "uncoordinated" student organization in campus history. Uncoordinated though SDS was, its "uncoordination" was surprisingly sophisticated.

Within SDS were four principal means by which "national policy" bound its then nearly 250 chapters into a semblance of a coordinated whole.

124

First, there was the *national office* in Chicago. If nothing more, it gave SDS national character, and worked to implement policy laid down at the organization's four major annual meetings. The national office was the voice of SDS. And in the fall of 1967 the national office urged its chapters to target on Dow.

SDS's and the Movement's second tier of coordination was *communications*—the myriad Movement newspapers that championed, guided, and instructed the New Left's college and high school activists. SDS's weekly *New Left Notes* was a powerful and persuasive link between the national office and its chapters. As both pragmatist and theoretician, *New Left Notes* talked jargoned theory and jugular tactics. That fall it published a tactical primer on Dow.

Then there were the *"travelers."* A "traveler" was an SDS field organizer. Operating from SDS national and regional offices, travelers visited the campuses, huddled with SDS campus leaders, sat in on chapter meetings, helped organize campus actions, and "carried the word" to the activist hinterlands. The "word" that season was "Dow."

Finally, and in many respects the most "coordinating" of all, were SDS's *national and regional conferences.* The most important was the annual national convention, usually held in June. At these conferences policy for the coming months was hassled out, position papers read and voted on, and the whole tenor and direction of protest set. Conference workshops that fall had minutely dissected the ways and means by which Dow might be confronted at the chapter level.

I remember the UCLA chapter meeting when someone announced that Dow recruiters would shortly visit the campus. In half an hour's time we'd put together a rough plan of action. Dow would be confronted in its lair: the UCLA Job Placement Center.

Nobody asked, "Shall we confront Dow?" The sole question was how and when. The decision had all but been made in absentia by SDS's conferences, by *New Left Notes,* by campus "travelers" during their frequent visits and by national office pronouncements.

I doubt whether SDS's national officers were even aware of UCLA's "Dow Days" until, like everyone else, they read about them in their morning paper. No "orders" ever filtered down from Chicago. None were needed. Had the national office "ordered" the demonstration, the order might well have been flouted. Still fiercely independent, though never as independent as they believed, of like mind though they often denied it, local SDS chapters made war on Dow in their own way, in their own time, and on their own campuses. But the point is, they made it.

Bluntly, confrontation is the name of the game.

It is not insignificant that while the American public, as a whole, has turned hawkish toward the campuses, it has turned dovish on many of the issues championed by the campus protesters it now denounces.

Almost single-handedly, confrontation first polarized, then turned public opinion nearly 180 degrees against any full-scale, long-term American commitment in Vietnam (or, for that matter, in Laos or Thailand). It heavily influenced Lyndon Johnson's decision to abandon the Presidency. It caused adult America to begin a searching reappraisal of the society it had largely created and to question the basic values of its own life style. It thrust into the headlines, into the courts, and into American consciences the plight of black and brown Americans, the inequality of justice as dispensed to the poor, the national scourge of pollution and, on every level of learning, the questionable relevancy of the American educational system.

For military-aged but voteless youths, protest and confrontation are the sole rostrums from which they, who must do the fighting, can contest their own heedless sacrifice in distant and meaningless wars.

But it is unnecessary to defend youths' or anybody else's right to protest and to confront. It is a fundamental right of free men.

Regardless, youths' thrust toward a more relevant society has carried a price tag: violence. Violence—the Movement has contended —is the inevitable consequence as confrontation is raised from impotent petition to potent protest. Though many parents and educators and law enforcement groups would disagree, it is my contention that you cannot have effective protest without violence or the threat of violence.

Most Americans who today cry out loudest against the "violence" of the young forget too easily that when youth was nonviolent—in the Movement's civil rights era—there was terrible violence. Then the

126

mayhem that was done was levied in the South against youth who stood passively against the bullwhip, the gun, the mob, and the White Man's law. The South—almost everywhere—turned peaceful, non-violent protest into bloody confrontation.

Nonetheless, there is a significant difference between calculated, escalated confrontation—and anarchy. The first is the muscle of protest. The second utterly destroys it.

The proponents of these conflicting philosophies of confrontation collided on the University of Indiana campus at SDS's now legendary National Council (NC) meeting during Christmas vacation, 1967. I was there as UCLA's voting delegate.

Like a cancer victim who finally faces up to the evidence of his own X rays, SDS for the first time—there at Bloomington, Indiana—admitted it had a malignancy. The cancer was Progressive Labor and its "thoughts of Mao." By that Christmas, PLism had spread from the campus chapters to SDS's vitals. And so, too, had PL's revolutionary fever.

At Bloomington, PL for the first time had the numbers (nearly 25 percent of the four hundred delegates) it needed to contest openly SDS's national office leadership. What developed was a split along philosophical lines, something previously unheard of within SDS.

On one side stood the Maoists and their friends who declared that SDS must carry "the revolution" to the "community"—to the American working class—by establishing off-campus worker-student alliances.

Against them stood SDS's national office supporters, most of whom were neither Communists nor revolutionaries but rather, as they labeled themselves, "independent radicals."

"What revolution?" they demanded of the Maoists. SDS, they further insisted, should work solely within its own "community"— the campus.

PL, the minority, came close to being the majority in the voting. Incredibly, PL and its revolutionary Maoism had, in only a handful of months, gained respectability within SDS. It was winning the votes —if not yet the philosophical support—of campus kids who wouldn't know a Maoist if they saw one, much less Mao's little Red Book.

Vote after vote on future SDS policies and positions was breathlessly close. PL won none of them that time. But it had shown its hand and strength.

At Bloomington, too, PL boldly established an instrument of internal subversion within SDS: the Worker-Student Alliance, a caucus of PLers and their supporters. In time, the Alliance would reach for control of SDS and, in doing so, destroy it.

SDS's anti-Maoist leadership was terrified. The most up-tight of all was big Mike Klonsky. A staffer from SDS's Los Angeles regional office, Klonsky—come SDS's June convention—would be elected its 1968–69 national secretary, but only to preside over SDS's breakup.

I knew Klonsky well, as I did his brother, Fred, who only that October had launched SDS on the Los Angeles City College campus.

Everywhere at Bloomington, we anti-Maoists huddled to answer one question: "How do we beat PL?"

PL's threat wasn't its insistence on worker-student alliances nor, at the moment, even its Maoist ways. The threat was PL's all-or-nothing power grab. PL was perilously close to putting SDS in its pocket.

My own belief, shared by many anti-Maoists, was that PL could be beaten in open debate. Draw out PL and its straight-from-Peking Maoism was bound to show. Revealed, it would almost certainly doom PL to defeat. But we "debate them" advocates lost out.

SDS's leadership—with Klonsky in the vanguard—panicked. They decided that PL could only be beaten at its own game—by being "out-radicaled." Behind so seemingly desperate a decision was the obvious fact that PL's radicalism was winning supporters. The way to win them back, contended SDS's national office people, was to appeal to their radicalism by being more radical even than PL.

To pave the way for its headlong rush toward radicalism, SDS at Bloomington abruptly renounced its social democratic heritage and even its own founding statement of principles.

It was an astounding turn of events.

One delegate aligned to the Klonsky faction rose to declare, "SDS is today an organization of campus radicals."

Another denounced SDS's founding "Port Huron Statement" as "a social democratic document which no longer reflects SDS's radical-left nature . . . or intent."

Abjectly, SDS had made its commitment to radicalism. With far less hesitancy it would in time commit itself to lead the "second American revolution."

8. Up from Revolution

MARCH 12, 1968, was a day to remember.

That day Senator Gene McCarthy scored his New Hampshire primary upset over President Lyndon Johnson and headed, in political innocence, down the road to nowheres-ville. With equal innocence, the campuses joined his march to oblivion.

It wasn't McCarthy, the candidate, most youths championed. Rather, it was the cause he had come to symbolize: youth power and its moderate but muscular new role in electoral politics. Both the candidate and his cause would dead-end in disillusionment at Chicago. Thereafter, radicalism would rule the Movement.

One of the prime factors responsible for pushing its moderates toward radicalism was the televised image of a single rotund man, his pudgy fists directing his own chorus of self-acclaim: Mayor Richard Daley of Chicago. The sweaty image of the boss Democratic kingmaker in action proved to millions of watching youths what they had only vaguely suspected: not that the Movement's moderates had been so wrong, but that its radicals had been so right. The system seemed all but impregnable to evolutionary change.

That same day I dropped out of UCLA—but not, strictly speaking, out of school. The Party had chosen me—along with seventeen other "most promising" youths from across the nation—to attend the "Oxford" of U.S. Marxism: its ten-week High Party school in New York City.

It was a left-leaning "Rhodes" scholarship which, though awarded by the Party, in my case was funded largely by the Federal Bureau of Investigation and, ultimately, by *every* U.S. taxpayer.

I remember one day down in Greenwich Village (where the

131

school was in session) plunking coins into a cigarette machine. As the pack came sliding out, I murmured, "Thank you, Governor George Wallace." I figured *that* pack must have come out of ole George's income taxes. I can't remember ever smoking a pack slower, or enjoying it more.

Here he was preaching his gospel of racism around the country, red-necking from behind that bulletproof shield of his, and promising to preserve the good ole White Power Structure against the campus "radicals." And he'd even gone so far as to say that if he was elected, he'd run over the first "anarchist" who "lies down in front of my automobile." And now ole George had gone and bought a "campus radical" a pack. But he didn't buy my vote or get it that presidential year. Neither, for that matter, did the Communist party or Peace and Freedom candidates.

The comical thing was that the Bureau and the Party's Southern California District were at odds over my attending that High Party school, though the Party, of course, didn't realize the FBI had an almost equal interest in furthering my Marxist education.

The Bureau was elated when it learned of my being picked to matriculate in the Party's highest (and most elusive) school of Marxism.

Considerably less elated was the Party's own Southern California District. Dorothy Healey, its chairman, didn't even mention the possibility of my attending until a couple of weeks before the school was to start. When she did, she made almost certain I'd say no.

One Saturday morning, at a District Committee meeting, Dorothy took me aside. "By the way, Bill," she said casually, "do you want to go to the National School [as it was called in Party circles]? Helen Winter [a member of the Party's national secretariat] wrote, requesting that we send you."

For a moment I didn't know what to say. Obviously, I'd been the only one selected from the entire district. And High Party school wasn't something that came along every day.

The school I'd been tabbed to attend would be only the Party's third in nearly thirty years. But going would mean I'd have to drop out of UCLA for a quarter.

"Let me have a few days to think about it," I stalled. But Dorothy said, no, she'd have to know immediately.

I was on the spot. But so were Dorothy and the district. I'd have to make the decision strictly on my own. There wasn't time to consult the Bureau, much less go through channels to Washington.

As for Dorothy, she was on a spot of the Party's own making. What with the differences being what they were between herself and Gus Hall's New York bunch, and with Party national headquarters using its High Party school to indoctrinate and win away some of the Southern California District's most promising youth, Dorothy was hoping I'd say "no, thank you."

Instead, I said, "Okay . . . tell them I'll attend."

The result, you might say, was a joint venture, and proof that under cover, at least, capitalism and communism *can* work together. And often do.

The Party's Southern California District dug up $100 for my ticket (youth fare) to New York. Party national headquarters eventually came through with the return fare, plus a weekly spending stipend of $15 (the same as other High Party schoolers received), with housing provided, besides. The Bureau, for its share of the venture, chipped in $10 per diem for my living expenses ($700 for the seventy days I'd be in New York), another $150 for incidental travel, and my salary. By then, it was $225 a month.

Just before I left, Ted A'Hern met with me for a final briefing. He'd brought along $1,000 in cash, the only way I was ever paid. He also gave me the name and phone contact of the agent who would be my handler while I was in Manhattan.

"Here's the Bureau's share," Ted grinned, handing over nearly the whole ball of wax in advance. "The rest of it your Communist friends can ante up."

I arrived in New York, checked in at Party national headquarters (23 West 26th Street in Manhattan), and was assigned the family with whom I was to stay. The next day I met my fellow High Party schoolers at the Ukrainian settlement house in the East Village which was to be our classroom for nearly three months.

Of the eighteen of us brought in from all over the country, sixteen were "youths." About a third were from the campuses. The school's two other enrollees were older Party staff people.

Five of those High Party kids worked in SDS. Typical, I suppose, was Susanne T., a slender, dark-haired coed of about twenty-one from Rhode Island, who was an activist, though not a top leader, in her college's SDS chapter.

Susanne was cast in the SDS role preferred by the Party, which had never particularly sought—as did Progressive Labor—to push its youth into SDS leadership. For the Party, activism within SDS was enough. The Party continued to view SDS as a maverick at best, and unwieldy, organizationally, in the extreme.

Even with its own DuBois club all but dead, the Party chose not to pick up the pieces when, in 1969, SDS itself shattered. Instead, early in 1970, the Party launched a completely new youth organization of its own: the Young Workers Liberation League (YWLL). Nonetheless, the Party sometimes found itself thrust almost inadvertently into the high councils of SDS.

Mike Klonsky, SDS's maximum leader and 1968–69 national secretary, always considered himself "a communist" (the small "c" variety). But Communism with a big "C" also ran in Mike's family. His father, Bob Klonsky, was a Party member and sat on our Southern California District central committee.

Five other of my High Party schoolmates were DuBoisers, including twenty-two-year-old Rocque Ristorucci, a volatile, hard-lining Puerto Rican youth from New York City, who had been DuBois' educational director when Franklin Alexander was national secretary. DuBois' headquarters staff was also represented—in Jack Rady, a DuBois organizer. Of late, he'd been pressed into service as Gus Hall's personal chauffeur.

Three of my Party school chums were deeply involved in their labor unions. One was Juan Carlos Lopez, the Mexican-American youth from San Francisco against whom I refused to testify when, in September, 1969, the Department of Justice and Subversive Activities Control Board brought action to have Juan adjudged a "certified" Communist.

There was just one black militant: Kendra Alexander, one of the girls I'd "grown up" with in the Party on the West Coast.

134

Now she and Franklin, DuBois' former national chairman, lived in Chicago.

Backgrounding the school's rigorous nine to five thirty, five-day-a-week routine was a tragic death, a capitalisticlike investment, and a live-in experience.

The first was the assassination of Dr. Martin Luther King, Jr., during the first week in April. Black America had lost its Gandhi.

The second was the $12,000, or roughly $700 per student, the Party was spending for those ten weeks of schooling. I had come by my cost estimate firsthand. I had been the one selected to dole out the $15 weekly stipend given each student. That bit of largesse alone, over those ten weeks, added up to $2,750. As dispenser of the Party's dole, I was in a position to talk costs with Helen Winter, the school's director.

"We're spending a lot of money," she conceded, "but, in the long run, we think it'll be worth it."

The Party was gambling that from the eighteen of us would come "some dedicated people . . . and future Party leaders."

As for the live-in experience? It was the nearly three months I spent as the house guest of two of the Party's stalwarts: a well-known attorney and his wife. My host was an American attorney who acts for the Soviet Trading Company AMTORG, which handles Soviet-American trade. He, in turn, handled AMTORG contracts between the USSR and various U.S. companies. He and his wife made me feel completely at home, invited me to join them and their guests for dinner, gave me free run of their Manhattan apartment, and an open invitation to its well-stocked refrigerator.

I vowed then—against the FBI's insistence otherwise, for I was in weekly contact with my New York handler and twice met secretly with him—that I would never turn informer on people who had welcomed me, a stranger, into their home.

I have never violated that pledge. In truth, there was nothing to report. The relationship of my host with his Russian employer was the same as that between any lawyer and client. Only rarely did he or his wife mingle socially with AMTORG's Russian staff.

One of those rare evenings, however, did occur during my visit when an AMTORG official and his wife came to dinner. The Russian,

135

who had spent years in the Soviet Foreign Service, including a stint in England, was my host's legal-counterpart in AMTORG.

So, on my way home from High Party school that evening, I stopped by a little Jewish bakery. I told the lady who waited on me that "some Russians are coming to dinner" and asked if she had a dessert they might like.

Since it was almost Easter, she brought out some little holiday cakes. "Wonderful!" I exclaimed. Then I noticed their decorations. Spelled out atop each in white frosting was the Russian symbol meaning "Christ Is Risen."

"They won't do," I told her dismally, "*these* Russians are Communists."

Suddenly, I was seized by inspiration. I asked to borrow the little squeeze tube bakers use to decorate cakes, had it filled with red frosting, and set painstakingly to work. Over each little cake's "Christ Is Risen" symbol, I frosted a big, red hammer-and-sickle.

When my cakes were served after dinner that evening the place just came apart as I explained how I'd found the cakes and "communized" them.

"But really," the Soviet attorney said, still laughing, "we'd gladly have eaten the Christian ones, too."

Right there, I decided, was one difference between most Party people and the Communist McCoy. Our Russian guests weren't all uptight over dogma. Never, during that entire evening, did a word of politics creep into our conversation. By contrast, all Party people in America seem to devote most of their talk to politics and revolution.

I got back to Los Angeles the first week in June, and immediately headed for the beach. It wasn't sunshine I needed, but seclusion—a place where I could tape my Bureau reports. I spent an entire day at it. Transcribed, those tapes ran to nearly fifty pages.

The next day I looked up Walter Crowe. For some odd reason our conversation turned almost prophetically to Sirhan Sirhan, whom Walt had recently seen. It had been their first real get-together in nearly three years.

"He's completely changed," Walt reported. "We haven't anything in common any more."

136

Less than twenty-four hours later Robert Kennedy lay mortally wounded in the moment of his greatest political triumph—his sweep of the California presidential primary.

"My God, Walt, it was Sirhan!" I gasped the next morning when I got through to the county offices where Walt was a social worker. "Sirhan shot Bob Kennedy."

The news had just broken. Sirhan, though seized at the scene, gun in hand, had for hours refused to identify himself. Now his younger brother, Munir, had come forward to say that the youth they were holding was Sirhan.

For a long moment it was as if that phone had gone dead. Then Walt spoke a single word, "Why?"

It was a question the Bureau (whom I'd alerted, thinking Walt's insight on Sirhan might be helpful) and the Los Angeles Police were to ask Walt time and again during seven interrogations and, unbelievably, a lie detector test.

Personally, I've never believed the police were serious in their fragile attempt to link Walt, who had once belonged to the Party, and Sirhan, who had dabbled in Marxism, in an "assassination conspiracy." It was an act of police desperation in the frantic hours following Robert Kennedy's death.

It didn't help matters having Sirhan tell investigators that Walt was one of his closest friends. Sirhan, the angry, volatile loner, had no close friends. Less elusive, however, were his closest companions: hate and fear.

Sirhan was traumatized by the fear that his growing "Americanization" was robbing him of his cherished Arab accent. When he first joined the radical Organization of Arab Students at PCC, he was fearful of speaking out lest fellow Arabs take him for other than what he was—a Jordanian national. Proudly he declared, "I'm not an American." Still, he was afraid to return to Jordan, where his father lived.

His hatreds were equally ambiguous. Fiercely pro-Arab and anti-Israel, he hated Jews but regularly played Chinese checkers with an elderly Jewish neighbor. He called blacks "niggers" but admired the Black Muslims and, on occasion, read the Muslim newspaper,

137

Mohammed Speaks, even while openly scorning Mohammed's teachings.

Though born a Greek Orthodox Christian, he had taken up the mystic Rosicrucian cult, but filled his diary with Marxist ramblings. Sirhan's hatred for the rich was all-pervading. Still, the big thing in his life—even while managing to get himself fired from one job after another—was to make a million bucks.

Once at PCC, Sirhan stormed backstage after a guest speaker from Saudi Arabia had put down Nasser, whom Sirhan worshipped. Instead of berating the Saudi Arabian for his anti-Nasserism, Sirhan's attention had drifted to a couple of Arab students who were discussing the Koran. Sirhan burst suddenly into their conversation, cursing, "To hell with the Koran." There was no understanding Sirhan. But, then, Sirhan had never come close to understanding himself.

But why Robert Kennedy?

Better than any evidence revealed to date, Walt's own conversation with Sirhan, two weeks before the tragedy, provides some startling insight.

Walt had found Sirhan even more distraught than usual. Since March, when his aversion to taking orders had cost him his last job— as an errand boy for a Pasadena health food store—Sirhan had been doing absolutely nothing. He had simply been hanging around the house. Walt suggested that he get interested in something, if only "politics," meaning the radical campus kind.

"Naw," Sirhan replied, "I couldn't get involved in politics or anything like that halfway."

Others, Sirhan shrugged, might get their jollies just protesting. But not he. Bluntly, he told Walt if he ever "got political," got interested, say, in the anti-Vietnam movement, "I'd want to do the whole thing."

Sirhan's concept of the "whole thing" was organizing a guerrilla band, holing up in the mountains somewhere, and waging a shooting war against the Establishment.

In that, if nothing else, Sirhan seemed consistent. Back in junior high he and Walt had carried rival paper routes. They'd gotten into an argument one day. Sirhan challenged Walt to a fight. Since they

138

were both lean, short, the same age, and evenly matched, Walt suggested they wrestle.

"Are you kidding?" Sirhan snapped, and suggested they settle their differences "like the Americans and Russians do"—meaning for real and with guns.

But that day in May, 1968, Walt took Sirhan's "all or nothing" threat as merely Sirhan's excuse for doing what apparently he now did best—nothing at all.

When Sirhan—who hated Robert Kennedy because he was everything Sirhan wasn't and pro-Israel besides—finally decided to get "interested in politics," he didn't content himself with merely writing a letter of protest. He'd gone "the whole way." He'd borrowed a rare 8-shot, .22 caliber snub-nosed pistol. He'd loaded it with equally uncommon killers—mini-magnums, the most powerful ammunition made for a .22. Three of those eight bullets had struck their target: Robert Francis Kennedy.

As stricken was the Movement itself. Physically, it was exhausted by the fury of its 221 major demonstrations—Columbia's siege included—that had struck 101 colleges and universities during 1968's first six months. Emotionally, it was prostrated by the stark and repressive events of history. Cut down by bullets or ballots in a span of four short months were its champions of moderation: King, Kennedy, McCarthy, and McGovern.

More ominous were the savage put-down by the Soviets of the Czech youths' modest demands for a breath of freedom; the brutal repression of West Berlin's young who, like their American counterparts, were demanding changes not simply in education but in society itself; and, finally, the bloody "battle for Paris" which, at its conclusion, once more relegated youth to what de Gaulle bluntly called "its proper place"—voiceless, powerless oblivion.

The Movement, in pained reappraisal, looked to its own image in the fall of 1968 and was forced to agree with the judgment of John R. Seeley, dean of the Center for the Study of Democratic Institutions.

"The young," Dr. Seeley concluded in a special report to *Encyclopaedia Britannica,* "have succeeded to the title of 'public enemy number one.' "

For all these reasons, Montreal's "Hemisphere Conference to End the War in Vietnam," held over Thanksgiving weekend, was a milestone in the Movement's march toward militancy.

Like our Poor People's Convention of 1966, the Hemisphere Conference of 1968—attended by well over two thousand delegates from North and South America—began and ended as two different things.

It began as a stage-managed show of hemispheric solidarity for "peace"—as defined by its sponsors, the Canadian and U.S. Communist parties. As such, the conference was to be a rubber-stamp affair. After the usual speeches, applause, and resolutions, everybody would acclaim their solidarity for "peace" and depart for home. Behind them they would leave what the conference was all about: a declaration of hemispheric support for North Vietnamese and Viet Cong negotiators who, if agreement could be reached on the size and shape of the Paris "peace" table, might yet sit down with Averell Harriman, the U.S.'s chief negotiator. North Vietnamese and Viet Cong officials were to be flown to Montreal from Paris and Hanoi as the conference's special guests.

What actually ensued more resembled a riot.

At Montreal, the conference's Old Left sponsors were to be shoved rudely aside by militant New Leftists. A Black Panther would commandeer the microphone and accuse the astounded delegates—some, from South America, as dark-skinned as the Panthers themselves—of "racism."

Panther boss Bobby Seale, flanked by a retinue of bodyguards, was to emerge the conference's leader and moving force. Blatantly, from the podium, he would call for armed revolution. And, toward the end, the conference would literally go up in smoke as scores of draft cards were burned—all with the smiling approval of the visitors from Hanoi.

The Party old guard had permitted one mistake to mar their otherwise flawless plan for tranquillity and moderation at any price. They'd invited the New Left's militant revolutionaries: the Panthers, SDS's Maoists, and the equally maverick Third World Liberation Front.

Five hundred strong, the militants had descended on the conference. On its second day they physically stormed the rostrum and brashly took over. After that, "peace" was trampled underfoot.

Clear to those of us who watched was the future course of the Movement. Whatever the wishes of the campuses' New Left moderate majority, they were foredoomed—organizationally—to fall before the militants. Campus kids could scarcely be expected to do what the far cagier Old Left itself had failed to do—cope with the activist likes of the New Left's revolutionary "crazies."

Flying back from Montreal (where I'd been UCLA's only SDS representative), I doodled three words: "moderate," "radical," and "revolutionary."

Over Chicago I inked out "moderate." Before Denver, I'd scratched out "radical." What remained was "revolutionary." It described then, as now, the Movement's activist leadership. Visibly widening was the ideological gap between the Movement's many and its revolutionary few. An organizational breakdown between leaders and followers was plainly in sight. It would come six months later, at Chicago, with the dissolution of SDS.

Yet, as Rev. Donald P. Merrifield, S.J., president of Loyola University, would analyze in early 1970, the "campus revolution," with or without organizational structure, was not about to just fade away.

Dr. Merrifield called "false security" the older generation's hopes that most collegians, given time and maturity, would "come around to the Establishment point of view."

Quite the contrary seemed far more likely.

For many students on American campuses there could be no "return" to the Establishment view because, since young adulthood, they had never subscribed to it nor felt a part of it. But neither were they yet committed to radicalism or prone, as Dr. Merrifield said, "to becoming rock-throwing revolutionaries."

Rather, they teetered undecided and uncommitted.

"They are moderates . . . who could go either way," concluded Merrifield, a Jesuit educator with a sure feel for the mood of the campus.

How they "go" could decide, as well, the direction of the nation.

9. Breakup

I WANTED out.

I felt dirty inside. For more than four years I'd been living a lie. I'd slept with the Movement, taken to my bed its most fervent philosophy and some of its most passionate women, and when the encounters were concluded, I had been guilty of betrayal. Like an addict going for the needle, I had reached for the Bureau's tape recorder, inserted one of the Bureau's tapes and told all. It was as tawdry as an errant husband recounting the details of an affair just concluded with his mistress, five minutes after sneaking home and climbing into his own connubial bed. My mistress—the Movement—had become my wife. I was wedded to it spiritually and psychologically. I wanted a divorce—from the FBI.

Our breakup had begun the previous fall at the start of my senior year at UCLA. Sometime during that fall quarter I had told Ted A'Hern, my handler, that this would be my final year. At graduation, the following June, I was quitting. I wanted to break clean, cut my ties with the Bureau as casually as they had begun, and simply lay our relationship to rest.

Subtly, Ted had tried to dissuade me. "We were thinking," he'd say, "that when you went on to graduate school you'd want to continue."

But my own turn of mind as to where America and the Movement were and where both were headed—our clandestine meetings now had become verbal jousts—had apparently convinced him. Word that I would quit after graduation had filtered through channels to J. Edgar Hoover's headquarters in Washington; to the Attorney General; to the Department of Justice.

One day, in mid-January, Ted remarked casually, "A fellow from

Justice wants to talk with you. He'll be in town in a week or so and I'd like to set up a meeting."

We met downtown, near McArthur Park. It was raining when I parked at the place Ted had suggested. A few minutes later Ted drove by with a passenger beside him and parked farther down the block. I got out and walked to the car.

"This is Bob Crandall of the Department of Justice," Ted said, introducing his companion. "Why don't you sit in here with Bob and I'll wait in your car?" So I slipped into the car beside Crandall and Ted went to sit in mine.

A'Hern was still maintaining the fiction of interagency independence which, outwardly at least, exists between the Bureau and the Justice Department. By the rules of this easy arrangement, Justice is Justice and Bureau is Bureau, and never the twain shall meet—openly. No one from Justice supposedly sits in on an FBI interview. Nor vice versa. Of course, once Crandall and I had chatted, A'Hern and I would sit down to recap, word for word, what had been said.

The game, silly on its face, was in the case of A'Hern and Crandall just a bit ludicrous. Ted and Bob were long-time friends. Both had graduated from the same FBI class. For the first few years Crandall had been an FBI agent himself. But while Ted had continued to carry his attaché case and pack his pistol, Crandall had gone back to the law—on the Department of Justice's legal staff.

Now Robert A. Crandall was one of Justice's top legal guns. Fiftyish, with thinning gray hair and a developing bureaucratic pouch, Crandall's jowls and a hint of buck teeth made him look a bit like a worried chipmunk. But there in the car he came to the point more like a ferret.

"Would you be interested in testifying?" he asked, and quickly outlined what he had in mind.

The Attorney General had a couple of "people"—Crandall said "people," but I knew he meant "campus commies"—he wanted to nail. To do it, the Attorney General proposed calling on the services of one of the Establishment's more unique and least used henchmen, the Subversive Activities Control Board (SACB).

The Board, a quasi-court of five members appointed by the President and confirmed by the U.S. Senate for terms of five years, was vested with a singular duty—to conduct hearings and determine, solely upon petitions submitted to it by the Attorney General, whether an organization singled out by the Attorney General was, in fact, a "Communist-action," "Communist-front," or "Communist-infiltrated" group. And, in the case of individuals, whether they were members of such groups.

If, after hearings, the SACB branded them as such, the findings and names were published in the *Federal Register,* putting them on public record as declared subversives under the law. The Attorney General, then, could also add them to his subversive list.

The SACB just has to be the cushiest job in the Establishment —and the costliest to taxpayers. Its five Board members each draw $36,000 a year. Most years they work hard at doing just that—practically nothing at all.

Though the SACB had been in the subversive business for something like nineteen years, it could report—as of mid-1969—that it had officially "nailed" only one "Communist-action" organization (the obvious: the Communist Party/USA); put the finger on only seven "Communist-front" organizations (most of them years-since defunct) and as yet not a single individual "Communist" (although, admittedly, some forty-four of its cases against individuals named as members of "Communist-action" organizations had been kayoed by the courts).

But then, in early 1969, the Board lacked what every team in the government's commie-catching Big League really needs—a super star. Shortly, the Board would get one—Otto F. Otepka, the ousted one-time director of the State Department's Office of Security. Otepka was one of the more controversial figures in government intelligence.

On September 23, 1963, Otepka had been suspended—and later fired, but still kept on the payroll—from his State Department job. He had faced thirteen charges involving his alleged turn-over of confidential documents to a Senate internal security subcommittee. Twenty volumes of Senate committee testimony alone had grown out of the Otepka case. In 1967, Secretary of State Dean Rusk, acting after a departmental hearing, found Otepka guilty as charged ("of conduct unbecoming an officer of the State Department"), reprimanded Otepka, but demoted rather than dismissed him (he was still on the payroll at something like $20,000 a year). Richard Nixon's new Secretary of State, William P. Rogers, likewise refused to reinstate Otepka, who had taken a leave of absence, absenting himself—for the first time since his suspension—from the government payroll.

Early in 1969, the Otepka affair reached what some (his friends) called a "vindication" and others (his enemies) termed a "compromise." President Nixon appointed Otepka to the SACB's $36,000-a-year Board, a salary that came close to doubling the best he had ever earned when he was the State Department's chief security evaluator.

But that day when Crandall asked me if I'd be interested in testifying, I knew next to nothing about the Subversive Activities Control Board and less of its history. Much later I was to learn a lot about both and why the Attorney General, through the SACB, had singled me out as a potential witness. And why, from thousands of campus activists, he'd picked two of the more obscure—and a third, no longer even a Party member—whom, with my testimony, he hoped to "nail."

The most patently obvious reason for the hearing the Attorney General proposed was to make headlines and carve a notch, before the conclusion of fiscal year 1969, in the SACB's rusting red blunderbuss. Armed with a new law (Public Law 90-237, Act of January 2, 1968), which no longer required those found by the SACB to be "subversive" to register as such—a requirement declared unconstitutional by the U.S. Supreme Court—the Board had gone hunting again, both for sport and to test the new law. That's why they finally rushed the hearings, at which Crandall proposed I testify, scheduling them for mid-June. It was to get them into the record before June 30, the conclusion of the Board's fiscal year. In that fashion its Nineteenth Annual Report to the President could, with just a little bureaucratic juggling, make it appear that the SACB's high-salaried Board members were earning their keep.

Less obvious on the face of it may have been a second reason: by inference and innuendo to brand most SDSers as Communists—or potential sympathizers.

I had been set up as the man with the hot iron—as the one chosen to apply the indelible brand "subversive" to the rumps of thousands of kids whose sole crime was their growing disenchantment

146

with the American Dream. Plainly, I was being used. At the time, however, I didn't know it. I knew only that I wanted out.

"So," Crandall had concluded, "we'd like you to testify."

"No . . . no," I gasped, the full impact of what Crandall was saying—and what he'd come close to demanding—getting to me for the first time. "The understanding was that I would just quit. I've known these people all this time. They're friends of mine. I simply couldn't face them."

"What about Walter Crowe?" he asked abruptly.

"Walter," I exploded, "is my closest friend and you damned well know it."

Of course, I knew why Crandall had suggested I testify against Walter. On the stand they'd get me to testify that Walter had been a member of the Communist party. Then they'd bring out the fact that Walter had once palled around with Sirhan Sirhan. The public would be left to draw its own—and obvious—conclusion. Millions, having wanted to believe it all along, could now tell themselves, "So those commies *were* behind the assassination of Robert Kennedy."

It wasn't Walter they were after, but headlines. I could read them now, "SIRHAN SIRHAN PAL NAMED AS COMMUNIST." Factually, the headlines would be correct. The conclusions drawn would be utterly and totally false. And Crandall knew it.

What's more, with just a little interpolation, one might link Walter with the campus activists, and they, in turn, with anyone to the left of the Attorney General himself.

I still don't know whether Walter was Crandall's idea or if it came from higher echelons—from Attorney General John Mitchell or from the White House itself.

"No," I told Crandall, "I certainly wouldn't testify against Walter. If you force me to, I'll take the stand in his defense."

At that, Crandall backed off. But a moment later he came up with two other names: Clifford Fried and David Utter Mares.

Cliff Fried, then about twenty-five, was a member and past chairman of SDS on the sprawling San Fernando Valley State College campus. Blond, married, and goateed, he was a graduate student in microbiology, and working toward his master's. As an activist he pretty well ran SDS on the Valley State campus. Lately he had

147

branched out, helping to organize SDS chapters in San Fernando Valley high schools as well. He was not only a Party regular and one of its leading youths, but had taken over the post of Youth Director for the entire Southern California District.

Dave Mares, though a member of SDS at Los Angeles City College, where he was an undergraduate, worked mainly among his own people: deprived Mexican-American youths on Los Angeles' blighted east side. Quiet and slender, with sharp, inquiring eyes, Mares had been the brightest student in my Marxist theory class. He, too, was a Party member, and more: At the Party's next national convention, in May—the last I attended—he would be elected to the Party's ruling, eighty-three-member National Committee.

I knew both Dave and Cliff well from Party, DuBois, and SDS work, and admired Dave Mares especially. Both had appeared, with frequency and in considerable detail, in my Bureau reports.

"Look," I told Crandall, almost desperately now, "I've known these guys a long time, too. I don't see how——"

He cut in, "But this might be your *last* opportunity [he emphasized the "last"] to *clear yourself.*"

I was stunned. Almost from the Movement's inception I'd been one of the Bureau's (and, by association, the Department of Justice's) most valued student informers. I had filed more than eight hundred reports, thousands of analytical pages. And I had named thousands of names. I had done the Bureau's bidding—joined DuBois, wormed into the Party, seduced SDS. I had penetrated and betrayed them all.

And now Crandall, like some cheap DA swapping a felon's freedom for a confession, was offering me the opportunity to "clear" myself.

The implication was plain. In the years ahead I might be hounded by the red-baiters, perhaps by the Bureau itself, and maybe fired from one teaching job after another for my Party activities of years past. I'd be stuck with the accusation, and out on the dole, because I'd have no proof—no FBI sheepskin—to hang on my wall attesting I'd graduated *Nauseum Cum Laude* from FBI Undercover School. I'd have nothing to prove that, all along, I'd been working for the Bureau. Unless, of course, I finked under oath and got myself declared, on the public record, an "official Communist for the FBI."

148

I could visualize it happening. It would start as a whisper or, perhaps, as a note anonymously sent to my prospective employer.

"How about it, Mr. Divale?" he'd ask gravely, having called me into his office.

Of course, I would suggest he check with the FBI. He'd do just that and draw a blank.

You don't just go to the Bureau and ask, "Did a fellow named William Tulio Divale ever work for you as a spy?" Cut yourself off cold-turkey from the Bureau, simply drop out as naïvely as I intended doing, and insofar as the Bureau is concerned, you're a nonperson. You don't exist, never have existed. The business transaction with Wayne Dixon, once I called it quits, would be terminated.

Terminated, perhaps, but my file wouldn't necessarily be "closed." More likely—as one of my handlers once hinted the Bureau sometimes did—they'd merely substitute my real name for my code name and transfer my file from their "active informant" section to the security section, under "campus activists." From a watcher, I'd become the watched. Nor would I be the first student informer who, in working for the Bureau, had, in fact, worked to build his own file.

Right there, I should have said, "No, I won't testify." But I didn't. In all fairness, Crandall's coercion had been by implication only. The decision, one way or the other, we agreed, would rest with the FBI.

"Let's see what the Bureau thinks about it," I concluded. And we left it that way.

That was in January. In my mind, at least, the thing was ended. In June, I'd quit clean. During the next couple of months, Ted and I met nearly every week, as always, but Crandall's conversation never once came up.

Then, in early March, just as we sat down to lunch, Ted said right out of the blue, "Well, it's been decided. The Bureau says okay. You're going to testify."

I nearly choked on my coffee. In January, Crandall and I had had a casual conversation. Now, nearly three months later, it was "decided." Just like that.

Now A'Hern, obviously under heavy pressure from Washington,

began applying the screws. The way he made it sound, the government had been doing practically nothing else, during these intervening months, except build its case. The Attorney General, Ted said, had already filed his petitions against Mares and Fried, declaring them Party members. They'd be served in the next few days. The Justice Department and the SACB were depending on me.

"The hearings," Ted concluded, "are set for June seventeen and eighteen here in Los Angeles."

From that day on, right through my final exams and on to graduation—which I didn't attend—it was all a kind of stream-of-consciousness existence, not really real but so real I'd wake up sweating. Awaiting me was that witness chair. It wasn't electric, but condemned as I was it might just as well have been.

By the end of May, with the hearings only three weeks off, I was really sweating it, but trying to keep my cool. At SDS affairs, in the Co-op, at weekly Party club meetings, in my UCLA classes, I just managed to hang on. I'd sit there, staring around those roomfuls of familiar faces, reaching out with my eyes, almost desperately, to the people who trusted me. Then with a shudder, I'd recoil, knowing that in a matter of days they'd know. All they knew now—once Fried and Mares had been served their subpoenas—was that somebody was going to fink. The Attorney General's case, they were certain, would rely on an "insider's" testimony. That meant someone in the leadership, an activist, and probably on campus.

It wasn't that campus kids were defending Fried or Mares for their alleged Party memberships. Until the Attorney General's petitions, probably not half a dozen people on their campuses even suspected that Mares and Fried might have ties with the Party.

Rather, to most campus youths, Fried and Mares were symbols of the Establishment's shotgun repression, and its opening blast on the Movement itself. A lot of people didn't like Fried. Still, they rallied around him, not because they supported communism (less than one in one hundred likely did) or even subscribed to Marxism (a relatively few did), but because the Attorney General's petition was a reach from Washington itself into the campus.

Right up to the end, to the very moment I stepped into that hearing room, I participated in Movement affairs as I always had.

At the Bureau's urging, I even flew to New York to attend the Party's Nineteenth National Convention.

Ted phoned scarcely a week before the convention. "The Bureau thinks it would look good—your attending the Party's national convention just a couple of weeks before you testify. How about it?"

I hadn't expected to attend and didn't want to. By then I had a pretty acute case of double alienation and bitterness: at the Bureau and Justice for conspiring to have their last pound of flesh. And at the dogmatism of the Party's New York leadership which, known only to a few insiders, such as myself, had recently fired Dorothy Healey from her twenty-year chairmanship of the Southern California District.

For two decades she had scrimped along, never earning more than $65 a week—her highest salary as District chairman—while fighting for better pay (and paychecks often double and triple her own) for others. I earned more from the FBI for spying on the Party than Dorothy did running it.

Now, because she insisted that the Party should heed its majority and because she staunchly refused to retreat from her public criticism of the Soviet Union, made at the time of the Czechoslovakian invasion—she had called the Soviet action "a violation of Communist principles and a setback to the cause of socialism"—she had been sacked. But, then, so had been Dubcek.

The Party's Nineteenth National Convention—in May, 1969—was shaped from the same mold as others I had attended: Gus Hall and his New York bunch ran the show. This time, though, I missed the first act and most of the others, too. I simply didn't have the heart for it.

I didn't even bother attending the convention's first-day sessions. The second day I sat in on a youth workshop where most of the talk zeroed in on how to reactivate the old pre-1940 YCL (Young Communist League) to replace the defunct DuBois clubs. The national leadership had finally got around to acknowledging that the DuBois clubs had failed dismally.

I spent one day at Columbia University's library on a research project—in my major area of undergraduate study—which, eventually, would convince me that Marx had been better at researching his

151

theories on "economic slavery" in the modern world than in the ancient.

Marx and Engels had theorized that the development of early civilization—and in particular its accumulation and concentration of "capitalistic" surpluses—was based on slavery. Slavery, both argued, formed the economic base of ancient economies. I determined to prove the point one way or the other.

To do it, I devised what seemed a novel and valid research stratagem: Quite literally I censused the number of slaves a son might inherit from his father.

The chief source of my data became the "inheritance texts" of the ancient Mesopotamians—clay tablets, inscribed in cuneiform language. These ancient "wills" described in detail a father's wealth and how it was to be passed to his sons. Many thousands of the Mesopotamians' clay bequests had been recovered by archeologists.

I chose for my study the ancient Mesopotamian city of Nuzi, which had flourished around 1400 B.C. Many of its "inheritance texts" had been collected and translated from their original cuneiform. Carefully, I constructed a sampling of family units—father, mother, their sons and their wives. From the same ancient tablets, I established a *population ratio* of free men to slaves, the first of its kind for that prebiblical era.

Slaves, I discovered, comprised only about 15 percent of ancient Nuzi's labor force. Marx had been wrong. Obviously, slavery could have had no dominant economic role in so early—and typical—a civilization. Ancient slavery, then, did not become economically important until the age of Greece and Rome when slaves made up almost half the population.

So, throughout much of the Party's Nineteenth National Convention, I'd sat things out—mostly in Columbia's archives.

The second week in June—with the SACB hearings only a week away—the sack was simply shoved over my head. For months now, ever since Cliff Fried and Dave Mares had been petitioned by the Attorney General and served their subpoenas, campuses throughout Southern California had been boiling. Everywhere, defense committees were forming. Now, it was announced that all of them were getting together for a defense committee strategy meeting to be held at the Unitarian church in downtown Los Angeles. The meeting was scheduled for 8 P.M., Monday, June 9—and I went.

Cliff Fried was there. "Hi, Bill," he said grimly, friendly as always, but scared.

You could read fright all over his face. I suppose, had anyone studied mine, they'd have read the same thing—but for a different reason. I hadn't anticipated anything like this. Cliff and Dave, and maybe their attorneys, I could face. But a united front of perhaps a thousand campus kids—just about everybody who was anybody in the Movement—was something different.

And that was what they were planning. The strategy was to pack the SACB hearing chambers, with the overflow picketing the Federal Courthouse building outside. The Movement, as one, had risen in defense of Mares and Fried—SDSers, the Coalition people, the BSU, just plain campus kids, even a sprinkling of the Third World Liberation Front, and Party people, too. They would all be there. Just to make sure they would, the defense committee's action group was printing leaflets for distribution on dozens of campuses.

I was clammy. If Dave Mares had been there, had he come up to me with those big, dark, trusting eyes of his, I'd have cracked up right in front of him. But Dave didn't attend his own defense strategy meeting. Dave, one of the Party girls told me, had gone into seclusion.

I went out of there into the night in a daze. I can't remember how I found my van, or the way back to the Co-op. I was sick to my stomach. Now I knew how it was going to be. I wouldn't be facing just Mares and Fried, but just about everybody in the Movement I knew in Los Angeles.

Early next morning I phoned Ted.

"I can't testify in Los Angeles," I told Ted bluntly. "Get the hearings moved. I don't care where—twenty-five miles out of town. Move them back to Washington. I just can't handle meeting all those people."

Ted said he'd try. The SACB would be urged to consider moving the hearings. Meantime, Bureau agents, scouring the West Coast, were engaged in one of their less publicized manhunts. Their quarry was a second-string witness—like myself, a Bureau undercover informant

153

—whom the Bureau hoped to ring in as my substitute if the SACB refused to move the hearings out of Los Angeles, and if I, just as stoutly, refused to testify.

But my hoped-for stand-in had simply dropped out of sight. He had loaded his wife and kids into the family camper, and taken off into the piney woods for a two-week vacation. FBI agents had scoured the eleven western states, put out all-points bulletins, alerted hinterland wardens and sheriff's departments, and poked into hundreds of sylvan campsites. But as yet they hadn't found their man. And the hearings were only a week away.

The following day Crandall phoned from Washington. He told me what I already knew. The Board's decision was no. The hearings would be held in Los Angeles.

But it was Crandall's parting words that really got to me—like a rapier driven clean through the kidneys.

"Don't worry," he soothed long distance, "there'll be other hearings . . . other opportunities for you to get a trip to Washington."

I put down the phone, incredulous. Here I was, torn to bits, just living confetti, and the level of Crandall's thinking—and that of the Bureau and the Attorney General, for that matter—was that all along what I'd really been angling for was a free trip to Washington.

When you get an inside reading like that into the Establishment mind, you begin to understand why America's youth are angry. And why the polarization of anger is leagues wider than any mere generation gap.

I went to bed that night telling myself I'd never walk that last mile to the SACB's witness chair.

But the next day—for the first time in our nearly two years' association—Ted came out to the UCLA campus to see me. It still wasn't FBI policy, where undercover work was involved, to set foot on a campus. Ted had broken a Bureau rule in coming.

"I'd have phoned," he explained, "but I was afraid you'd say no."

The Bureau, he said, hadn't been able to locate my stand-in. Now Crandall was due to arrive the next day and some of the Board's members were already in town. The hearing was scheduled for first thing Tuesday morning. And here it was Thursday.

"The whole thing," Ted said, almost plaintively, "rests with you, Bill. We simply haven't anyone else."

I knew, then, that somehow I'd have to go through with it.

Those next four days—beginning early Friday morning when I met with Crandall in his Bixel House hotel room in downtown Los Angeles to rehearse my testimony, through Saturday when we met again to run through the "script," and right up to the morning of the hearings when I ducked out of the Co-op early to avoid any of my friends—were more like a bad trip than anything resembling reality.

At that first meeting with Crandall he'd laid out the entire procedure. To back up my testimony he had selected seven or eight of my Bureau reports—some of them of an "establishing" nature (they established my credentials as an FBI informant), some "accusatory" fixing the time and place of Party meetings and functions directly involving Mares and Fried.

The script Crandall proposed we follow was necessary, he explained, because of the type of hearing the SACB conducted. Legally, all the direct testimony—that linking Mares and Fried to the Party— would have to originate with me, the star witness, who had been personally involved. By the rules, Crandall would not be allowed to link the defendants to any Party activity about which I hadn't testified up to that point. Unless, for example, I had brought up the fact that I had been a member and later chairman of the Southern California District's Education Commission and had, in August, 1968, taught a class in Marxist history, Crandall couldn't specifically refer to that Party school, as at the hearings he did, and ask, "Was the respondent David Mares present during the session that you taught?" I would then be able, as I did, to answer "Yes."

That was one reason for my two meetings with Crandall. The second was to brief me on attorney John J. Abt, the able lawyer for Communist causes, who'd flown out from New York City to represent Mares and Fried.

"Abt is a first-rate constitutional lawyer and very, very sharp," Crandall warned. "He's going to try to discredit you. If he can discredit you, he can discredit your testimony."

Perhaps one of the SACB hearing's more incredible paradoxes was that, though there John Abt stood against me, defending those

I had been forced to defame, less than six months later, in November, 1969, I would ask Abt to *defend* me—and before the same Senate Internal Security Subcommittee he had faced in 1953. The obvious conflict of interest prevented him from handling my case, but he was kind enough to turn me over to an associate who did.

And so, my day of reckoning drew near. Still, I might have faced up to myself and to that hearing room if, on Sunday, June 15, scarcely forty-eight hours before I was to take the witness stand, I hadn't blown my cool. That Sunday all of the Party's leading youths in Los Angeles were having an all-day get-together to reorganize the Party's youth section. I attended. And both Dave Mares and Cliff Fried were there.

I'd come to say my last goodbyes. For this was the last Party function I would ever attend. The others, of course, didn't know *that*. But *I* did. That's why I was just bits and pieces when those kids— some of whom I hadn't seen for a long time—expressed their pleasure in seeing me.

"Bill, you look great," one of the guys said.

He remembered me from the summer before when I'd weighed eighty pounds more. Now I'd slimmed down to 230 pounds. And one of the girls I'd known for years flew at me from nowhere with a big hug and kiss. In the kitchen, where everybody was batching hot cakes—we'd made that meeting a Sunday brunch fun-thing—it was just too much, what with the batter and banter all going at once.

Jim Berland, the Youth Commission's chairman, had thrown open the apartment he'd rented in UCLA's student housing complex to the crowd. Kids had gathered from half a dozen campuses, kids who maybe hadn't seen one another for months. We were plain enjoying each other's company.

But inside I was going to pieces. It wasn't just the talk about Dave and Cliff, who were as friendly and admiring of me as they always were, or even the more somber speculation as to the identity of the person who was going to fink. The thing eating on me was me. Inside, I was jelly.

Late Monday night I gathered up from my Co-op room all the things I wanted to save—a couple of cartons full of research notes I'd spent four college years accumulating. Once I had finked, I felt sure feelings against me would run high in the Co-op. While I was away—the Bureau had reserved a motel room for me during the hearing's two days—somebody was almost sure to say, "Let's get that fink, Divale," and they'd ransack my room.

And that's just what happened. Fortunately, I'd managed to save all my research material.

I rose early the next morning. I stopped by the kitchen to say goodbye and to shake a few hands. I said I was going away for a couple of days. That was my pretext for shaking hands.

Downtown I met Ted, parked my van in the FBI garage, and with a couple of other agents climbed into a Bureau car. We drove to the U.S. Federal Courthouse's subterranean garage and went in by a back way. Hustled to the eighth floor, I was ushered into an ante-chamber. Beyond its massive oaken door—now guarded by two FBI agents—was the hearing room.

For what seemed hours—though it was only forty minutes or so—I sat there sweating. Bureau agents kept coming and going, and with each report from "in there" the thing got worse. The hearing room was already packed. The Movement was out in force. And those who couldn't squeeze in had taken up posts as pickets outside. I could hear the murmur of voices every time one of the agents opened the door a crack to see if the Board was about ready to call its star fink.

"Where are Mares and Fried sitting?" I suddenly asked Lee Oliver, one of the government lawyers. It was Oliver I was going to follow into the hearing room once my call came.

"I'll check," he promised.

Moments later he was back.

"They're at the respondents' table on the other side of this door. Walk out there, and you all but stumble into them."

"And Dorothy Healey?" I asked, the shock really setting in.

"She's sitting right beside them, at the defense table."

Oliver drew me a little sketch of the hearing room. The defense table was to the left of the SACB's rostrum, and only a short distance from the door. Walking out I'd practically collide with Cliff and Dave. The witness stand was way over to the right. To get to it was going to be a regular parade.

"Look," Crandall said, trying to make things easier, "there's no

157

reason to look at them. Once on the stand, look straight at me. You won't see them at all."

"No," I replied quietly, "I'm going to look at them . . . at Cliff, Dave, and Dorothy . . . look them all straight in the eye. I owe them that much."

Suddenly there was a hand on my shoulder and Oliver was saying, "The Board's ready for you, Bill. It's time to go."

Then, like a bad dream, I was following Oliver out.

As I stepped through the door, I was conscious that everybody was standing . . . that every eye was on that door . . . three hundred pairs of eyes. The Movement itself was watching, waiting, to see who would step out to testify against it.

The first person I saw was Dorothy. I saw her blink. Then anguish, like something alive, flushed over her face.

"Oh, no!" she gasped, as if it couldn't be.

For a split second, like an animated moment caught by a high-speed camera, there was only silence. It was followed by a tremendous upwelling of sheer disbelief.

"Not him!" the murmur of incredulousness told me they were thinking.

I followed Oliver, my eyes meeting eyes, my jaw set, following the blob of gray that was Oliver's suit, past the respondents' table where Dave sat, just blinking, and next to him Cliff, his face as fixed as a death mask.

Herbert Philbrick, in his book *I Led Three Lives,* had recounted that identical moment when, after years of undercover work for the Bureau, he had "surfaced" at a hearing not much different from mine. He'd felt exalted, as he described it, as if, finally, he'd got the last laugh. He'd strode "briskly"—I remember the word—to what, for him, had been one of life's most triumphant moments.

I felt like the condemned as I took my seat in the witness chair. If, at that moment, there had been an executioner with his hand on the death lever, I'd have wanted him to pull it.

Then Crandall, straining as he lifted a sealed box of my reports, placed it, unopened, in evidence before the Board.

After that, Crandall led me through the script. I recounted how I'd gone to work for the Bureau, how I'd joined the Party and the

158

DuBois clubs and how I'd risen to leadership in both. Then, as we'd rehearsed it, I got more specific, naming meetings and events I'd attended. I identified Cliff and Dave as having been there and pointed them out.

It was Abt's turn, then. Mostly, that first day, because he hadn't yet had time to study my Bureau reports, copies of which had been handed him, he talked about money—the $14,596 the Bureau had paid me over those years and how much for salary, raises, and travel I had received. He was trying to show how, having finked for the buck, I'd compromised myself and my credibility as a witness.

And then that first day was over. The hearing was adjourned until the following morning. The Bureau got me out of there, undetected, but by a different route from the one we'd used coming in, and back to my van. Alone I drove out to Santa Monica to the motel room they'd reserved under my code name.

I was distraught. I got the newspapers (they were full of my testimony), went to a pier place for dinner and returned to my room.

That night I phoned Walter Crowe. Compulsion made me do it. I wanted to hear Walt's voice, and what, now that he knew, he'd say.

Slowly, fumbling, I dialed the number. It rang, it seemed, forever, and then he answered.

"Walt," I said, "this is Bill."

On the other end there was silence. Then Walt was saying, "Man what a thing . . . wow." Walt was dead drunk. He just kept "man . . . man . . . man-ing" me. He was out of it.

"I called," I said, as shaken as he was but stone sober, "well, just to tell you I was sorry."

I told him I'd phoned because I had to talk with him . . . to talk to someone.

"Not tonight," he said. "Maybe later, but not tonight." He paused, then added, "We'll still be friends . . . don't worry."

I hung up. Really, I guess, that's what I'd called to hear. That somehow, after it all, Walt and I would still be friends.

Next day, the hearing was all desperation, but not as much for me as for John Abt and his defense. My testimony couldn't be refuted. So what Abt attempted to do was to refute me as a Marxist. He led up to it by recalling my own testimony about the Marxist

159

history class I'd taught. Adroitly, he worked me into an obvious trap. He'd make me play the fool by asking me to do in that courtroom what I'd claimed to have done in class—teach Marxist history. Not many Marxists themselves can do that. And certainly, Abt figured, not an FBI undercover informer.

Carefully, cunningly, he led me into the credibility snare he was setting. The questioning went like this:

ABT: What aspects of Marxism did you lecture on in that class?

DIVALE: It was the historical aspects. Mainly, the transformation from primitive to ancient society and also the changeover to feudalism.

ABT: You dealt with the transition from primitive communism up to the period of feudalism?

DIVALE: Yes. I don't recall if we dealt with the later period.

ABT: In that particular class?

DIVALE: Yes. It was just one session.

ABT: You testified yesterday—let me have that report back. You testified yesterday that in 1968, August, 1968, you attended a school of the Educational Commission of the Southern California District of the Party.

DIVALE: Yes.

ABT: And you testified yesterday that at that school you taught a session on historical theory.

DIVALE: Yes.

"All right," Abt, in effect, said suddenly as he sprung his trap, "so teach us."

There, from the stand, in a U.S. Federal courtroom borrowed for a U.S. hearing on subversives, I conducted what must have been the first government-sponsored course in Marxism. By the end of the first minute, Abt knew his trap had sprung open—not closed. Another five minutes and he called it quits.

But he still had one trick left. Perhaps he couldn't shake any testimony or test my credibility by ideology, but there were always my morals. I'd halfway expected him to take that tack, too.

The thing was, a year or so before I'd taken a fun kind of fling in a magazine called the *National Swingers Directory*. They ran pictures and descriptions of "swingers." I joined the fun. In the center spread of one issue they had printed a photo of me captioned "Single

160

Swinger," and under it my description with the added note that, to quote the magazine, I was "well-mannered and discreet; seeks single gals and couples for excitement; also would like to exchange photos."

Now, as Crandall rose to object, Abt entered the magazine in evidence. Of course, it was irrelevant. And Abt, under fire from Crandall, admitted it. He also conceded I didn't have to answer his questions about my alleged "swinging" life. But I did—in just one sentence of testimony that closed the case, concluded the hearings, and made it easier for headline writers that evening to get their papers off to the presses.

"I don't," I told Abt from the stand, "see what my sex life has to do with my politics."

With that, the SACB could pack up and head back to Washington. I'd delivered their pound of flesh. Now our breakup was final. I'd bought my freedom—from the FBI.

10. The Angela Davis Affair

THE *Angela Davis Affair*—which would make headlines across the nation, provoke Governor Ronald Reagan's hand puppets (the conservative-dominated Regents of the University of California) to their rashest challenge yet of academic freedom, and coalesce the university's nine sprawling campuses as had occurred only once before and that during the "Loyalty Oath" purges of the fifties—had its beginning in a most unlikely place: my cubbyhole room on the Co-op's first floor, and scarcely four blocks from the offices of UCLA's *Daily Bruin.*

From that room I was to fire the first verbal shot in the Angela Davis case. But it was the *Daily Bruin* which, unknowingly, loaded the gun. The *Bruin* did it on June 24, 1969. That day—precisely a week after my cop-out before the Subversive Activities Control Board —the *Daily Bruin* de-gutted me across its front page.

Had the *Bruin*'s editors attacked me politically, I'd have understood. I had committed the New Left's most unpardonable crime. I had finked. But character assassination—as the *Bruin* chose to practice it—was an entirely different matter.

The Bureau had tried to prepare me for what was almost certain to come.

"You won't find it easy returning to the campus after this thing, Bill," one of my handlers warned just before the hearings. "You'll be facing some pretty strong music."

I really hadn't anticipated UCLA's marching band turning out to greet me. Finks are seldom accorded a hero's welcome.

The activists—most of them former friends or acquaintances— would, at the very least, I was sure, apply social ostracism, a brutal political penalty first devised by the ancient Athenians and as punishing today as it was in the fifth century B.C. Revived by the student movement, it is a vengeful weapon turned against the most flagrant of its defectors. Outwardly, it leaves no marks. Inwardly, it can do terminal damage.

I returned to the Co-op ostracized. Former friends turned their backs at my approach. Scrawled obscenities, even veiled threats, were shoved beneath my door. In the dining room, I ate alone.

Scarcely had I returned to the Co-op, after the hearing's final day, than somebody slashed the right front tire of my van camper and heaved a fist-sized rock through the windshield. Then, a couple of days later, right after supper, I was given my moving notice—verbally.

In full view of half a dozen other students, the Co-op's activist president told me how, insofar as he and most of my fellow Co-opers felt, it was going to be.

"Divale," he said, "I suppose you'll be packing your things and moving your finking ass out of here before the week's up?"

He asked me, because he really couldn't order me out. But the implication was plain. They'd make it so rough I'd want out.

But the *Daily Bruin* had gone for the genitals. The females of the species generally do. The writer of the *Bruin* front-pager was a girl—Liza Maddison, a *Bruin* staffer, a liberal, and a former classmate. She lived in the building just across from mine. We were passably acquainted. Her chief tool of personal vendetta was the razored quote and misquote.

She'd assembled a baker's dozen of both, all attributed to anonymous "fellow students" and former "co-op buddies of Divale," but hadn't seen fit to interview me personally.

"Why," she asked, "did he do it?"

"For 'coin and kicks,' " she reported one student, identified only as a Co-oper, as saying.

She quoted another as nicknaming me "Bourgeois Bill." She went on to say that, "hardly representative of [the] oppressed working-class, Divale enjoyed expensive clothes, lotions and cream. He bought special foods for himself and drank only certain brands of coffee. He owned a Morris Minor and a Honda, then sold them both and bought a camper from a friend. He also owned stock in oil companies."

It was Brand X bullshit. But against my acknowledged $14,596 FBI earnings, of which the *Bruin* took particular note, it sounded like the living-it-up McCoy.

Even my Co-op cooking chores came under fire. The *Bruin* put it this way:

> Divale had weekend cook at the co-op and had a tendency to dye cookies, rice and mashed potatoes red or pink, and at breakfast the residents were treated to a round of "Communist Pancakes."

She concluded her diatribe with a little ditty she claimed was frequently heard around the Co-op. It went, she said, like this:

> Bourgeois Bill
> Sitting on a hill
> Never works, never will.

A day or so after the *Bruin* attack, I phoned one of its editors. I told him I wanted to reply to the article. He agreed that I should.

So I sat down to write what, in time, would trigger the *Angela Davis Affair*—a confrontation so basic to academic freedom that it is sure to be carried all the way to the U.S. Supreme Court.

The article I eventually wrote—and which the *Bruin* carried in its July 1 edition—was not, however, a direct response to Miss Maddison's personal attack. Rather, it was a statement of principle which increasingly had motivated my reports to the FBI, my own openness within and outside the Party, and my public appearance before the SACB: As a Marxist I believed—and still believe—that communism and Communists should be aboveground and aboveboard. If you are a Communist, you should say so, publicly if necessary, privately if asked.

None of this was idle preaching. I'd been practicing it all along.

Ever since the SDS National Council Meeting on the Berkeley campus in December, 1966, I had been an "open" Communist. I'd at-

165

tended as both UCLA's SDS representative *and* as the announced spokesman for the Southern California District of the Communist party.

In the same context I'd testified against Cliff Fried and Dave Mares. It wasn't simply that they were Communists and Party members, but because they had concealed from their fellow students and followers the fact that they were. That, I felt, was their deceit, not their Party membership.

But I draw a fine line, just as I did at those SACB hearings. Politics, I believe, is a man's most profound personal affair so long as he is not a "public person." That your grocer is a Republican—or a Bircher—affects neither the quality of his service nor his products. He is not a public person. Campus leaders—like elected city, county, state, and national leaders—are. So too, by the very nature of the courses they lecture and teach, are instructors and professors in the social sciences: in courses where political perspective pervades course content.

In these courses, the instructor's political perspective—if he has one—should be plainly visible. And just as plainly labeled if he doesn't. It is the instructor's academic obligation to his class to do so. But having stated his perspective, that should be the end of it.

As I wrote my *Bruin* rejoinder, a striking example of what I was talking about—the personification of my "truth in lecturing" principle—came startlingly to mind: *Angela Davis.*

Angela was black, beautiful, brilliant, and was soon to teach on the UCLA campus. At the moment, she was a graduate student, completing her doctorate in philosophy at the University of California's new San Diego campus.

A dedicated student and provocative female, Angela was every bit a scholar and very much a woman. A Phi Beta Kappa at Brandeis University, where she'd earned her B.A. degree, she'd won a scholarship to Paris' renowned Sorbonne and had gone on to advance study at the University of Frankfurt.

At UC/San Diego she was the protégé of the campus's only self-declared Marxist professor—Professor Herbert Marcuse, one of the elder statesmen of the philosophical New Left and the perennial target of the Reagan reactionaries, not the least of them being California's

166

Superintendent of Public Instruction, Dr. Max Rafferty, who, because of his elective office, was also a member of the Regents of the University of California.

San Diego's right-wingers had declared open season on Marcuse. Their avowed intent was to drive him from the university. Personal threats on Marcuse's life had caused him to absent himself in Europe. There he'd become the darling of the Continent's youth generation and in particular its activists. At seventy-two, Professor Marcuse was both the "youngest" of campus activists and among the Movement's best-read (and best-selling) philosophers. *Time* had once described him as a kindly man with a "Kris Kringle smile, Katzenjammer accent, and snow-white hair."

Professor Marcuse was no Communist. He considered the Communist party doctrinaire. Long before most other American leftists, he had proclaimed Soviet communism a revolutionary failure. Nonetheless, he was an avowed and declared philosophical Marxist. But then, by 1969, so were the majority of campus activists.

What Marx, a hundred years removed from the American scene, had failed to envisage, Dr. Marcuse and most New Left thinkers perceived only too well: that as capitalistic society evolved technically, its owner-managers would succeed—through higher pay, fringe benefits, and better working conditions—in "buying off" their workers and lifting them economically and philosophically into the middle class. Seemingly shattered was the "industrial working class" base upon which Marx, in his day and stratagem, had relied for agitation and as an agent for social revolution.

Marcuse contended that the base had not been erased, only elevated. For while "workers" might now call themselves "technicians," and while they might have exchanged the white worker neighborhoods of their fathers for the white look-alike box-houses of Suburbia, unchanged was their true status within capitalistic technology itself.

Wage earners no different from their fathers, they had ascended to the ranks of the "middle-class poor." Pitifully, they had become slaves to a New Materialism whose chains were wrought from designed-for-obsolescence automobiles they could ill afford, mortgages that kept them in middle-class poverty, and easy credit that held them in life-long chattel. They possessed everything that money and credit could buy save one: happiness. In that, they were poorer than church mice.

Angela was one of Dr. Marcuse's proudest protégés there on the UC/San Diego campus. Awarded her M.A., she'd pressed on toward her Ph.D. Now, still under Dr. Marcuse's tutelage, she was writing her doctoral thesis on German idealism, a philosophy rooted in Hegel, Nietzsche, and Marx. She had, in fact, already been hired by UCLA's philosophy department as an acting assistant professor, and would begin teaching her first classes on the UCLA campus during the winter quarter, 1970.

Scarcely twenty-five, Angela had risen from Alabama racism and squalor to a professorship in one of America's great universities. But Angela, I knew, was more than merely a philosophical Marxist. She was a member of the Communist party.

I'd learned of Angela's appointment to the philosophy faculty from Rich Healey, Dorothy's son, only a few weeks before the SACB hearings.

"Say, did you hear about Angela? Kalish has hired her to teach in his philosophy department," Rich said over coffee one day.

I hadn't heard. But then, in the late spring of 1969, it wasn't generally known that the philosophy department had hired its first black professor. Nor that Dr. Donald Kalish, the department's chairman and as stormy a petrel on the UCLA campus as Dr. Marcuse was on his, had made it possible not only for Angela to teach but, at the same time, to pursue her doctoral thesis.

Angela's appointment would begin with the upcoming summer quarter. It was to run for one year, with the tacit understanding that if she did well it would be extended at least through a second year. Technically—and because she hadn't yet earned her Ph.D.—she wouldn't be a member of the faculty. Her contract was the nontenure, provisional variety. Under it, she would pursue her doctoral research during the summer and fall quarters of 1969, getting acquainted with the UCLA campus in the meantime. Her first teaching assignment in the philosophy department would come with 1970's first quarter.

"That's great news," I told Rich. "Angela deserves it."

168

I'd first met Angela at a Youth Commission meeting in the summer of 1968. At the time, she'd been a Party member only a few months. She'd joined earlier that spring while I was in New York City at the High Party School. The Youth meeting was one of the first I attended after my return, and I'd scarcely arrived before I noticed Angela. She was hard not to notice. I managed to strike up a conversation. As I remember, it was about thirteenth-century medieval philosophy. It wasn't difficult, since she was carrying a paperback book on Aquinas.

After we'd disposed of Thomas Aquinas and the Catholic Renaissance, Angela told me she was working on her Ph.D. In fact, she was just then preparing for her oral examination, the final step before the doctorate's thesis.

"It must be quite a hassle," I said, "your living in Los Angeles and going down those one hundred and twenty miles to San Diego to class."

"Oh, it's really no bother," she lilted. She made the trip, she said, twice a week, on the days she had classes.

I was impressed then and on several other occasions when we'd met. Here was a really fine-looking girl, a black girl working on her Ph.D. The black movement and the student movement were lucky to have her.

Now as I began my rejoinder to the *Daily Bruin,* Angela came once again to mind. Here, made-to-order and in the very context of the principle of intellectual honesty I was critiquing, was an on-campus example of a Party member soon to take her place on the faculty.

But should I involve Angela? Had I the right?

Only a handful of the campus's most active student Communists knew of Angela's Party membership. Rich Healey, though never himself a Party member, knew—after all, his mother was the Party's district chairman. And the Federal Bureau of Investigation knew. Thinking back, I was certain I hadn't included Angela in any of my reports. By the summer of 1968, when I'd first met her, I had begun to weigh carefully every name I included.

Still, once or twice in passing conversations with my agents, Angela's name had cropped up. "Name dropping" with the Bureau is never mere casual prattle. It is an admission that the Bureau has the person in "active file," is building a dossier, and is seeking still additional data to cram into it.

The Bureau had a file marked "Angela Davis." I had no doubt about that.

Yet in Angela's case I doubted whether the Bureau, bound as it is by law against divulging information except to other government agencies, and then only through Department of Justice channels, would violate Congress' restraint merely to expose a single faculty member—Angela or anyone else.

Paradoxically, on June 25—the day following the *Bruin* attack and only a day or so before I wrote my rejoinder—Sergeant Justin Dyer of the Los Angeles Police Department's Intelligence Division had named Angela during his appearance in Washington before the Senate Permanent Subcommittee on Investigations, chaired by Senator John L. McClellan (D.-Ark.).

Almost in passing, Dyer had tentatively linked Angela with the Communist party.

In discussing an on-again, off-again Los Angeles SNCC chapter, Dyer related that on June 21, 1968, several members were removed from the SNCC rolls, primarily because they were Party members or Party prospects. Angela Davis, Dyer stated in his Senate testimony, was one of those who "went into the Communist party."

Dyer's testimony, however, wasn't published until October. By then, the Angela Davis case was out in the open.

As I wrote my rejoinder, I knew that inevitably Angela must figure in it. I began with a simple statement of fact: UCLA was my university and my community. That, I explained, was why I'd chosen the *Daily Bruin* in which to make my statement—the first since my widely publicized testimony before the Subversive Activities Control Board.

Then, in what may have seemed an unprecedented turnabout for a former FBI undercover informer and star government witness, I said:

"I think the Communist party has a legitimate role and function

170

and should participate in this necessary process of social change. It is not my purpose to deny them this right. However, I think they should be open and frank in their political activities and beliefs. I also have ideological differences with them which I should be able to express without being accused of red-baiting."

I went on to document the objectivity that had ruled most of my FBI reports. I quoted directly from several of them to illustrate how I'd become a kind of devil's advocate: reporting a damning incident, I'd interpret its meaning in the context of the Movement's evolving philosophy.

"I always attempted to report objectively," I stated. "I did this because of my attitudes as a social scientist and also because of my respect and emotional feelings toward the people involved. In this country Communists have been subjected to much unjust persecution. I oppose this. But Communists also have the responsibility to be open in their beliefs and political activities."

Then came my bombshell.

"I will now give one example," I wrote, "where a Communist will be involved in our community, UCLA, and where not only the general student body, but even most Communists will not be aware of it."

(In my first draft, which went into my wastebasket, I cited Angela by name. In the second—which went to the *Daily Bruin* and was blazoned across its front page on July 1—I did not. I merely revealed that an unnamed professor—a Communist party member—had been hired to teach at UCLA. No useful purpose, I concluded, would be served in naming her. I had made my point. To have named Angela would merely force the Regents to repressive action. That, I most assuredly did not want.)

As printed in the *Bruin* my charge was purposely veiled:

"The philosophy department has recently made a two-year appointment of an acting assistant professor. The person is well qualified for the post and is also a member of the Communist party. I do not question this person's right to teach at UCLA or anywhere else. This person will probably be a fine scholar. . . . I commend the philosophy department for making the appointment. . . . The university needs more Marxist professors if we are going to carry out a real dialogue with Marxism. . . .

"The only issue I raise here," I concluded, "is that the faculty and students should know that this person is a Communist party member. My argument is not based solely on the fact of his or her membership (in the Communist party) but because the person's work at UCLA will be discussed in Party meetings, and at that point it becomes political activity. It is in this context that we have a right to know of the membership. . . ."

The bomb that would demolish the farce of academic freedom had been planted. The explosion wasn't long in coming.

It came, in an urgent call from Ted A'Hern, my handler during my final two undercover years with the Bureau. The Regents of the University of California, Ted said, wanted to talk with me. He gave me a name and phone number in Berkeley to call collect.

The number turned out to be the office of the Regents' legal counsel. The name was that of the Regents' assistant counsel, attorney Donald L. Reidhaar.

Reidhaar opened the conversation pointblank. "It's about this Communist professor thing and your *Daily Bruin* article," he said. "We want you to know that we're very sure the person you mentioned is Angela Davis."

So the Regents knew. They'd known July 9, eight days after the article's appearance. That day the San Francisco *Examiner* had broken the story that Angela Davis was the person to whom my *Bruin* article referred. Oddly, the *Examiner*'s story had never made the Los Angeles papers. Or, if it had, I'd missed it. The Regents, obviously, hadn't.

Regardless, Ed Montgomery, the *Examiner*'s Pulitzer Prize-winning reporter (for his 1951 exposure of scandal in the Bureau of Internal Revenue's San Francisco office), scarcely merited another Pulitzer for his spade work. The most cursory inquiry into UCLA's philosophy department would have established that the department had hired only *one* new professor that quarter—Angela.

But Montgomery—following a tip—had done better than that. He'd phoned Angela directly on the UC/San Diego campus. She'd

172

confirmed her hiring by Kalish, but declined to comment on her political affiliations.

Montgomery's minor scoop was to precipitate a major confrontation. Nothing less was at stake than Academic Freedom—the "Fifth Freedom" of intellectual man. The first four had been proclaimed by President Franklin D. Roosevelt, in perhaps the most memorialized of his speeches, on January 6, 1941: Freedom of *Speech and Expression,* Freedom of *Worship,* Freedom from *Want,* and Freedom from *Fear.* To America's collegian young, the fifth—*Academic Freedom*—was every bit as dear as FDR's (and the past generation's) revered four.

"Montgomery's avalanche"—so-called by some because the pebble he'd tossed had unleashed a philosophical landslide—would bring UCLA's youthful new chancellor, Charles E. Young, to the brink of dismissal; evoke voter recall movements against two California Superior Court judges caught up, through judicial happenstance, in the Angela Davis case; and trigger a revolt among the nearly nine thousand professors and instructors of the world's largest university.

On July 11—just two days after Montgomery had tossed his "pebble"—the Regents, dominated by its conservative campus-phobes, ordered UC's administration to find out whether, in fact, Angela was a member of the Communist party.

Reidhaar's call was a first undercover feeler in the Regents' then undercover campaign against Angela herself and ultimately against the university.

I told Reidhaar in some pretty tough terms my feelings. The article spoke for itself, I said. It needed no amplification. "It was my parting shot in campus politics," I conceded. "I have nothing more to say."

But Reidhaar, obviously a man with a mission (and likely on direct orders from Governor Reagan himself), wasn't about to be put off that easily.

"The Regents," he soothed, "were thinking that perhaps you'd be willing to testify as to her Party membership."

"Tell the Regents," I retorted, "that I won't testify. If it comes down to testifying, I'll be for her, not against her."

That jarred him a little. For the next ten minutes he recited the

Regents' policy statements on the hiring of Communists, dating back to 1940. He concluded with the Regents' most recent Standing Order, adopted only two weeks before (on June 30, 1969), in which the Regents had unilaterally reinstated their power to be final judge and jury over university tenure appointments.

Conveniently, he neglected to quote a corollary resolution, adopted at the same time. In it the Regents pledged that *"no political test shall ever be considered in the appointment and promotion of any faculty member or employee."*

What the Regents had done was to proclaim their word the divine final judgment over "life" (tenure) appointments to the faculty. As a sop, they'd sworn that in exercising their newly usurped control over faculty promotion and hiring, and presumably firing, neither a political test nor a faculty member's political views would color their final decision. The Regents' pledge was about as meaningful as a cannibal's vow to turn vegetarian.

That's why I laughed when Reidhaar, sluffing over the Regents' "no political test" pledge, got down to the nitty-gritty. If it was established, through my testimony, that Angela was a member of the Communist party, the Regents would forthwith fire her.

"Count me out," I told Reidhaar. "And that's final."

Anything but final was the basic issue—academic freedom.

Vaguely, I was aware of the series of rulings by the Regents—going back to 1940—which made membership in the Communist party tantamount to dismissal from the faculty.

Then, as today, the Regents' aim was not the removal of a few admitted or even suspected Communists. It was an apparent usurpation of that most sacred of faculty prerogatives: freedom of thought within the university and, by extension, throughout the U.S. itself.

That the University of California had become the often bloodied battlefield in a last-ditch and losing battle to save America from itself, and from the real enemies of freedom—those who sought to abridge it—was no accident.

UC epitomized the zenith and the corruption of the American educational system. It was the giant among universities with a giant-sized Achilles' heel. It was totally beholden to the whim of the legislature (and ultimately, upon the capriciousness of the governor), and to corporate, government, and foundation grants for its year-to-year financial survival.

As the world's largest university, with more than 106,000 enrolled on its nine campuses, UC was the General Motors of American higher education. Only nineteen of America's five hundred largest corporations (headed by GM itself) had more employees than UC had students. The products of UC's academic assembly lines managed (and often chaired) the industrial giants of America (Ford Motor Company's vice-chairman and former president, Arjay Miller, had graduated in the class of '37); spearheaded the thrust of U.S. scientific achievement (UC's roll of Nobel Laureates read like a Who's Who in Science); masterminded the U.S. worldwide espionage net (the CIA's former director, John McCone, had earned a UC degree); and sat in the highest councils of government.

If the University of California and its campuses—in particular Berkeley, its activist and intellectual epicenter—were loud in their protestations for "peace now," it was because they had had more to do with the business of war than any other educational/industrial complex in the nation.

In a very real sense UC had fathered the nuclear age—a fact many of its students, if not much of the world, had come to regret. History's first atomic explosion, fired at Alamogordo, New Mexico, on July 16, 1945 (and the two A-bombs dropped on Hiroshima and Nagasaki three weeks later), was largely a product of the Los Alamos Scientific Laboratory, still one of the AEC's most top-secret atomic hatcheries, and then as now a veritable appendage of the University of California. UC operates still another of the nation's most formidable nuclear complexes—the E. O. Lawrence Radiation Laboratory, with facilities at Livermore and Berkeley, California.

Now the same minuscule-minded Regents who railed at UC's student protesters for blighting the university's image were only too ready to brand it, in the minds of voters, as "Commie infiltrated" in their zealot's search for a single fledgling professor teaching an obscure, undergraduate class in philosophy.

"A bunch of dirty old men raising old issues," Regent Frederick

175

G. Dutton would say later, in characterizing the Reagan witchhunt, and his own fellow Regents.

The brewing conflict over Angela Davis, though rooted in the headline-making UC "Loyalty Oath" purge of the early fifties, went back even further, to 1940, when Kenneth May, then a teaching assistant in mathematics on the Berkeley campus, was fired for being a member of the Communist party.

In dismissing May, the Regents issued the first of a series of policy statements, declaring that "membership in the Communist party is incompatible with membership in the faculty of a state university."

In June, 1942, the Regents went further, requiring all university employees to sign an oath swearing to uphold the U.S. and state constitutions.

While most faculty members chafed at so transparent an affront to their loyalty and patriotism, they dutifully pledged their constitutional allegiance. Not, however, until 1949—when the Regents radically upped their loyalty ante—did festering faculty resentment explode into open rebellion and lead to the famous purge of 1950. The spark that touched off the revolt was the Regents' demand—made in March, 1949—that in addition to their written allegiance to the Constitution, employees must also swear to a philosophically limiting oath.

Henceforth, declared the Regents, university employees would have to state, "I do not believe in, and I am not a member of, nor do I support, any party or organization that believes in, advocates or teaches the overthrow of the United States government by force or by any illegal or unconstitutional methods."

The Regents had reacted precipitately to two unrelated incidents occurring on UC campuses more than five hundred miles apart.

One was the appearance on the UCLA campus of Professor Herbert Phillips, who had been dismissed from the University of Washington faculty for his alleged membership in the Communist party.

The other was a scheduled lecture by the British Labor party's brilliant political economist (and former Harvard instructor), Harold J. Laski. Labeling Laski a left-of-left liberal, if not a Communist (he was neither, but rather one of the architects of the brand of socialism being practiced by the British Labor party, then in power), the Regents denied Laski the use of university facilities.

Three years later the Laski affair would return to haunt the more perceptive of the Board's members.

"We were a bunch of grubbing damn fools," one Regent would concede.

What prompted such introspection among even the Board's ruling conservatives was the disclosure, in 1953, of the Laski–Holmes papers. Perhaps UC's voiceless students and cowed faculty had been denied access to Laski's brilliance, but not one of the stalwarts of constitutional liberalism, U.S. Supreme Court Justice Oliver Wendell Holmes. Holmes and Laski—it was revealed three years after the Regents' Laski ban—had for years probed the depths of one another's intellects.

The disclosure came with publication by the Harvard University Press of the hitherto unrevealed two-volume exchange of Laski–Holmes letters—a dialogue of intellectual first magnitude and admiration, though of differing political philosophies—that had spanned two continents, nearly two decades, and an age difference of more than fifty years.

Time magazine was to call the now legendary pen-palling between such poles-apart minds, begun when Laski was twenty-three and a Harvard instructor in government and Holmes, at seventy-five, still an associate justice of the U.S. Supreme Court, "perhaps the longest and most scintillating correspondence of the 20th century."

Faculty reaction to the Regents' imposition of a political oath of allegiance (far different from an affirmation of loyalty to the Constitution) was immediate. While the majority of the faculties' academic senates (the faculties' self-ruling body on each of UC's campuses) supported the Anti-Communist hiring policy, nearly 14 percent of the university's then four thousand instructors and professors refused, as a matter of principle, to sign the Regents' belittling pledge of political purity. For their part, the Regents withheld the employment contracts of those who would not sign.

What followed was a Regent doublecross and political purge unequaled in the history of American higher education.

177

Early in 1950, faculty representatives believed they had reached an accord with the Regents. Evolved was a gentleman's agreement. The academic senates would, by resolution, endorse the Regents' anti-Communist policy (in effect, making it faculty policy as well), after which the Regents would rescind their loyalty oath.

By March 21, 1950, all of the University's academic senates had voted, by mailed ballots, to sustain the Regents' policy. At this point, the Regents would abandon the oath. No one would be forced to sign against his principles. No one would be fired.

But on March 31—ten days following the faculties' vote of compliance in carrying out their part of the bargain—the Regents pulled their doublecross. By a 10-10 vote, they refused to abolish the loyalty oath. Later the Regents did abandon an outright oath. But they inserted it as a clause in the university's employment contract.

Forty-five members of the faculty still refused, on principle, to sign. Of these, thirty-nine declared they were not Communists, nor sympathizers, and never had been. Most were willing to sign affidavits to that effect, but not the contractual stipulation—whether an oath appended to their contract or a clause inserted in it—insisted upon by the Regents.

Before it was over, thirty-six faculty members, including several with major reputations, were fired, along with 157 other university employees. Many who had signed but saw in their capitulation the end of free expression at UC packed up and left. They were snapped up by universities and corporations throughout the world.

"Rather than having caught Communists, you have caught the free and independent spirits of a [great] university," one faculty representative told the Regents to their faces.

The issue, then as today, ran far deeper than a signature of loyalty, whether by oath, clause, or proclamation. In humbling its faculty, the Board of Regents had attempted to assert its control over almost all university matters. That was the nub of the issue: who runs the university—the Regents or its faculty?

Two 1967 high court rulings, as well as the Regents' own "no political test" pledge of June 30, 1969, had clearly set new guidelines. No longer could membership in the Communist party be used as grounds for dismissal from the faculty, whether at UC or any other American university.

In the 1967 New York case of *Keyishian v. Board of Regents,* the U.S. Supreme Court had invalidated New York State statutes making membership in the Communist party grounds for disqualification from teaching in a public institution.

Again that same year, and based on the New York decision, the California Supreme Court, in *Vogel v. County of Los Angeles,* had ruled unconstitutional the section of California's constitution that required public employees—including faculty members—to sign an oath denying membership in any organization advocating the "violent overthrow of the Government."

The clincher was the Board of Regents' own resolution of June 30 in which its members publicly pledged that never again would a political test be used in the appointment or promotion of any faculty member or employee.

Angela, I was convinced, could with impunity openly declare herself a member of the Communist party without fear or risk of reprisal. The courts and the Regents themselves had said she could.

Then Reidhaar had phoned. "If we can prove she's a member of the Communist party, we'll fire her," he had declared.

Six weeks later came another call, this time from John Sparrow, an associate counsel for the Regents, and Reidhaar's legal superior.

Sparrow said he wanted to come down to the UCLA campus for a chat with me.

"What for?" I asked, incredulous that the Regents were still intent upon Angela. But I agreed to see him.

At lunch Sparrow got down to the business at hand. He explained how he and the Regents had set Angela up for the kill.

The Regents (who, at the time, were contesting only her summer employment, not her teaching assignment to come) had sent Angela a letter. In it they'd asked her to state whether or not she was a Communist. If she replied that she was, they intended to fire her. If she failed to answer or, more likely, replied that her politics were none of the Regents' business, they planned to fire her anyway, on the grounds of "noncooperation."

179

The Regents had mailed Angela their two-faced letter a few weeks earlier. As yet, they hadn't heard from her.

Sparrow's real worry seemed to be that Angela might simply quit—and cheat the Regents of the game they were after. He had come, he explained, to sound me out on Angela's probable response.

"Angela's answer," I correctly predicted, "will be 'yes.' She's going to come right out and say 'I'm a member of the Communist party.' It's a matter of principle with her. She won't hedge. You can bet on it."

Ten days later, on September 5, Angela answered the Regents' challenge.

In a letter to UCLA Chancellor Young, she readily acknowledged her Party membership.

The Regents had their answer. The second great battle for academic freedom at the University of California was joined.

The Regents did the expected. By a 19 to 2 decision, they voted to fire her and ordered UC President Charles J. Hitch to notify Angela of her dismissal, pending the usual routine of a hearing before the UCLA Academic Senate's Committee on Privilege and Tenure.

The committee's only duty would be to determine whether Angela was a member of the Communist party. For that—as President Hitch conceded in his dismissal letter—was the sole ground for her firing.

Since Angela had freely admitted her Party membership to the Regents (and would make her politics a matter of public record at a press conference on September 23, two weeks before the opening of UCLA's 1969 fall quarter), the faculty's findings were foregone. In fact, they were uncontested by Angela herself.

Foregone, too, as the powerful and middle-roading Los Angeles *Times* saw it, was the new course of faculty confrontation being pursued by the Regents.

"Seven years ago," wrote the *Times*, "the University of California Board of Regents received the Alexander Meiklejohn Award of the American Association of University Professors for defense of academic freedom, especially for lifting a ban against Communist Party speakers on UC campuses.

"Last week the Regents started down an altogether different road,

180

voting to fire Angela Davis, a newly hired UCLA philosophy professor who acknowledges membership in the Communist Party."

But for the Regents' associate counsel, John Sparrow, it was by now a familiar road. Once more he flew down to Los Angeles to see me. This time, he explained, it was to get my views on the legal tack the Regents proposed to take in their efforts to oust Angela.

The Regents' legal attack, Sparrow confided, would be based on the grounds that, as a Communist, Angela could not be an "independent person or thinker." She was bound, Sparrow contended, by the Party's long-held doctrine of "democratic centralism": once a policy or decision was adopted, it bound all Party members to adherence.

"Party people," I corrected Sparrow, "do have differing views. When they disagree with a policy, they simply don't carry it out. They ignore it."

I reminded him of the Czech invasion controversy. Officially, the national Party sided with the Soviets. Most Party people didn't.

"I don't pretend to be a lawyer," I shrugged, "but you won't win trying to prove Angela is a pawn of 'democratic centralism.' When you get to the California Supreme Court, you'll be slaughtered."

"We don't expect to win in the California Supreme Court," Sparrow replied matter-of-factly. "It's the U.S. Supreme Court—and Dick Nixon's new appointees—we're banking on."

He meant, of course, Judge Clement Haynsworth, whom Nixon had nominated to the High Court in August. Though Haynsworth's Senate rejection—the first for a High Court nominee in nearly forty years—would come in late November, both the Regents and the President batted better, if belatedly, with Judge Harry A. Blackmun.

But even as we talked, in the making was a script for confrontation that would become a classic of the campuses and of the Movement, itself. Its cast of thousands—the whole of the University of California's 106,000 students and 9,000 faculty members—was in the best Hollywood tradition. So was its principal setting: the shrubbed and multi-storied UCLA campus, whose population density per square mile (58,000 students, including an extension enrollment of more than 30,000) rivaled that of most American slums.

The script's heavies were UC's twenty-four Regents, sixteen of them (the majority representing powerful corporate and political interests) appointed by Governor Reagan or his predecessors; the Regents' lawyers; and those campus-phobes among the state's politicians.

If, indeed, there was an authentic hero in the drama that was to follow, it was Chancellor Charles E. Young, at thirty-seven one of the youngest university chief executives and by all odds the most candid. At UCLA's helm only a little more than a year, he had managed to win the affection of much of the campus, and even the grudging respect of its rebels.

It had been a year to test Young's cool—and he'd kept it.

He had defused a potentially explosive take-over of his own administration building's second floor by two hundred militant demonstrators protesting the presence of Dow Chemical recruiters on campus. Rather than resort to force (in the building's basement a riot squad of police awaited only Young's word to move against the invaders), he'd told the students, "Let's all go home and talk about it tomorrow." And the rebels had.

Young's most dangerous—and personally most embarrassing—test had come the previous January. Two Black Student Union members had been gunned down at a campus BSU meeting. The victims as well as two of the five black US (United Slaves) members arrested for the murders were enrollees in Young's pet and newly set up "High Potential" program for disadvantaged, but promising, minority students.

Young had moved swiftly not simply to quell rumors and allay fears, but to assure minority leaders, on campus and off, that the "High Potential" program would in no way be affected by the tragedy.

Through it all, Young had lost none of his usual aplomb, although privately he conceded, "Sometimes I feel as if I'm being picked apart slowly but surely by a big flock of birds."

Seemingly imperturbable in turtleneck shirt and sports jacket, Young had been caught unawares by Angela Davis' hiring. Now he found himself the man in the middle.

Clearer than most, Young perceived in the script not merely a drama of confrontation, but of stark pathos.

"This has been a Greek tragedy from the beginning," he was later to reflect. "Everyone is playing a predetermined part. Everybody speaks the lines he is supposed to speak and we go plodding on to the inevitable outcome."

The outcome, as Young foresaw it then in late September, 1969, would be the eventual overruling by the courts of the Regents' dismissal of Angela—with the windup that she would retain her teaching position at least until the conclusion of her one-year provisional contract. But in the postmortem, Young anticipated a grisly, if only figurative, body count. His own, he conceded with his usual candor, might well be found among the victims.

The Angela Davis Affair, as it was to play itself out through the months ahead, had all the twists and turns of a soap opera, and a cast to match.

The cast—in order of their appearance:

Angela, playing herself. Breaking public silence at a press conference on *September 23,* she freely admitted membership in the Communist party's all-black Che-Lumumba Club, and stated she formerly was also an activist in the Black Panthers.

Dr. Donald Kalish. September 26. Only ten days before the start of UCLA's fall quarter, he assigned Angela to take up her teaching chores immediately, although originally she hadn't been scheduled to begin teaching until early in 1970. Angela's assigned course was "Recurring Philosophical Themes in Black Literature," a regular UCLA catalog course.

Governor Ronald Reagan. September 27. He angrily charged Kalish with malicious mischief.

Chancellor Young. October 1. Before an overflow meeting of UCLA's faculty he stood against the Regents, declaring, "The very concept of a university demands a freedom of inquiry which is incompatible with the application of political tests." He promised the faculty he would not prevent Angela from teaching despite the Regents' dismissal order.

UCLA faculty. October 1. It voted 551 to 4 to rescind its nineteen-year support of the Regents' anti-Communist hiring policy.

The Regents. October 3. Meeting in emergency session in San Francisco, the Regents decided not "at this time" to attempt to remove Angela from her teaching post. Instead, they voted to withhold credit from her course.

183

Angela. October 6. As two thousand faculty and students jammed UCLA's largest auditorium, Angela lectured her first class. Milling pickets outside carried signs reading "Davis, YES; Reagan, NO."

UCLA's student body. October 15. In a referendum, 81.3 percent of those students casting votes declared themselves opposed to Angela's firing. The vote was 7,410 against dismissing her, 1,389 in favor.

Superior Court Judge Jerry Pacht. October 20. In a strongly worded opinion, he declared unconstitutional the Regents' three-decade-old policy against employing Communists.

Chancellor Young. October 22. Obeying a court decree, he reinstated credit for Angela's philosophy course.

State Assemblyman Floyd L. Wakefield. October 27. He launched a voter recall drive to oust from the bench Judges Pacht and Robert Kenny, both of whom figured in the Angela Davis case.

UC faculty. December 16. Tabulation of a secret, mailed ballot among faculty on all nine University of California campuses revoked the faculty's long-standing support of the Regents' anti-Communist hiring policy. A faculty spokesman explained that to have continued to support the policy would, in the faculty's view, have been an endorsement "for political tests . . . as a basis for university employment."

Appeals Court. December 22. A three-judge tribunal, headed by Judge John J. Ford, overruled Judge Pacht's decision on a change-of-venue technicality.

Angela. January 7, 1970. With the start of the 1970 winter quarter, her teaching load in UCLA's philosophy department has now doubled. Angela now teaches two courses.

The Regents. May 15, 1970. Following UC President Charles J. Hitch's recommendation that Angela be rehired for a second year, the Regents broke a fifty-year precedent. They relieved both President Hitch and UCLA Chancellor Charles E. Young "of any further authority . . . in the Davis case." The way was cleared for the Regents themselves to fire Angela.

UCLA faculty. May 18, 1970. In angry defiance, UCLA's all-powerful Academic Senate voted to retain Angela in her teaching job

—and pay her full salary out of their own pockets, if necessary— should the Regents fire her.

The Regents. June 19, 1970. They voted (15 to 6) not to renew Angela's teaching contract, in effect firing her. Their action, the Regents declared, was based on four "extreme, anti-ethical" speeches they accused Angela of making, one on the seething UC/Santa Barbara campus, which they contended were "inconsistent with qualification for appointment to the faculty of the University of California."

Angela. June 20, 1970. She vowed to carry her dismissal to the U.S. Supreme Court, if necessary.

The curtain fell on what could be but Act I in *The Angela Davis Affair.*

ACT II opened to the staccato of gunfire. The date was August 7, 1970. Four heavily armed blacks, three of them convicts and one on trial for murdering a San Quentin guard, burst from Marin County (California) Hall of Justice with five hostages—Superior Court Judge Harold J. Haley, Assistant DA Gary Thomas, and three women jurors. In the wild fusillade that followed, Judge Haley and three of his kidnappers were slain.

The four guns that had been smuggled into that San Rafael courtroom were quickly traced to Angela. Even then, I could not bring myself to believe the mounting evidence: that Angela might personally be involved. And in an apparent Latin American-type plot to take hostages in the hope of bartering them for the freedom of the so-called "Soledad Brothers"—three black inmates accused of murdering a Soledad State Prison guard.

Angela, I knew, had helped organize the Soledad Brothers Defense Committee. She'd worked tirelessly in their behalf. But kidnapping and murder?

When the news first broke, I was sure the guns Angela had purchased had been loaned or taken and used without Angela's knowledge. I couldn't imagine it being otherwise. Then police dropped their bombshell: The shotgun used in the courtroom takeover had been purchased just two days previously—on August 5. Angela was the purchaser.

Swiftly, the evidence—condemning on its face—linked Angela

185

as more than a casual observer to the Marin County shootout. Witnesses claimed they'd seen her in the rented Ford van—the getaway vehicle—the day before the escape attempt. Others put her near the scene (she'd bought the shotgun in nearby San Francisco) in the frequent company of militant, seventeen-year-old Jonathan P. Jackson. Young Jackson—whose older brother, George, was one of the Soledad Brothers—had smuggled the weapons, all of them Angela's, into the courtroom. Jonathan, in fact, had visited his brother in San Quentin two days before the takeover, the same day Angela purchased the shotgun. The following day young Jackson had been seen in Judge Haley's courtroom. The next day he'd come bearing Angela's four guns. If her guns under California law had aided the commission of a major crime, she could be judged legally as liable as the actual participants. Now Angela, charged with murder and kidnapping, was a fugitive. And had been, said police, from the moment, some three hours after the shootout, she'd boarded a plane in San Francisco bound for Los Angeles International Airport. In her possession was a valid passport.

As the FBI added her name to its "ten most-wanted" list (Angela is the third woman to make the list in its twenty-year history), one of UCLA's most respected professors spoke for the academic community everywhere. He echoed my own shock and dismay.

"The question here," he dolefully concluded, "is neither academic freedom nor the right of political dissent. . . . We [faculty and students] have gone to the wall . . . to make this distinction between the advocacy of unpopular ideas and unlawful activity. This principle offers no protection from . . . the legitimate consequences of illegal action."

In fighting UC's regents and gathering to her support the majority of students and faculty, Angela had shown political maturity. But her involvement in violence—if proved—could be only an act of abject immaturity. And one which played into the hands of those most vocal in seeking to bar her from teaching.

Uncertain as *The Angela Davis Affair* remains, there is one certainty. Academic freedom has been dealt another blow. And this time not by its enemies, but by one of its own soldiers and once staunchest defenders—Angela herself.

186

11. Days of Rage—and Roses

SDS did not come apart quietly. Like a man on a rack of his own devising, the Students for a Democratic Society tore itself apart excruciatingly, in screaming agony, a limb at a time.

The screaming and the agony were the grisly sound effects of SDS's "Days of Rage"—five unscripted days of retribution and, at the last, self-disembowelment, staged in Chicago's dingy, morguelike Coliseum, on the fringe of the black ghetto. There, on June 18, 1969, fifteen hundred SDS delegates from nearly three hundred campuses gathered for what would be SDS's Ninth National Convention—and in all probability its last as a representative voice of student protest.

At Chicago, sweeping principles for change in America were drowned by raucous minutiae; reason was to fall silent before the drumbeat chorus of "bullshit," "shame," and "motherfucker." The once-reasoned philosophy for betterment was to crumble into bits and pieces snatched uncomprehendingly from Marx, Mao, Castro, and Lin Piao—and thrust like blunted daggers at the cowering delegates.

Before it was over the convention *minority* (SDS's Revolutionary Youth Movement faction—RYM—allied to SDS's national office staff) would "expel" the convention's *majority*—the Worker–Student Alliance (WSA)—supported by the Maoist Progressive Labor (PL) party.

Leaders from both factions would take to the podium protected by their own handpicked bodyguards. For the first time in SDS's history, delegates would be frisked at the door by a green armbanded security force (which would lead Jeff Gordon, spokesman for the PL faction, to protest loudly from the convention floor that "women's breasts are being felt and their legs are being felt close to their vaginas").

187

Another first was the barring of the Establishment press—something most SDSers would be thankful for, considering what went on.

If you've watched the so-called "sane" conventions of Republicans and Democrats on television, you would have found SDS's Chicago convention insanely incredible. But much of it wouldn't have been televised. It would have been censored right off the tube.

On its surface, the fight between opposing factions was over such issues as the *status of blacks in the "revolution"* (RYM held them to be an "oppressed colony within the U.S.," while the PL/Worker–Student Alliance maintained blacks were just "workers," like other workers championed by PL); *who, when the revolution arrived, should hold ultimate power within the U.S.* ("the people," said RYM; "the workers," countered PL); *who should lead the revolution* ("whites should follow black leadership," insisted RYM; "the workers, white and black, should lead it," said PL); *what should be SDS's tactic on campus* (RYM: "demand the admission of black students as a tactic aimed toward the shutdown of the campuses"; PL: "working-class students shouldn't go to college. College merely twists their minds and diminishes their 'working class' perspective").

On one issue—"male chauvinism," a piece of rhetoric lifted whole from Marx—both sides seemed in agreement. Male chauvinism described women for what SDSers saw them to be: an oppressed class, looked down upon and used by males as little more than personal property. That women's status was still mostly horizontal was, both sides loudly agreed, the fault of the American male's "chauvinistic" (blind) attitude toward females and their rights as females. So everybody was against "male chauvinism." Yet it was this one issue of "agreement" which, ultimately, would precipitate the split in SDS.

One whole bundle of issues that never made SDS's convention agenda concerned possible changes in the American system. Nobody at Chicago was talking about "reforming the system," "working within the democratic framework," and least of all about "electoral politics."

On the agenda was only one serious proposal: violent revolution.

But even this was surface stuff. Beneath lay the basic battle for control of SDS.

When the shouting, the vituperation, and divisive scheming were over, the Students for a Democratic Society would lay in pieces. Where, at the outset, there had been one SDS, now there would be five. In reality, there would be no SDS at all. Nor would the Students for a Democratic Society any longer truly represent the campus or the Movement. It had, in fact, ceased to represent either long before Chicago.

The paradox was almost too easily explained. While the activist hard-core leadership of the majority of SDS campus chapters by 1969 were Marxists of one brand or another, most rank-and-file SDSers were not. They still are not.

Over-all, my own guess is that less than 10 percent of the SDS's nationwide membership were revolutionary Marxist-Leninists. Within the Movement itself, there are even fewer "revolutionaries"—less than 1 percent, by my estimate.

Some authorities have put the "wrecker" element just slightly higher. The Educational Testing Service, which works closely with the campuses, has estimated the revolutionary "wrecker" element at 2 percent. It classified another 8 percent as "militants." Activist "protesters" (but not necessarily militant ones) added up to another 20 percent. Finally, Educational Testing found that at least another 40 percent more of the campus were "concerned students"—students concerned about the drift of the American system. They, like the vast majority of "protesters" and certainly like many of the "militants" themselves, were for change, not revolution. Any way you figured it, the "wrecker" revolutionary element came to less than 5 percent.

Yet the "wreckers" controlled SDS's Chicago convention because they controlled SDS's campus chapters. That they did was the fault of the Movement's great silent majority.

My own "election," as UCLA's only voting delegate to SDS's 1967 National Council (NC) meeting on the Indiana University campus, was typical of the way it happened on most campuses.

I *wanted* to attend that Bloomington, Indiana, NC meeting and so did Walt Crowe. One night at our Student (Party) Club it was decided that we should try to get UCLA's SDS chapter to elect us its delegates. At the very next chapter meeting we simply proposed ourselves as delegates.

"You're elected," was the response of most of the SDS kids there

I LIVED INSIDE THE CAMPUS REVOLUTION

who really didn't have the time or money to go. Besides, who wanted to traipse two thousand miles back east in mid-winter to a convention? Most of the chapter kids had far more compelling plans over that Christmas vacation—like skiing. Anyway, most of them weren't all that interested in SDS politics. But Marxist-minded SDSers *are*. They eat, sleep, and fornicate politics.

Thus it was that UCLA's SDS sent two delegates—both Marxists and both members of the Communist party—to Bloomington. Neither Walt nor I were "wreckers," granted. Even so, we were more attuned to philosophical Marxism than the majority of UCLA's SDSers. The chapter wasn't Marxist. Neither were the majority of its members. The worst that could be said was that they were "inactivists"—kids who willingly permitted a handful of super-activists, who were Marxists, to speak for them. The same kind of thing was happening in SDS chapters all across the nation.

Eighty percent of the fifteen hundred campus delegates who showed up at Chicago for SDS's crucial convention were revolutionary Marxists. The only real question was which kind of revolutionaries— firebrand "independents" or equally rabid "wrecker" Maoists, aligned with Progressive Labor (PL)—would emerge in control of SDS come the convention's adjournment.

In tenuous control, at the convention's call to order, was SDS's Chicago national office hierarchy which included strapping, twenty-six-year-old Mike Klonsky, SDS's national secretary; Bernadine Dohrn, SDS's twenty-seven-year-old interorganizational secretary, a graduate (in 1967) from the University of Chicago's law school and a professed revolutionary Communist; Mark Rudd, leader of Columbia University's 1968 shutdown, whose politics were closer to Bernadine's than to Klonsky's; and a scattering of others, including Robert Avakian, a Maoist "expert" and leader of the then newly organized BARU (the California Bay Area Revolutionary Union).

Arrayed against them were the forces of the Maoist-leaning PLers—headed by tough, owlish Jeff Gordon, an SDS activist from Brooklyn; John Pennington of Harvard; and, of course, behind the scenes, Milt Rosen, chairman of the Progressive Labor party. Rosen had masterminded PL's tactical infiltration of SDS back in 1966.

Gordon and his PLers, who formed the Worker–Student Alliance

190

within SDS's delegate ranks, were the unknown quantity. PL's influence both at a chapter level and within SDS's leadership had grown enormously since SDS's last national convention, in 1968, at East Lansing, Michigan. The question to be answered was, how much?

The scene was tense with expectation, stifling with smoke (there was a hint of pot in the air), and laden with danger: the chairs, the folding type, were also the throwing kind . . . and every one of them, as every delegate-veteran to violence was well aware, was a potential weapon in the opposition's hands.

On the podium, the convention's chairman pounded for order (using a rock rather than a gavel).

Minutes later big Mike Klonsky and his SDS staff knew they were in the minority and inevitably would lose their grip on SDS. The revealing clue lay only partially concealed in one of those "unimportant" convention floor fights which, in reality, proved to be a test of voting strength.

The issue, raised by Klonsky himself, was whether to admit the Establishment press—provided that, as big Mike suggested, each reporter divvied up $25 and signed an oath promising not to testify later against SDS members present, or about the convention itself.

Suddenly a PL delegate rose in opposition.

"I say bar them," he thundered (to huge applause). "We don't need the capitalist press. The capitalist press isn't going to print the truth, anyway. We have our own press [meaning the Movement's "underground" papers]."

More huge applause followed (and an uneasy rustling of those untethered chairs), and then the chairman gaveled the debate to a vote. The decision of the delegates came swiftly and decisively.

PL's position—to bar the press—won by a 3 to 2 majority.

And so the die was cast. Klonsky and SDS's national office leadership sensed that they were licked. PL obviously had more delegates, and more convention votes.

Still, about a quarter of the delegates, many of them women, remained uncommitted. Some belonged to small factions of independent socialists or even anti-Communist labor groups. Others were just straddling the ideological fence.

With the gals apparently holding the slim difference between

191

abject defeat and some semblance of victory (and control), Klonsky decided to press hard for women's liberation, an issue calculated to woo the uncommitted females. Klonsky's strategy almost worked. The factor that upset it was his dealing from his deck of tricks still another issue—racism—and his trump on the racism scene: an angry Black Panther.

The Panther was Rufus "Chaka" Walls, Deputy Minister of Information for the Illinois Panthers. Tough, blunt, and profane, once Walls had the convention microphone—and the delegates' ears—he refused to let go.

It wasn't Walls's profanity that incensed the female delegates. Profanity, after all, is part of the lexicon of activism. What did annoy them was Walls's sudden switch to an issue almost as close to his heart as racism—women's liberation.

"About all this 'male chauvinism' jazz," Walls roared, his voice booming across the convention floor. "I'm for Pussy Power myself."

As SDS's revolutionary puritan females cringed ("You can call them almost anything to their faces and they won't bat an eye, but 'pussy power'—that hits them below the belt," one delegate said later), Walls ranted on.

"Revolutionary women have a lot to contribute," he bellowed. "I'm glad to see there are enough women around here for all the revolution. The way women contribute is by getting laid."

From the four corners of the Coliseum's vast, dingy arena, a chant of anguished protest went up, "Fight male chauvinism!"

The chanting eventually drove Walls from the podium. Reluctantly, he handed the microphone to another Panther, Jewel Cook, the Chicago Panthers' field secretary. Cook pleaded first for quiet, launched into a diatribe on the PL delegates (which had been Walls's actual assignment), then reverted to Walls's unfinished theme.

"I'm with my brother. I'm for Pussy Power myself," Cook declared. "The *position* of women in the Movement——"

Chanting boomed out again—"Fight male chauvinism"—as that arena full of delegates sensed what Cook was about to say.

"The position of women," the Panther snarled back at them, "should be prone!"

The place turned into bedlam. In disgrace, and with the chants

192

of SDS's angry Marxist delegates pounding at them, the Panthers slinked away from the podium.

In any event, SDS's fate and that of the Klonsky faction was sealed. Far from winning the convention's uncommitted females, Klonsky and his Panthers had succeeded in driving them into PL's fold.

Next day, with Bernadine Dohrn leading the way, SDS's national office faction walked out of the convention. Behind barred doors (in one of the Coliseum's barnlike assembly rooms), they voted to "expel" the PL faction, though it held the clear majority of delegate strength. They also named their splinter group the Revolutionary Youth Movement (RYM) or "The Weatherman," the moniker taken from the lyrics of a Bob Dylan song.

On Saturday night, the convention's last evening session, the RYM delegates strode back into the convention hall, but only long enough to read the majority PL/Worker–Student Alliance out of SDS. They trooped back, led by ten Black Panthers and a column of green-armbanded "security men" who ringed Klonsky and Dohrn on the podium. It was Bernadine who, having led the walkout, now made it final.

"We in the next room," she shouted, "have been discussing principles. We support the national liberation struggles of the Vietnamese, the American blacks, and all other colonials. We support all who take up the gun against U.S. imperialism. We support the governments of China, Albania, North Vietnam, and North Korea. We support women's liberation."

As startled PLers tried to drown her out by chanting, "Read Mao . . . Read Mao!" Bernadine continued relentlessly:

"All members of the Progressive Labor Party/Worker–Student Alliance and all who do not support these principles are no longer members of SDS."

Thus SDS had become two separate groups: the RYM ("The Weatherman") and the PL/Worker–Student Alliance. Within months SDS would be three as Klonsky and Avakian pulled their people out of RYM, and labeled themselves the Revolutionary Youth Movement II (whereupon "The Weatherman," headed by Mark Rudd and Bernadine Dohrn, added an "I" to make it RYM I, differentiating themselves from Klonsky's new "II" group). The Klonskyites had split from "The Weatherman" whom they regarded as a "bunch of adventurist crazies." Nonetheless, all were Marxist Maoists.

Two other groups eventually set up on their own. One was a small faction calling themselves the Labor Committee, and the other was a group of anti-Communist leftists—the Independent Socialist Clubs. From one unified organization, SDS had splintered into five conflicting groups.

SDS had, in fact, come to grief. The chanting, sweating, scheming young revolutionaries at Chicago spouting quotations from Chairman Mao certainly did not represent their campuses back home. In truth, they represented only themselves.

After the split, both "The Weatherman" faction under Rudd and the PL/Worker–Student Alliance, headed by John Pennington, its newly elected national secretary, loudly proclaimed themselves to be the "real SDS."

In Chicago, "The Weatherman"/Rudd faction (which in the wee hours of the convention's final day had laid claim to SDS's bank account, membership roster, and list of contributors) declared itself the "winner" and continued to publish *New Left Notes,* most of whose thinning pages were devoted to castigating the PL faction.

In Boston, stronghold of Progressive Labor and also home of the Pennington-led PL/Worker–Student Alliance, the PL version of the "real SDS" published its own version of *New Left Notes.* Most of its pages were given over to diatribes against the Rudd faction.

It was hard telling, at a casual glance, the origin of these rival *New Left Notes.* Both pictured the clenched, upraised black fist of anarchy and revolution on their front pages. Both claimed to be published by the "Students for a Democratic Society." To sort them out it was necessary to note their differing publishing addresses. PL's was published in Boston; "The Weatherman's," in Chicago.

There were, of course, other more significant differences.

The worker-allied PL splashed its version of *New Left Notes* with stories headlined, "Ally With Campus Workers" . . . or, again, "Students Help Workers Fight Racist Boss."

"The Weatherman"/Rudd version of *New Left Notes*—proclaiming "All Power to the People" (*not,* you'll note, power just to

194

"workers")—was, if anything, more frantic and even more Maoist. Whole pages were devoted to Cuba and Castro (in which "The Weatherman" announced recruitment of its now well publicized "Venceremos Brigade" of youthful Yankee cane cutters—in the service of Fidel). Uncle Ho commanded a front cover—under "The Weatherman" pronouncement (and belief) that "Vietnam Has Won!" Meaning, of course, the North Vietnamese. And under a photograph of a dozen bearded and bra-less collegians fiercely engaged in calisthenics (and trying hard to look fierce while doing them), it proclaimed in all seriousness that this was "The Red Army . . . training in parks in Cleveland."

It was all pretty silly. Worse, it was plain sick.

As 1970 dawned, the Rudd/"Weatherman" faction gave up any pretense of being either "the real" or any other kind of SDS. So, in the end, PL had won. In just a little more than three years it had succeeded first in penetrating, then in infiltrating, then in subverting, and finally in capturing SDS. But in winning, PL had achieved an empty victory. It had won a corpse.

Just as the Communist party had suffocated the DuBois clubs with its Marxist embrace, PL had destroyed SDS with Maoist affection. Thus had both wings of the Communist party, though by different routes, annihilated the student organizations they had attempted to build and control. PL had done it through infiltration, the Party by high-handed bureaucracy.

The "crazies" might still be winning headlines, but largely they had lost the campuses. They had taken to playing revolution mostly with themselves.

All too apparently some few were also playing with dynamite. While doing so early in March, 1970 (making bombs, police bomb squadders would say), one group of "Weatherman" crazies blew themselves up and almost took with them the next door Greenwich Village town house of actor Dustin Hoffman (*The Graduate*).

Police found the bodies of three mangled "Weatherman" SDSers in the rubble. Moments after the blast, two young women had run from the building. One was Cathy Wilkerson, former editor of *New Left Notes,* one of three top SDSers who had accompanied David Dellinger on a futile mission to North Vietnam in November, 1967, and a bomb of a girl whom I'd met on several occasions. But I certainly had had no inkling then that Cathy—the daughter of a prosperous radio station executive—would take to making them. And, of all places, in her father's own $250,000 Village town house.

One of the crazies—Bob D.—once showed me his standard text: a plain, untitled pamphlet. It described in do-it-yourself detail a dozen bombs put together from stuff you can buy at any hardware store or make in a school's chemistry lab.

One was a light-bulb bomb. It was a childishly simple and vengeful device, capable of setting off a charge of dynamite.

How far from the mainstream of the Movement—and the campus—SDS has really strayed was never more evident than during Moratorium Day, 1969. While millions across the nation chose that October 15 for the greatest outpouring of antiwar sentiment in the nation's history—with most schools and colleges shut down, with 100,000 massed in Boston Common, 50,000 parading before the White House—PL, which was now SDS, not only sat out Moratorium Day, but boycotted it.

"Moratorium Day," headlined PL/SDS in its newspaper, "Is a Cover, Not a Solution."

With true Maoist rhetoric, SDS's leadership pictured Moratorium Day as a kind of capitalistic trick.

"The Moratorium," said SDS, "sees the Vietnam War as an 'American tragedy'—as a tragic mistake. We disagree. It is not an accident. We think that it is part and parcel of the system of U.S. imperialism, a system based on the driving need of big business to maximize profits. . . . We think that the U.S. has no right to negotiate anything in Vietnam. U.S. businessmen have exploited the human and natural resources of the Vietnamese for twenty years. This has meant lousy wages, miserable conditions and starvation for the people of Vietnam, and huge profits for U.S. firms and their local allies."

It was hardly the campuses, or even most SDSers, talking. It was even less most American youths talking. It was the wholly Maoist Communist SDS leadership talking.

It was further proof of the assessment the independent radical newspaper *Guardian* (which plays neutral observer on the Left) had made after witnessing SDS's breakup convention at Chicago.

"The base of [SDS's] membership," concluded the *Guardian,* "still remains incredibly distant from the center of decision-making in the organization. If this trend continues, the distance may become unbridgeable."

By Moratorium Day, 1969, that distance had widened to the infinite. If anything, the gap between the campuses' SDSers and SDS's leadership was wider than the generation gap itself.

Thus, while fifteen thousand students gathered in solemn protest on the University of Wisconsin campus, while twenty thousand lighted candles at UCLA, and Mayor John Lindsay of New York, economist John Kenneth Galbraith, and even actress Lauren Bacall spoke out for peace, SDSers in the main stayed home. The fact that they did and that Moratorium Day without them became a legend in campus history belittles SDS's role these days in the Movement.

During the months following that first Moratorium Day, I made two personal marches on Washington myself. On November 6 I went voluntarily to be interviewed at an executive session of the Senate Internal Security Subcommittee. The second time—on December 19—I returned in anger, under subpoena from the subcommittee's chairman, Senator James O. Eastland (D.-Miss.).

Eastland was attempting to force me to swear into the public record the more than two hundred pages of commentary I had given—detailing my years of undercover work for the FBI—at an off-the-record executive hearing of the previous month. Once back in Los Angeles following that first session, I'd had serious second thoughts. I simply did not want my comments to become public testimony, and possibly be used against those I had named. Originally, I had been scheduled to return to Washington on December 4 to swear in my testimony. I simply didn't show. Senator Eastland had then commanded my appearance by subpoena.

When the U.S. marshal delivered it he'd said curtly, "This is the highest order of subpoena we serve. It isn't something you'd better let slide."

He was right. Eastland held the trump—the power to hold me in contempt of the U.S. Senate. But I wasn't about to play the senator's game. A few days earlier I'd gone on television in Los Angeles to explain why I no longer would.

197

In that televised interview, I said I now felt I'd been wrong in working for the Bureau. I said it was morally corrupting for the FBI, or any government agency, to recruit one citizen to spy against another. It corrupted all citizens. It corrupted the nation. Most corrupting of all to democracy was the use of one citizen's testimony against another, and especially when used as a bludgeon by repressive government bodies, as Eastland's Senate Internal Security Subcommittee.

I stood as a tawdry symbol of that corruption. For none had been more corrupted than I.

The basic wrongs in American society, I went on to say, weren't going to be corrected by jailing or harassing a handful of students. If anything, that was compounding the wrongs. My testimony—before both the Subversive Activities Control Board the previous June and again, in November, in closed session before the Internal Security Subcommittee, could lead only to government repression.

Even then, in November, 1969, Vice President Spiro Agnew's attack on the press and television media, the then-in-progress "Chicago 7" trial and the shrill cry from those on the right for "law and order," all pointed toward an eventual suspension of American freedoms.

It would be months before William L. Shirer, dean of journalist-historians (*The Rise and Fall of the Third Reich*) would publicly reach the same conclusion. He predicted a "legal dictatorship"—a dictatorship by approval of middle-of-the-road Americans. The Movement had been saying the same thing since late 1968.

I wanted no part in driving America toward fascism—or toward the inevitable revolution of youth that a turn toward fascism would surely ignite. I would no longer play fink.

That was why I stood on my constitutional rights when, on December 19—in answer to the Senate's subpoena—I stood before a special executive session of its Internal Security Subcommittee, in Washington, chaired that day by Senator Strom Thurmond (R.-S.C.). At my side was Washington attorney Henry Schoenfeld. He had been recommended by John Abt, who had been my inquisitor at the SACB hearings in Los Angeles, and to whom in desperation I'd turned for help.

198

That day in Washington I simply refused officially to acknowledge the two hundred pages of commentary I'd already given the committee unofficially. That was the crux of the matter. I could not prevent my thousands of words of testimony from being used on a purely informational basis by the subcommittee or various government agencies. But without my commentary's being put "on the record," it could never be used against my peers. I was determined to prevent my words from being used as bludgeons against those I had exposed. The only solution was to stand on my constitutional rights.

An hour of badgering by Thurmond, and the matter of William Tulio Divale versus the U.S. Senate was laid to rest.

Perhaps, in my own way, I'd helped to serve blunt notice on the Establishment and on the world of my elders of youth's new mood in the seventies.

We are no longer impressed by the society they have created. We no longer hold their values either necessarily valid or necessarily meritorious of preservation. We do not believe in their pious righteousness because they, themselves, know it to be fraudulent. We do not look to them as models for our own daily lives because theirs are no better and no less imperfect than our own.

No longer will we be pilloried by archaic authority, repressed by a justice that is often unjust, or held to obedience of laws made for an earlier generation in a past era.

Never will we permit the kind of "law and order" fascism that Shirer and many Movement leaders darkly envisage. Six million unprotesting Jews may have gone as lambs to their slaughter. But America's youth generation is neither lamblike nor meek. Those who would make fascism in America will make it at their own risk. Nor will youth stand still for repression—political, parental, or police. Neither will it much longer tolerate the hypocrisy of the American Dream.

Those who imagine otherwise are deluding themselves.

They forget that by the mid-seventies (whether or not 1970's eighteen-year-old voting rights bill, signed by Richard Nixon on June 22, withstands the constitutional test), youth will have its say—and likely its way—by the ballot. *Each year*—beginning now and reach-

199

ing to 1984—nearly four million youths will turn twenty-one. Whether as eighteen- or twenty-one-year-old voters, they will vastly swell the "youth vote."

They forget that every element of the U.S. armed forces—the National Guard included—is largely composed and cadred by youths who largely feel the same alienation from society as do most other youths.

They forget that nearly twenty million blacks—a high proportion of them youths—will not permit the clock to be turned back or equality meted out in conciliatory drips and dabs. Nor will they permit the President the luxury of a period of "benign neglect" on race matters, as recently suggested by Presidential Assistant on Urban Affairs Daniel P. Moynihan.

They forget that more than twenty-two million college and high school youths, becoming increasingly polarized against the Dream of their fathers, demand not a more abundant but a more meaningful and life-rewarding America.

Today's youth is not about to permit any combination of government, any coalition of voters, or any cadre of command to dictate away its freedoms. Anyone who believes that youth will permit itself or the nation to be sentenced to the repressive Dark Ages—whether labeled "fascism," "McCarthyism," or "status quo-ism"—has not correctly taken the pulse of the youth generation.

But hard-nosed, poll-watching political experts have. Recently, Representative Rogers Morton of Maryland, national Republican chairman, candidly told a conference of top Republicans, "We have to groove with youth . . . or we are going to be turned out of office at the end of this decade."

I am not at all certain that America has that much time: a decade in which to do the things youth demands be done today or the day after tomorrow, at the latest.

For the challenge of youth to America is blunt and uncompromising.

"Change it or lose it. Time and the ballot are on *our* side."

12. Who's Who in Campus Activism

WHO speaks for American youth?

The answer—as of now—is that no single activist group does. Yet each has set for its task the shaping of tomorrow's young voter—and some, who would take up arms rather than the ballot, of tomorrow's revolutionary.

Whether it will be voter or revolutionary, or something in between, each activist group is spurred by the certain knowledge that today's collegians (as well as those youths who do not enter college) will by their very numbers hold the power in a few years to change the political course and image of America. Bluntly, this is the impact of the activism now engulfing campus and ghetto, city and suburb, the main streets of America and its dingy back alleys.

The rivulet demand for change in the fifties has become a mighty river of protest in the seventies.

The question is not "Will there be change?" Rather, it is "What kind of change—evolutionary or revolutionary?"

In nearly every case the campus has become the focus for change, whether for little more than a restructuring of the status quo or for a revolutionary, even violent, revision of the American system.

That is why the roll call of campus activism I have gathered here deserves more than casual reading. In a relatively few paragraphs I have tried to call the roll of activism, group by group, and to explain where each has been, where each is today, and to provide some inkling as to where each may be going tomorrow.

The roster of campus activism, grown from a handful of campus-active groups in the sixties, has become a legion in the seventies. It spans the political and philosophical spectrum, from the radical right NYA (the newly formed National Youth Alliance which espouses racial inequality, and is antiblack, anti-Jewish, and antimoderate) to the revolutionary left—perhaps best represented by RYM I, the Maoist-revolutionary "Weatherman" offshoot of the Students for a Democratic Society.

I have included only those groups that are campus-based (or have strong campus ties) and that, either because of their present and future impact, or because of their cogent past, seem most likely to influence the future course of the nation.

STUDENTS AFRO-AMERICAN SOCIETY

This organization has various names and is sometimes called the eastern BSU. Some of the names are as follows—at Harvard: Organization for Black Unity; at Yale: Black Student Alliance; at Vassar, Cornell, Rutgers, Wesleyan, others: Students Afro-American Society; at Colgate: the Association of Black Collegians; at the University of Wisconsin: the Concerned Black People; at Ohio State: the Black Student Union. Elsewhere, Black Liberation Front or Association of Black Students.

They are essentially leaderless, campus-to-campus organizations of black students—a number of them recruited to the campuses they attend from among ghetto or urban youths who financially or scholastically might not otherwise qualify. Some are enrolled in newly established black studies departments.

Black students find themselves the minute minority (less than 3 percent) on most campuses. Even when their own scholastic backgrounds do not put them at a disadvantage academically (as is frequently the case), they feel socially segregated, tend to stick together —on campus, in living quarters; off campus, socially. Disillusionment among recruited star black athletes is often greatest (they quickly learn they have been recruited to play ball and the coach often couldn't care less if they graduate. And many don't). Many complain their college courses are irrelevant to their backgrounds and taught in the "white context." Others are hard-pressed, even with partial scholarships, to get along financially.

Thus have arisen numerous confrontations, usually aimed against the college and its administration. In recent confrontations black students have demanded: (1) more black students; (2) more black instructors; (3) black studies courses—and control over them and their faculties; (4) special tutoring; (5) segregated living quarters—including all-black dorms; (6) more scholarships and more financial aid; (7) more black athletes.

Often backed by white campus activists, and sometimes by the general student body, black confrontations have ranged from the thirty-six-hour armed take-over of Cornell's Student-Union building to the seizure, in February, 1970, by black students from five nearby Connecticut valley colleges of seven buildings on the all-girl Mount Holyoke College campus. The buildings were held for fourteen hours.

On December 5, 1969, seventy-five members of the Organization for Black Unity (OBU) occupied Harvard's administration building for six hours. Among the OBU's demands: more black workers should be employed on Harvard construction projects. OBU demanded that the percentage of blacks on such jobs be raised from the then approximately 5 percent to "at least 20 percent." Harvard did better than that. It ruled that 19 to 23 percent of workmen on the contested projects would henceforth be black or Puerto Rican.

At Vassar on October 30, 1969, black coeds (members of the Afro-American Society), aided by black male students, filed into the college's administration building at 3:25 A.M. and occupied it, demanding an all-black dormitory and upgrading of the college's black studies program to full degree status. The program, previously, had been experimental and on a pass-fail, nondegree basis.

BLACK PANTHER PARTY (BPP)

Though ostensibly an off-campus organization (with units in some thirty-seven U.S. cities), the militantly revolutionary Black Panthers began on campus (at Merritt College, Oakland, California). The two-thousand-member organization (known also as Black Panther Party for Self-Defense) grew out of a BSU (Black Student Union) chapter started there by then Merritt student Bobby Seale, who would become BPP's chairman, and Huey P. Newton, BPP's Secretary of Defense.

The BPP has maintained close, sometimes controlling ties with campus BSU chapters, a number of whose leaders are also Panthers.

The Panthers' ties with SDS's "The Weatherman" RYM I wing have been close, too. Both share the Panthers' credo—"Power to the People." Both appraise black America as an oppressed colony within the United States which must be liberated—by force if necessary.

By contrast, SDS's other Marxist wing—the Progressive Labor-controlled Worker–Student Alliance—has fallen out with the Panthers over their failure to have a "working class perspective." But PL's opposition to the Panthers goes deeper. PL is fundamentally opposed to the Panthers' "nationalism," which runs contrary to PL's "international" working-class view.

The BPP, as organized by Newton and Seale in Oakland, California, in October, 1966, had as its founding goal the defense of the local black community against alleged brutality by "pigs" (Oakland police), whom Panthers "stalked" (trailed), both to observe any acts of "brutality" and to advise arrested blacks of their constitutional rights.

The Black Panthers took their name (and stalking panther symbol) from the original Black Panther party which SNCC's Stokely Carmichael and John Hulett had organized in Lowndes County (Alabama) as a refuge for black voters barred from the county's white Democratic and Republican organizations. During 1968's brief SNCC–Black Panther merger, Carmichael stood third in the Panther hierarchy, with the title of Prime Minister.

Two 1967 incidents brought the Black Panthers to headlined national attention. On February 21, twenty armed Panthers (openly —but legally—carrying pistols and shotguns) met the widow of Malcolm X at San Francisco's International Airport and escorted her through terminal crowds. The other incident, on May 2, was more dramatic: twenty-six heavily armed Panthers marched into the chambers of the California state legislature, in Sacramento, during a debate on gun control laws. There was no gunfire.

Since then, the openly revolutionary, often gun-toting, now increasingly Marxist-lined Panthers have:

(1) Been involved in numerous shoot-outs and confrontations with police, including a running gun battle in Oakland, California, on

April 7, 1968, in which a Panther party secretary, seventeen-year-old Bobby James Hutton, was killed.

(2) Earned the enmity of U.S. Attorney General John Mitchell and his Department of Justice, whom Panthers accuse of instigating a nationwide Panther purge, aimed at exterminating the Panther leadership. Two of the most notorious raids in the government's alleged "kill Panthers" campaign occurred over a four-day period in Chicago (on December 4, 1969) and in Los Angeles (on December 8), during which two Panthers were killed and seven wounded.

(3) Won the support of much of the hitherto uncommitted and moderate black community. A *Wall Street Journal* survey of blacks in four cities (Cleveland, Chicago, New York, and San Francisco) in January, 1970, showed that sixty out of one hundred blacks interviewed expressed *full support* of both the Panthers' philosophy and armed tactics. Only twenty-six of the mostly middle-class black Americans interviewed flatly opposed the Panthers. Ghetto youth, especially, have become fervent Panther-philes.

Whether concerted or not, police, court, and government action has decimated the Panthers' leadership. Panther chairman Bobby Seale (who was bound and gagged at his "Chicago 7" trial, and slapped with a stiff contempt penalty) was charged with the torture murder of Panther Alex Rackley, who allegedly had turned police informant. Huey P. Newton, twenty-seven, Minister of Defense, was jailed on a murder rap. Minister of Information Eldridge Cleaver, thirty-four, fled the country and went into exile. His wife, Kathleen Cleaver, Minister of Communications, fled with him. David Hilliard, Panther Chief of Staff (and, because of attrition in the leadership, the recent high man in the Panther hierarchy), is under a federal indictment growing out of his declaration that "We should kill President Nixon" —made at a November 15, 1969, Moratorium Day rally in San Francisco.

Of the police raids, many of them nocturnal, *Newsweek* magazine said recently, "The campaign has taken a fearful toll of the Panthers. They have probably never been so fearsome as the ferocity of the drive against them suggests."

As of mid-1970, no less than one hundred Panthers were in jail.

Court action was pending against another three hundred to four hundred. A massive May Day (May 1, 1970) New Haven, Connecticut, demonstration in behalf of Seale and fellow defendants in the Rackley case was all peace and pizza, thanks in part to Yale president Kingman Brewster and the Yale Strike Steering Committee which fed and housed the demonstrators.

For their part, the Black Panthers make no secret of their hatred —and contempt—of police, and of the government itself. The Panthers made "pig" a synonym for "police" in the vocabulary of campus activism. *The Black Panther,* the BPP's weekly national newspaper, often warns the "pigs" to beware.

When San Diego, California, police raided a Panther pad, ostensibly seeking a fugitive, *The Black Panther* printed this warning: "We . . . remind the Pig Power Structure once again of what our Minister of Defense, Huey P. Newton, said some time ago, 'The racist dog policemen must withdraw immediately from our communities, cease their wanton murder and brutality of Black people, or face the wrath of the armed people."

But the Black Panthers can be just as scathing in their opinion and handling of their own as of outsiders. Regularly, *The Black Panther* purges Panthers who have failed to measure up.

Under a headline, "The People's Pimp From New Haven," the paper announced that Panther Theodore Spurlock, "the most reactionary counter-revolutionary madman to ever hit the set here in New Haven [Connecticut], has been expelled from the Black Panther Party." New Haven chapter leaders accused Spurlock of eight sins, including "liberalism," "consciously cashing false checks in the Party's name," and "selfish departmentalism."

BPP's view of Vietnam is equally blunt. The cover of one issue of *The Black Panther* showed a black GI whose helmet was inset with brutal race riot photographs, including a lynched black man. The cover's capition, "OUR Fight Is *Not* in Vietnam."

BPP's ever-growing closer ties with Arab guerrillas (BPP's Minister of Information in exile, Eldridge Cleaver, found sanctuary in Algeria) and its near reverence for the philosophy of Malcolm X have turned many BPPers anti-Semitic. One of the Black Panther party's ten planks calls for "an end of the robbery by the capitalists of our Black Community." Many take this as a veiled reference to ghetto area businessmen, a number of them Jewish. The BPP views Arab guerrillas as "revolutionary brothers." It considers the state of Israel as merely another capitalistic establishment.

Other BPP "planks" include: (1) freedom—and the black community's power to determine its own destiny; (2) full employment for blacks; (3) education that "exposes the true nature of this decadent American society"; (4) exemption of "all black men from military service"; (5) justice—by juries composed of the black man's "peers" (fellow blacks); and (6) self-determination for America's "black colonials" through a United Nations-supervised plebiscite "to be held throughout the black colony in which only black colonial subjects will be allowed to participate, for the purpose of determining the will of black people as to their national destiny."

The Panther "Breakfast Program" for feeding ghetto children has won it wide acclaim in the black community. So, obviously, has its martyrdom.

No single force in black America has, in recent years, contributed so strikingly to the polarization of the black community as have the Black Panthers.

BLACK STUDENTS UNION (BSU)

The BSU—the largest, most vocally militant of campus black student activist groups—was born on the San Francisco State College (SFSC) campus. However, this did not occur in March, 1966, as even many BSU members erroneously believe, but nearly three years earlier, on September 19, 1963. On that date a group of San Francisco State black students, most of them deeply involved in the civil rights movement (and many of them only recently returned from participating in the sit-ins and marches in the South), petitioned the college's student government for the right to form a Negro Students Association (NSA). At its inception the NSA was divided within itself on the question of integration. While spearheading the drive on campus (and in the San Francisco Bay area) for black rights, not all NSAers agreed about the virtues of integration. As one NSAer of

207

those days recalls, "Integration wasn't our scene. It was okay some-where in the distant future, but black was beautiful . . . that was our bag."

Almost single-handedly, one student shaped the NSA into the image of the BSU: James Garrett.

Brilliant and dynamic, the then twenty-four-year-old Garrett was a black student from East Los Angeles City College. In February, 1966, he transferred to San Francisco State College. Garrett had been a SNCC organizer in Watts and a SNCC field worker in the South. As Garrett was later to tell an interviewer from the National Commission on the Causes and Prevention of Violence, "The reason I came to the campus [SFSC] was to try to do some organizing. I wasn't interested in going to school for any other reason than to organize the students."

Jimmy Garrett turned the formerly loosely knit, civil rights-oriented NSA in a new direction: on the road toward militancy and self-pride. Now its student members would declare, "To hell with it—we'll be black, dammit, because black is beautiful."

In March, 1966—only a month after Garrett arrived on the campus—the Negro Students Association voted to change its name to the "Black Students Union." And the BSU was born.

By May of that year, Garrett (who by summer was elected the BSU's chairman) and a BSU task force had done some "sorting" out. They made a power analysis of the college, identified the group that controlled the college's Associated Students (the student governing body that controlled student funds), and came to the conclusion that they were part of the same power structure with which blacks every-where were contending.

"We began," Garrett said later, "to find out what classes were racist. What teachers were racists. We began to set up internal education programs. We were seeking identity. A lot of folks [black students] didn't even know they were black. A lot of people just thought they were Americans."

A number of things in 1966 were to make San Francisco State's black students and BSUers know they were black. One was Stokely Carmichael's cry of "Black Power." Another was the Meredith March.

208

On June 5, James Meredith, who had integrated Ole Miss (the University of Mississippi) in 1962, set out alone on a 220-mile march from Memphis, Tennessee, to Jackson, Mississippi.

He had barely crossed into Mississippi when he was felled (though only injured) by three shotgun blasts.

That summer, too, James Garrett led some of San Francisco State's BSUers through Mississippi, Alabama, and Georgia "to let them see what was happening." The experience was to prove radicalizing.

Wrote Garrett: "We worked hard trying to be white folks and found out we couldn't . . . now our goals are revolutionary."

One thing the BSU did was to establish a ghetto tutorial program. Its aim was not simply to teach reading and writing to black elementary-school children (the BSU was convinced there was something basically wrong with white-oriented, white-taught schools), but to instill them with a consciousness of being black.

The first tutorial program—begun in a Baptist church on San Francisco's Fillmore Street—was launched with a $20 grant from the SFSC's Associated Students fund. Before the four-month-long student strike, which would close down San Francisco State in December, 1968, the BSU's tutorial program had expanded to twenty-two centers. Involved were more than five hundred college students, many of them engaged as tutors.

A second radicalizing project—this one aimed at older black students and blacks in the community—was BSU's experimental black college. The BSU hoped to "reeducate" blacks who had been identifying with the white community.

It would be an oversimplification to say that racism was the only tenet in the BSU's growing-more-revolutionary philosophy. If there was one blanket under which all of the black militants' views might fit, it was simply this: that everything in the predominantly white American society was white-oriented and interpreted from white self-interest. This applied to the Vietnam War, to the college administration, to the content of courses.

BSU's experimental college taught the harder facts of history: that many signers of the Declaration of Independence were slave-

209

owners (the "independence" they were proclaiming was obviously not for their slaves), and that Lincoln, in signing the Emancipation Proclamation, had done so not because he believed slavery wrong, but because abolition of slavery was to the economic advantage of the North. It prostrated the South's economy by abolishing its economic base.

Thus the militancy of BSU grew. In challenging the college's white administrators, its teachers, the content and context of its courses, the BSU eventually provoked a shutdown of San Francisco State College through often adroit and always escalated violence, including an attack on the offices of the student newspaper and its editors (for their editorial racism). And on November 5, 1968, a group of black students, most of them BSUers, presented SFSC President Robert R. Smith (the college's sixth president in eight years) a list of ten nonnegotiable demands. One of the demands was for the immediate establishment of a black studies department.

The weeks following the ten demands and strike have been called the most violent in the history of American higher education. Upwards of six hundred police were needed, daily, to keep the college open. By the end of January, 1969, 731 arrests had been made on campus. Eighty students and thirty-two policemen were injured. Damage to campus buildings exceeded $16,000.

Four months later the strike ended with a settlement put together by Acting President S. I. Hayakawa, the famed semanticist turned top administrator. While it was a tough settlement insofar as student discipline was concerned, the most important of the BSU's ten demands (as well as five demands made by the Third World Liberation Front—TWLF) were met. A Black Studies Department was established (it opened in the fall of 1969).

The San Francisco *Examiner* and *Chronicle* concluded that "When the bitter rhetoric finally dies away, it will become clear that the college has taken several strides toward bringing that much heralded relevant education within reach of larger numbers of non-white students."

Acting President Hayakawa had this to say: "The black radicals want a better America. And they may use revolutionary methods at

210

moments, but they are willing to give them up as soon as it's clear that the administration is willing to do something to improve the quality of their education and their opportunities within the system."

The BSU now claims chapters on some one hundred college and university campuses. Its high school recruiting program is growing.

In December, 1969, a black youth conference at Fresno, California, attended by BSU representatives from most of its state college and university chapters, drew up a loose charter of "The Three BSU Principles." Two of them were strongly working-class-oriented, showing the Marxist influences working within the BSU (supplied, in the past, by PLP—the Progressive Labor party—but more recently by the Communist Party/USA).

The Black Students Union's three principles are:

(1) Gain economic, social and political self-determination for "all oppressed peoples." (In discussing this principle, spokesmen said BSU advocated putting into the hands of the "working class" both political power and the production/distribution of material goods); (2) make educational institutions relevant to the needs of the people; and (3) intensify along socialistic lines the struggle against racism and capitalism.

The BSU has had a notably close relationship with the Black Panther party. A number of campus BSU leaders also claim membership in the Panthers. In recent years, Panther influence over the BSU's escalating militancy has been profound.

The Black Panthers' founders, Huey Newton and Bobby Seale, formed a BSU chapter on the Merritt College (Oakland, California) campus when they were students there.

While Newton and Seale saw in the student-oriented BSU a higher level of black militancy than had existed previously on campuses, it was still far less than the revolutionary organization they envisaged. They went on to form the Black Panthers. Nonetheless, BSU leaders concede that BSU's move toward revolutionary nationalism has been largely sparked by the Panthers.

The BSU's first off-campus office in San Francisco was something of an appendage of the Panthers' own San Francisco headquarters.

211

George Mason Murray, the twenty-two-year-old graduate student who with Garrett ran BSU's first tutorial program, was the Black Panther Minister of Education. Murray is also a leading voice in the BSU. The BSU's national organization—the Union of Black Students Unions—is headquartered at the same address in California as the national headquarters of the Black Panther party.

CHRISTIAN WORLD LIBERATION FRONT (CWLF)

Launched in 1969, the CWLF is essentially a fundamentalist Christian evangelical group gone hippie in an effort to reach campus radicals and to reform, in particular, those among them making the drug scene.

CWLF speaks in the vernacular of the hippie subculture, converting New Testament themes to the language of the New Generation, and steering a nonviolent, nonactivist path while opposing drug use and sexual relations outside the bounds of marriage. Its members often live communally, but with the sexes separated, in CWLF quarters newly established in Berkeley and Oakland, California.

While CWLF originated in Berkeley, it is spreading to similar high-density student areas of the Midwest and East.

The Christian World Liberation Front's founder-minister is forty-year-old Dr. Jack Sparks, a former associate professor of statistics and research design at Penn State who quit teaching to engage full-time in the student ministry.

"The only movement that was capturing youth was the radical left," he concludes, "and that seemed like a shame to me."

What the CWLF says, in essence, is that youth can live a "clean" (referring to mental, not bodily cleanliness) life, even though caught up in hippie or radical ways. The right road, believes CWLF, is to quit both the drug and sex scenes and get with Christ.

CWLFers joined San Francisco's November 15, 1969, Mobilization March, which called for the U.S.'s immediate withdrawal from Vietnam, although the organization itself takes no political stands. Its Mobilization Day paraders talked about peace (and Jesus Christ) rather than about war (whether Vietnam or elsewhere).

CWLF's "Christian hippie" approach and even its name—Christian World Liberation Front—are framed in the vernacular of the student movement.

One of its pamphlets—*Third Letter to the Street Christians*—is essentially a New Testament tract in hip jargon. Another—its *People's Medical Handbook*—contains nutrition, first-aid and personal hygiene tips, plus low-keyed descriptions of various of "the scene's" drugs. Typical CWLF bumper stickers read, "Jesus Is" and "God's Speed Doesn't Kill."

The Christian World Liberation Front, though fledgling, is one of evangelical (and fundamentalist) Christianity's attempts to regain the campus audience it was losing or had lost to radicalism.

W.E.B. DUBOIS CLUBS OF AMERICA (DBC)

Also known as DCA, DuBois Clubs of America, once the flourishing front of the Communist Party/USA (see text) was in the vanguard of the campus Movement, and vied with SDS for campus leadership. At its zenith, in early 1966, the DuBois clubs claimed about three thousand members in perhaps as many as eighty chapters, some on campus, some not. At the time, SDS had a national membership of only six thousand.

From its 1964 founding to 1967, DBC viewed itself as a socialist organization. Following the U.S. Attorney General's 1966 action, naming the DuBois clubs as a "Communist-front organization," DuBois openly acknowledged itself as "Marxist–Leninist." By 1967–68 it began to radicalize, in part to keep pace with SDS and other leading Movement organizations that were already radical, if not verging on the "revolutionary."

In 1970, the Communist party dropped active participation in DuBois and founded the new, fledgling Young Workers Liberation League (YWLL). The YWLL plans to take up where the Party's Young Communist League (YCL) of the 1930s–'40s left off, when it went defunct. As such, YWLL would be similar in structure to other YCLs organized throughout the world under various Communist party auspices.

The DuBois club grew from its San Francisco founding convention of June 19–21, 1964. Subsequent DBC national conventions (as

213

that in Chicago, June 17–19, 1966) invariably were held immediately prior to Communist Party/USA conventions or conferences, since many key DuBoisers were also Party members. Party "clubs," though their existence was often unknown to non-Party student members of DuBois, largely ran and manipulated the various DBC chapters.

The DuBois club took its name from Dr. William E. Burghardt DuBois, one of America's towering black intellectuals (a graduate from Fisk, Harvard, and the University of Berlin), who spent fifty passionate years fighting for black rights, and was a founder of the NAACP.

Born three years after the Civil War (his great-grandfather had fought in the American Revolution with the colonial army in New England), DuBois was a lifetime foe of Booker T. Washington. DuBois publicly blamed Washington for championing black freedom through education and economic progress, rather than through the franchise. More, DuBois publicly scored Washington as the "appeaser" who had largely paved the way for the U.S. Supreme Court's decision of 1896 which established the separate-but-equal doctrine—a doctrine not overturned until 1954.

By contrast, DuBois argued—and fought most of his life—for full integration at every level of society.

Lionized by some of America's greatest minds of his day, DuBois dreamed of creating a "talented tenth": the intellectual leadership needed to win full equality for the black man. His outspoken views led, in 1934, to his break with the NAACP and with Walter White, then its executive secretary.

One of DuBois's most famous declarations—titled simply, "I Won't Vote"—appeared in the October 20, 1956, issue of *The Nation*.

"In 1956," wrote DuBois, "I shall not go to the polls. I have not registered. I believe that democracy has so far disappeared in the United States that no 'two evils' exist. There is but one evil party with two names, and it will be elected despite all I can do or say."

DuBois was eighty-eight when the article appeared. By then he had not only abandoned the struggle for black rights in America but had turned toward the left. In later years he teamed with leftist President Kwame Nkrumah of Ghana, where he lived in his last years

214

and where, at ninety-five, he died on August 28, 1963. He had joined the Communist party, as he was to say, late in life: at age ninety-three.

Founded a year after his death, the DuBois clubs—though dominated by the Old Left—took a militant, New Left stance. It championed issues close to the community (black rights, worker rights) and the campus—draft resistance, anti-Vietnam, and the growing control of the campus through military-corporate research and funding.

The DuBois clubs' decline and now virtual eclipse can be blamed only in part on the Attorney General's petition to have it declared a Communist front organization.

More rightly, DuBois' decline can be blamed on its founder—the Communist party, whose increasingly top-down control and internal meddling cost DuBois its student support. New Left-minded students simply deserted DuBois, many to join SDS.

The DuBois club still maintains some semblance of organization and its headquarters in New York City.

NATIONAL STUDENT ASSOCIATION (NSA)

Also known as the United States National Student Association, NSA is the oldest, largest (based on its contention that because it represents the student governments on nearly four hundred campuses, it represents their entire student bodies), and most politically diverse of student organizations. In reality, NSA—perhaps because it has largely been a debating society among liberal, conservative, and moderate campus leaders—has never had any real power on the campuses.

Founded in 1947 by twenty-four U.S. campus leaders (including Douglass Cater, who was to become a White House aide to Presidents Kennedy and Johnson), NSA was conceived as the spokesman for American students in international student affairs—and, specifically, as a counter to such aggressive, Communist-subsidized international youth fronts as the International Union of Students (IUS). NSA grew out of the experience of American student leaders at 1946's Communist-dominated World Student Congress in Prague, where Soviet-backed student groups ran the show.

NSA's international program has always been especially strong.

215

Its representatives attend international student rallies and conferences. NSA has arranged hundreds of foreign trips and manages a world-ranging student exchange program.

But NSA's often liberal stance (it condemned U.S. policy in Vietnam and in the Dominican Republic, denounced nuclear testing, loyalty oaths, compulsory ROTC, backed civil rights and the southern sit-ins) made it suspect among ultra-conservatives.

NSA exploded into world headlines in late February, 1967, when the New Left-leaning *Ramparts* magazine, tipped by a NSA staffer, revealed that the U.S. Central Intelligence Agency had for the past fifteen years financed much of the student organization's operations. Tainted by CIA-ism and with its government funds cut off (by order of Lyndon Johnson), NSA found itself reduced to poverty and ridiculed. Conservatives accused it of radicalism. Campus radicals branded it a "captive" of the Establishment. Others—long frustrated by NSA's cross-purposes and indecisiveness—called it what they had always called it: a sleeping giant in student affairs.

Now the giant is stirring—radically. At NSA's twenty-second Annual Congress at El Paso, Texas, in August, 1969, black students charged the podium and in a wild melee took over the meeting. Blacks and their sympathizers demanded—and got—NSA's pledge of $50,000 (despite NSA's cumulative deficit of $120,000) to help black delegates launch a breakaway organization of their own—likely to be called the National Association of Black Students (NABS). One of NABS's demands: reparations from the campus community.

NSA's more radical turn is exemplified by its president-elect, David Ifshin, twenty-one, former student body president of Syracuse University, who in the spring of 1970 had led the anti-ROTC takeover of the school's administration building. Ifshin was the most vocal proponent of the 1970 NSA convention's "shut down Washington, D.C., on May Day" proposal.

NATIONAL YOUTH ALLIANCE (NYA)

National Youth Alliance is a hard-right, racist, ultra-conservative militant newcomer to campus activism (founded only in the spring of 1969). Born during George C. Wallace's third-party presidential campaign of 1968, it now claims a militant core of some twenty campus chapters (of five to twenty members each), whose philosophy, in part, derives from that of Francis Parker Yockey, whose 619-page book, *Imperium,* extols the virtue of Aryanism, and attacks Jews, Negroes, and Orientals as "culture distorters."

NYA unabashedly preaches white superiority and has one of the most simplistic of organizational structures. Its director—thirty-eight-year-old Louis T. Byers, who says he was booted out of his job as a John Birch Society coordinator (in western Pennsylvania and New York) because of his "publicly racist" views—makes all or most of the decisions and formulates all or most of the policy.

Robert Johnston, thirty-two, NYA's "militancy director," is charged with preparing courses in street fighting, judo, and self-defense. The organization's militant members are schooled to eject physically, if necessary, such recalcitrant students as might stage sit-ins or similar on-campus demonstrations.

NYA recently published the first issues of its newspaper, *Attack,* and a monthly newsletter, *Action* (claimed circulation: four thousand), and has staged a number of "Right Power" rallies.

In an interview, Byers outlined the militarylike chain of command he envisages for NYA.

"We shall not tolerate dissension," he said. "NYA is a fighting movement, not a talking one or a money-raising one, and, therefore, it is structured like an army."

Authoritarianism is necessary for NYA, Byers has claimed, to prevent "infiltration and sabotage."

PROGRESSIVE LABOR PARTY (PLP)

While the Peking-lining, ultra-radical, and revolutionary Progressive Labor party (also known as Progressive Labor Movement or simply Progressive Labor) is based off campus, PL's youthfulness (the average age of its membership is less than twenty-five), its disciplined cadre organization, and, since 1969, its control over the Worker–Student Alliance faction of the Students for a Democratic Society (SDS) make it among the campuses' most influential vanguard groups.

217

J. Edgar Hoover, testifying before the House Subcommittee on Appropriations on April 17, 1969, put PLP in some perspective.

"The PLP," Hoover said, "is one of several Communist splinter extremist groups formed during recent years to enunciate the tenets of Communist China and Mao Tse-tung. The majority [of such groups] have been ineffectual paper organizations. The PLP, however, is one group which has emerged with a broad-based membership making significant organizational strides in major U.S. cities and on a number of college campuses."

Born in 1961 (see Chapter 6) as the Progressive Labor Movement (PLM), but reorganized as a "party" (the Progressive Labor party) in April, 1965, PL was founded by Maoist-liners expelled in 1960 from the Communist Party/USA for their refusal to go along with Khrushchev's policy of co-existence with the West. They sided with Peking's implacable demand for violent revolution.

As the only made-in-America Marxist–Leninist group recognized officially (since 1967) by Peking as being "doctrinally correct," PL marks the first excursion of Maoist communism within the U.S. PL is not, however, controlled puppetlike from Peking. Rather, it is an indigenous species of Maoism which, though its root stock may have been imported from Peking, has grafted to itself some Marxist–Leninist theory which, at times, runs counter to Peking.

PL's ties with Red China are close, however. In October, 1969, PL's bi-monthly magazine *PL—Progressive Labor* (its cover sloganed, "Support Socialist China! Defeat Soviet Imperialism!") saluted Red China on its twentieth anniversary. In a full-page "open" letter addressed to the "Central Committee, Communist Party of China, Chairman Mao Tse-tung, Vice-chairman Lin Piao" and signed "National Committee, Progressive Labor Party," PL said in part:

> On the occasion of the 20th anniversary of the People's Republic of China, the National Committee of the Progressive Labor Party extends deep comradely greetings to the people of China and to their proletarian vanguard, the Communist Party of China. . . .
> U.S. and Soviet imperialists conspire to encircle and destroy socialist China. The focal point of their counter-

revolutionary strategy is to liquidate the People's War in Vietnam by obtaining a political deal in Paris which will protect the U.S. imperialist economic and military interests in Southeast Asia. . . .

This upsurge (in "genuine" Marxist–Leninist thought, Peking-style) gains momentum here in the U.S. With the militant Black workers in the lead, a broad worker–student alliance is being forged against the U.S. ruling class. Increasing numbers of revolutionary youth study Marxism–Leninism and the teachings of Comrade Mao to guide the class struggle for a new society.

Of those expelled from the Communist Party/USA in 1960 for their Maoist ways, a number were to go on to found PL. Among them were Milton Rosen, former Communist party labor secretary in New York State; William Epton, who had been deeply involved in the Harlem riots of 1964; and Fred Jerome and Mortimer Scheer, perhaps the best known of the four, who became PL's hard-driving West Coast organizer.

Though "puritanical" in the manner of the Old Left (PL frowns on smoking pot, decries loose morals), the Maoists swiftly became a force within SDS.

The circumstances surrounding PL's decision to penetrate and eventually to control SDS add up to an almost classic text for organizational take-over.

Almost from the day of its reorganization in 1965, PL decided that, like nearly every other political party of any consequence (though, with fewer than one thousand members, PL was hardly then a party of "consequence"), it needed a campus-based youth arm. Rather than start from scratch and attempt to organize one, PL took the easier route—adoption.

SDS was unaware either that it was up for adoption or about to be Maoist-infiltrated. Radical though SDS was, it was fiercely independent. Yet SDS's very organizational looseness made it an inviting and easy target for take-over. Moreover, SDS had made itself vulnerable to the kind of adoption PL had in mind when, in April, 1965—as it organized for its first March on Washington, scheduled for that month—it welcomed all who shared its anti-Vietnam views, Communists included, to join its ranks.

PL quietly accepted SDS's invitation.

Early in 1966, PL's ultra-radical leadership secretly ordered its collegiate members to join their campuses' SDS chapters—and to begin working toward chapter leadership. Control SDS's campus chapters, PL knew, and it would, almost by default, control SDS's national office and organizational staff.

Within three years PL was to achieve its goal.

Long before that, however, PL's influence began to be felt within SDS. Even by mid-1968, PL's SDS members—who owed first allegiance to PL, not to SDS—had (1) effectively silenced SDS's New Left outlook and philosophy; (2) begun to infuse SDS with PL's own hard-left, militant extremist Maoism—which embraces not only the *words* of Mao Tse-tung and the *anti-imperialism* and *national liberation* lines of Fidel Castro and the late Ho Chi Minh, but also the *guerrilla tactics* of the late Che Guevara.

SDS's abrupt change of view on the Vietnam War was indicative of PL's growing influence and persuasiveness.

When, in 1964, SDS switched from its primary interest in solely domestic issues (civil rights), and began to take stands on international issues, it viewed the Vietnam War merely as a major strategic blunder. SDS was for peace, and an end to the Vietnam conflict. By 1966, its stance on Vietnam abruptly switched from simply being *for* peace to one *against* the U.S. military—thus manifesting SDS's new antimilitarism line. By 1967 SDS began to view the war not merely as a military exercise, but as a provocation of U.S. "imperialism."

SDS's about-face—from its original stance for peace to one against militarism and finally against imperialism—was, ideologically, like night and day. In just three years SDS had succumbed to the Maoist view of Vietnam.

PL's instrument for SDS take-over was the Worker–Student Alliance caucus—a group within SDS supported by PL and composed largely of PL members or sympathizers. Some in SDS's non-Maoist leadership attempted to slow or halt the growing strength of the Worker–Student Alliance.

They were doomed to failure. By SDS's 1969 national convention it was obvious that the majority of convention delegates were PLers. When non-Maoist SDS delegates walked out, what remained in convention—and in control of SDS—was PL and its Worker–Student Alliance. The take-over was all but complete.

PL's chairman is Milton Rosen, one of its four original founders. Rosen backstaged the Worker–Student Alliance's capture of SDS.

Besides its bi-monthly magazine, *PL—Progressive Labor,* PL also publishes the quarterly magazine *World Revolution* (a digest from the world's revolutionary press), and the national English-Spanish-language, worker-oriented monthly newspaper *Challenge-Desafío.* Progressive Labor party headquarters is in New York City.

REVOLUTIONARY UNION (RU)

A new, rising, super Maoist-lining activist group, the Revolutionary Union's main base, until June, 1969, when it merged with a breakaway faction of SDS to form RYM II, has been San Francisco. It was the Bay Area (meaning the San Francisco Bay area) Revolutionary Union—the BARU—which joined with some Maoist SDSers in a split from "The Weatherman" RYM I faction just after SDS's 1969 convention. Result was the RYM II (Revolutionary Youth Movement II), which now constitutes the real strength of the RU.

The Revolutionary Union takes its name from its advocacy of "revolutionary collectives." It defines a revolutionary collective as "a relatively small number of highly dedicated, well-disciplined persons who are willing to subordinate individual preferences to collective decisions and who are capable of working in accordance with an equitable rational and efficient division of labor. The collective should be the focal point for intellectual activity, practical activity, and an effort to integrate the two." It defines "intellectual activity" as "study and analysis," and "practical activity" as "the formulation of tactics for day-to-day struggle and also the development of strategy which can place day-to-day tactics in a comprehensive revolutionary context."

RU's brand of revolutionary Maoism is, generally, to the left even of Progressive Labor's.

221

The Revolutionary Union bitterly opposed Progressive Labor's take-over of SDS. RU's opposition was based fundamentally on its philosophical differences with PL. Whereas PL believes revolution within the United States must come through revolutionizing American workers (thus, PL's concept of a worker–student alliance), the Revolutionary Union, while equally dedicated to a U.S. revolution, believes the revolutionizing force will, ultimately, represent an alliance between minority blacks and poor whites. RUers are outspokenly Maoists, support Red China and Albania, but oppose East Germany and Czechoslovakia. They look upon the Soviet Union as "evil."

Bob Avakian, RU's leader, is also second-in-command behind Mike Klonsky in RYM II. Klonsky had been SDS's 1968–69 national secretary.

Rooted on the West Coast and organized in San Francisco, RU's three original founders were Avakian, Bruce Franklin (who had organized Stanford's SDS chapter), and Steve Hamilton. The three compose RU's Correspondence Committee which promulgates "The Red Papers"—RU's statement of revolutionary principle. Another top RU (and RYM II) leader is Marvin Treiger, a former Communist party member. RU and RYM II are so intertwined in top leadership as to be one.

In "The Red Papers," RU advances its theory of a U.S. worker–black–poor revolutionary force, declaring in part:

It is not possible . . . for U.S. workers . . . to join the fight against American imperialism unless their class consciousness is heightened through the political work of revolutionaries. . . . Working people must have a consciousness of their own power to be the decisive force in the defeat of their class enemy, the monopoly capitalist ruling class.

Some believe that the Revolutionary Union will emerge, along with RYM II, as a leading force among the more revolutionary of former SDSers.

STUDENTS FOR A DEMOCRATIC SOCIETY (SDS)
The voice, fountainhead, strength, and central force of the New

222

Left since its founding in June, 1960, SDS—before its divisive Chicago national convention of June 18–22, 1969—had 317 chapters on college and university campuses and more than seven thousand national (dues-paying) members. It also had been active in radicalizing the nation's high schools.

But SDS's paid-membership strength has always been illusory. Many members, still clinging to SDS's old, hang-loose ways, simply didn't bother joining or paying dues, though they participated in SDS activism. SDS's activist strength has variously been estimated at between 35,000 and 100,000. SDS's secret strength (the philosophical, if not physical, support it received from the campus at large) has often been significant. A *Fortune* magazine poll published in January, 1969, for example, showed that two-fifths of all college students supported some or all of SDS's activist values.

SDS stands as a phenomenon in American political activism. It represents the youth generation's first reach for political power.

SDS's "founding father" is generally conceded to have been former University of Michigan student Robert "Al" Haber, SDS's first president and national secretary (and now the prime mover in the SDS-affiliated Radical Education Project—REP). It was Haber who called SDS's first convention, held at the Hotel Barbizon in New York City, in June, 1960. About thirty students attended. Most were from eastern colleges. At the time, there were just two SDS chapters— one at the University of Michigan and another at Yale (which called itself the John Dewey Discussion Club).

In fact, however, "SDS" had existed—if only as a letterhead organization—since the previous year. Then, in 1959, the Student League for Industrial Democracy (SLID), a moribund group of pro-labor liberals and social democrats who conducted discussions on the campuses, changed its name to Students for a Democratic Society (SDS).

The Student League for Industrial Democracy had been the youth arm of the prolabor, anticommunist, socialist-leaning League for Industrial Democracy (LID). For the first five years of SDS's existence, LID was its financial angel. Labor's break with SDS came in 1965. By then, SDS had not only turned against organized labor (it

223

accused Big Labor of being "racist") but had committed what, to labor, was an unpardonable sin: invited all student dissidents, *including* Communists, to join its ranks. At that, LID publicly severed all relations with SDS.

With labor's pull-out, SDS was on its own. But by then it was solvent. Its revenues in 1966—the first year after labor's breakaway —came to $86,624.90, from membership dues, donations, and literature sales.

Libertarian and social democratic in philosophy and makeup, SDS's first convention was a call to America's concerned youth—its alienated collegians—to work for changes within the society's democratic structure. The big issue was civil rights. And many of SDS's first leaders were already veterans from the "war" in the South.

Tom Hayden, of the convicted "Chicago 7," who had been editor of the University of Michigan student daily and was to become SDS's second president (1962–63), a leading spokesman of the New Left, and the author of SDS's famed declaration of principle, "The Port Huron Statement," was himself a veteran of the "southern wars."

Hayden's "Port Huron Statement"—named for the then fledgling SDS's June, 1962, convention site, an AFL–CIO summer camp near Port Huron, Michigan—first proclaimed the principles of the New Left. It called for sweeping reforms but not revolution in American society, appealed to the youth on the campuses to lead America out of their parents' hypocritical and basically undemocratic society, and spearhead the transformation of America toward true equality, liberty, and freedom.

The statement was the first to enunciate the basic theme of participatory democracy which, for nearly five years thereafter, would be one of SDS's guiding goals.

Participatory democracy, as Hayden visualized it, was to be a "democracy of individual participation" where each citizen participated "in those social decisions determining the quality and direction of his life."

Later, SDS would say that if youth is required to fight in Vietnam, then by the rule of participatory democracy, youth should have a share in making draft laws and formulating war policy. What Hayden and SDS were calling for was "Youth Power"—which would later underlie the campuses' cry for "Student Power," the student demand for a voice in university administration and curriculum.

Finally, the "Port Huron Statement" called for the youth generation to join with SDS in a New Left—as the means of achieving the changes SDS envisaged for America.

At the same Port Huron meeting, SDS's constitution was framed. Though amended in 1967, it remains unchanged—from the original of 1962—in its preamble and membership requirements. In part it declares:

> Students for a Democratic Society is an association of young people on the left. . . . Membership is open to all who share the commitment of the organization to democracy as a means and as a social goal. . . . SDS is an organization of and for democrats. It is civil libertarian in its treatment of those with whom it disagrees, but clear in its opposition to any antidemocratic principle as a basis for governmental, social or political organization.

Yet, by 1969, and though still organized under a democratic constitution, SDS would have embraced Marxism—including virulent Maoist Marxism.

SDSers did not hide the change of mind that had come over them or the change of goals that now ruled SDS itself.

"Our bitter yet powerful experience with American politics in the 1960s has moved us considerably away from our original Left-liberal stance," SDS declared in 1969. It conceded it had become "a mass radical and anti-imperialist student movement, advocating revolutionary politics for the New Left."

By then, too, SDS would have adopted much of the phraseology of Marxism. It was the sound, the fury, and the parlance not of the New but of the Old Left. By 1970, this was the *real* SDS.

SDS, which had set as its goal the transformation of America, had itself been transformed.

"We have discovered," one of its position papers would say in explaining the transformation, "our powerlessness, our unfreedom. Moreover, the social character of our oppression revealed the need of a collective struggle for liberation. . . . The contradiction between the brutal and dehumanized reality of advanced corporate capitalism and the liberating potential of its technology and productive organization has never been greater . . . from this viewpoint, all the world's people have never been more oppressed . . . nor has the potential for struggle [revolution] ever been greater. . . . The New Left will be at the center of that struggle."

SDS's thrust during the intervening years was for power to broaden its campus base so as to wield the kind of power with which it could force changes, and eventually revolution, in the American society.

In widely scattered, often little publicized attempts to extend its campus base, SDS reached out for allies and alliances:

With the poor, in such notable projects as its 1963 Join Community Union, an attempt to organize Chicago's unemployed youth; and the far more ambitious nine-city (Newark, Cleveland, Boston, Louisville, others) 1964–65 ERAP—for Economic Research and Action Project—which sought to awaken the political and community consciousness of slum and ghetto dwellers, and show them how (with rent strikes and demonstrations) to "fight City Hall."

With workers, in a wide-ranging round of projects that aimed to link the campus with the working man and his job. Typical was 1969's SDS summer "work-in" in which activists sought jobs in industry, then worked to radicalize blue collar and clerical employees. SDS aimed both to raise the "working class conscience" and ally itself with the industrial worker. SDS's proposed SLAP (Student Labor Action Project) was an over-all, national, chapter-by-chapter thrust to "get with labor." The clash in May, 1970, between New York City "hard hat" construction workers and students protesting the Kent State University "massacre" reveals the depth of SDS's failure to cement a worker–student alliance and portends increasing union labor action against SDS and its campus militants.

With GIs. Its aim has been to stir dissidence and insubordination among military personnel, especially those bound for Vietnam, and to build a base of strength within the military establishment (special targets: servicemen soon to enter college or the work force). SDSers helped set up antidraft information centers; actively participated in the October, 1967, Stop the Draft Week sit-in at the Oakland, California, Induction Center, and similar protests; supported the Fort Hood 3 (military noncooperators); participated in the Fort Dix, New Jersey, "invasion" of October, 1969, under the leadership of the "Committee to Free the Fort Dix 38" (GIs involved in a stockade disturbance the previous June); and, of course, protested on campus against the draft, ROTC, and military recruiting.

With the blacks. SDS has worked throughout its whole history for strong black alliances. SDSers participated in the 1961, 1962, and 1963 Freedom Rides, were the driving force behind "Friends of SNCC" chapters set up on northern campuses (in support of SNCC's efforts in the South), and flocked south to support SNCC's 1964 Mississippi Freedom Summer. Ties between SDS and BSU on the campuses are close. Growing closer is the working relationship between SDS and the Black Panthers.

With high schoolers. SDS's own campus experience had shown that four college years were not enough to thoroughly radicalize many students—thus SDS's reach into the high schools. Established within SDS is a High School Caucus—organized from high school delegates much as are SDS's campus delegates. In 1968, SDS's national council supported a motion to hire a full-time national high school coordinator. As one reason for high school recruiting, SDS's High School Resolution pointed out that "high school police training and ROTC are means to recruit future imperialist soldiers and prepare for aggressive wars."

Despite such seemingly never-ending activism, many SDSers saw scant progress toward the substantial changes in the American system they sought. Disillusionment set in. It caused some to look for shortcuts and for answers which they, themselves, seemed to lack.

One group, which by 1965 began to show up at SDS chapter and national meetings with the answers many SDSers were seeking, were those SDSers aligned with the Maoist-Marxist, Peking-oriented Progressive Labor party. Others with apparent answers to SDS's prob-

227

lems were Communist party youths who began joining SDS in 1966 mainly to thwart a take-over by PL (Progressive Labor).

By SDS's Chicago national convention in June, 1969, PL's penetration was complete. By then PL's cadres of hard-core activists had succeeded in dominating perhaps a majority of SDS's campus chapters. And it was from the campus that national delegates were elected. Rather than face a vote show-down with the stronger PL faction, SDS's national office followers (the "original SDSers") walked out of the convention, claiming to represent "the real SDS."

Eventually, SDS schismed into five parts. All of the parts save the breakaway anti-Communist Independent Socialist Clubs were Marxist-lining. The question most SDS leaders—and the majority of SDS's rank-and-file—were asking one another by 1970 was "What *kind* of Marxist are you?"

SDS had come the full philosophical circle. Now only the pieces remained.

UNRAVELING THE SPLIT-UP IN SDS

RYM I—Revolutionary Youth Movement I (or "The Weatherman"). The Maoist, ultra-revolutionary—and openly "adventurist"—faction of SDS, led by twenty-three-year-old Mark Rudd, who captained SDS's Columbia University shutdown of 1968, RYM I was one of the two original breakaway factions that splintered SDS at its 1969 Chicago convention.

RYM I—allied to SDS's national office—walked out of the Chicago convention taking with it (1) many of SDS's most fervent Maoist-lining student revolutionaries; (2) the key to and possession of SDS's national office in Chicago; (3) SDS's bank account and membership roster. RYM I left behind (and broke with) SDS's highly disciplined and likewise Maoist (and Progressive Labor party-dominated) Worker–Student Alliance (W–SA).

Since RYM I's spin-off, it, too, has split—with the less volatile of its leaders—forming RYM II, under the leadership of Mike Klonsky, SDS's former national secretary.

Until recently, both RYM I and the Worker–Student Alliance called themselves "the real SDS." Early in 1970, however, RYM I

228

officially relinquished its claim to being "SDS." The "real SDS" today is the Worker–Student Alliance, the youth arm of the Maoist-lined Progressive Labor (Communist) party.

RYM I, or "The Weatherman," works hard at "out-Maoing Mao." It proclaims "all power to the people," has already declared Ho Chi Minh the "winner" in Vietnam, and says frankly, "We are revolutionary Communists."

"The Weatherman" is pressing for an alliance with militant blacks and the poor as its revolutionary base. In the "socialist revolution" envisaged by RYM I, Amèrican blacks—which the Rudd group sees as an "internal colony of the U.S."—will rise, secede, and revolt. RYM Iers are pledged to follow black leadership in such a revolt.

During its Chicago convention breakaway, two principles were laid down which were to determine membership qualifications in the RYM I faction of SDS. The two points give considerable insight into the politics of Rudd's group:

(1) "We support the struggle of black and Latin colonies *within* the U.S. for national liberation and we recognize those *nations'* rights to self-determination (including the right to political secession if they desire it)."

(2) "We support the struggle for national liberation of the people of South Vietnam, led by the National Liberation Front and Provisional Revolutionary Government of South Vietnam. We also support the Democratic Republic of Vietnam [North Vietnam], led by President Ho Chi Minh, as well as the People's Republic of China, the People's Democratic Republics of Korea and Albania, and the Republic of Cuba, all waging fierce struggles against U.S. imperialism. We support the right of all people to pick up the gun to free themselves from the brutal rule of U.S. imperialism."

Bombs, more than guns, have been "The Weatherman" spokesman, particularly since its secret "national war council," held in Flint, Michigan, on December 27–31, 1969. There, "The Weatherman" formed into revolutionary "focals" (three-to-five-member tactical units), acquired the first of a number of dynamite and high explosives caches, boned up on explosive techniques (one of their purported

229

texts: a hundred-page article on explosives ripped from a technical book in Detroit's public library), and went underground.

In its revolutionary fervor "The Weatherman" prefers to fight the "opposition" (including "pig" police) rather than to fight for social change. It has concluded that combating social ills is a waste of time.

At the time of RYM I's walkout, Rudd was named national secretary; twenty-two-year-old Jeff Jones of New York, its inter-organizational secretary, and Bill Ayers, twenty-four, of Ann Arbor, Michigan, educational secretary.

Rudd and Ayers were among twenty-eight Weathermen named (thirteen of them as defendants) on July 23, 1970, in a federal indictment charging conspiracy to bomb a police association building in Detroit and corporate and government buildings in New York, Chicago, and Berkeley. Earlier, the two—along with Jones, Bernadine Dohrn, once SDS's national secretary, and other top Weathermen—had been indicted for conspiring to violate the new federal Antiriot Act during four "days of rage" in Chicago, protesting the "Chicago 7" trial. But none of "The Weatherman's" top echelon showed in court. They'd disappeared—underground.

RYM II—Revolutionary Youth Movement II. This equally Maoist-lined but less rash former SDS faction split from RYM I. The split, occurring sometime after the 1969 SDS Chicago convention, was based more on policies than on politics. Leadership opportunism also played a part.

Former SDS national secretary Mike Klonsky became head of the then fledgling RYM II, and promised to guide his group into revolution but with what he considers wisdom rather than rash adventurism. RYM II has joined in membership and in leadership with the San Francisco Bay area-based Revolutionary Union, an independent Maoist-aligned group of student revolutionaries. SDSer Bob Avakian, a Mao expert, former organizer of SDS on the Stanford campus and leader of the Bay Area arm of the Revolutionary Union (the BARU), is RYM II's second in command.

230

The RYM II is self-admittedly "Maoist." It believes North Vietnam *will* win. It puts greater stress on organizing black revolutionists than does the worker-aligned W–SA, and decries the radical actions of "The Weatherman." It was RYM II's demonstrators during the November 14–15, 1969, Moratorium march in Washington, D.C., who rallied outside the South Vietnam embassy shouting support for North Vietnam and the provisional revolutionary government. They also joined the confrontation with police outside the Justice Department building. In a word, RYM II has all the trappings of ultra-left activism, including the words of Mao, but is less apt to take to the streets or campus on a whim.

Besides Klonsky and Avakian, RYM II's leadership includes Carl Davidson, the SDS theoretician and staff writer for the independent radical newspaper *Guardian,* and Marvin Treiger, a former leader in the DuBois clubs.

W–SA—Worker–Student Alliance (also, the Progressive Labor party). For all practical purposes, the W–SA faction of SDS *is* Progressive Labor (PL) or, more correctly, is the Progressive Labor party's youth arm.

W–SA is a Maoist, tightly disciplined, well-organized cadre of youthful campus activists who in only three years reversed the whole direction of SDS (from social democratic radicalism to revolutionary communist Maoism).

The basic difference in W–SA's Maoist outlook, and the Maoist outlooks of SDS's other two major splinter groups, is Progressive Labor's "working class perspective." All of its views, policies, and actions are based on alliances with the American worker, whether black, white, or brown. PL, typically, looks at the black worker as just another "worker," not as a separate, "colonized" people, as does RYM I.

PLers and W–SAers say simply, "We are Communists." And with a capital "C."

Where RYM I says "Power to the People," the Worker–Student Alliance says, "Power to the Workers." Where RYM I looks upon the Soviet Union as "revisionist," the Worker–Student Alliance sees Rus-

231

sia as a capitalistic country, not really much different from the United States.

The Worker–Student Alliance publishes its own version of SDS's *New Left Notes* from its Boston, Massachusetts, headquarters. John Pennington of Harvard is national secretary. Pat Forman, San Francisco State College, is inter-organization secretary. Non-student (but former SDS New England regional staffer) Alan Spector is educational secretary.

STUDENT NONVIOLENT COORDINATING COMMITTEE (SNCC)

The Student Nonviolent Coordinating Committee sprang spontaneously out of the lunch counter sit-ins, the first of them peaceably staged at a Greensboro, North Carolina, five-and-dime store by four Negro college students on February 2, 1960.

For the first time the struggle for civil rights in the South had moved to the arena of private property. Students—blacks first, because most of the action was in the South, then more and more whites—had taken into their own hands a question that no longer could stand moot: Had the owners of private establishments, who welcomed the public as patrons, the right to discriminate?

On campus after campus, the answer was a resounding "no!"

During Easter Week, 1960, a hastily called conference of campus representatives met in Raleigh, North Carolina, and set up a Temporary Student Nonviolent "Coordinating" Committee. Its primary job was to act as an informational tie between the campus-scattered groups then forming under the SNCC banner. One outcome was SNCC's monthly newsletter, *The Student Voice*.

In October that same year, a second conference, this time in Atlanta, was called. It was there that SNCC took constitutional form.

From SNCC's inception through 1965—the organization's non-violent, civil rights phase—James Forman of New York was its black executive secretary, its public voice, and, behind the scenes, the shaper of SNCC policy. From the outset, SNCC did not characterize itself as a mass student organization. Rather, it was a highly staffed, highly efficient prime mover.

SNCC was the moving force behind the 1964 "Mississippi Summer Project," which brought more than one thousand volunteers (most of them northern students, many of them white) into Mississippi for voter registration work. To give Mississippi's new registered black voters candidates and a party of their own, SNCC created a new political force in the state: the Mississippi Freedom Democratic party (MFDP). It was the MFDP's integrated delegation that the 1968 Democratic National Convention recognized and seated at Chicago, bypassing Mississippi's white regulars.

SNCC's new militancy surfaced in May, 1966, when "Black Power," a slogan first enunciated by Stokely Carmichael (but used as early as 1953 by black novelist Richard Wright), became the new goal of SNCC. Carmichael, twenty-four, who had founded Alabama's all-Negro Black Panther party, replaced Forman as national chairman, and H. Rap Brown rose in the hierarchy to become a SNCC spokesman and later (1967) its chairman.

SNCC became a segregated force, ousting its white staffers and severing its ties with its white backers.

Briefly, SNCC and the new, fiercely militant Black Panther party merged early in 1968—a merger that ended with Carmichael being fired on August 22, 1968.

By June, 1969, SNCC had struck the word "nonviolent" from its name—now it calls itself the Student *National* Coordinating Committee—and H. Rap Brown, twenty-five, reelected its chairman, declared, "We do not accept unconditional nonviolence as a tactic."

SNCC's influence and stature, however, have waned noticeably within the past year. Militant community blacks have been attracted to the Black Panthers and its advocacy of armed activism. Black student militants have more and more gravitated to the BSU. Compared to either, SNCC might almost be classed a "moderate" among black power organizations.

SNCC's national headquarters remains in Atlanta, though its New York City office coordinates its seventeen regional offices.

Friends of SNCC. SNCC-affiliated groups, sometimes on campus, sometimes not, but with direct communications and coordination to SNCC national headquarters in Atlanta. Because SNCC itself is not a national membership organization, most SNCC members belong to a local Friends of SNCC chapter, many of them tied to campuses.

SOUTHERN STUDENT ORGANIZING COMMITTEE (SSOC)

Sometimes labeled the "SDS of the South," the Southern Student Organizing Committee was indigenous to southern campuses where SDS's northern radical taint made SDS unwelcome.

SSOC was organized during the weekend of April 4–5, 1964, in Nashville (which was to become its headquarters), with the blessings of SNCC, SDS, and later with the backing of a number of northern foundations.

Almost from the beginning, ill-fated SSOC wrapped itself defensively in the Rebel flag (and at the last, even unfurled it). In *The New Rebel,* SSOC's official publication, it pictured itself as a kind of middle-of-the-road campus voice standing between "the Goldwater Republicans on the Right . . . and the Negro Movement on the Left."

SSOC's liberal, not really radical stance made it the darling of northern foundations. The Field Fund alone contributed $50,000 from 1965 to 1968. The liberal New World Foundation came up with $10,000. Other contributors included the Taconic Foundation and the Aaron E. Norman Fund.

SSOC's view was inward, not outward, contrary to the prevailing aggressive philosophy of rebellion on northern campuses. The "cause" SSOC undertook for itself was explaining the South to northern campuses. In short, SSOC was still enmeshed in the Civil War when northern campuses were enmeshed in civil rights.

It was SSOC's thesis that the south was a kind of underdeveloped colony struggling for self-determination against the North. When a merger was proposed with SDS, SSOCers shrank back.

"SSOC," they argued, "grew out of southern, agrarian, conservative society . . . with strong ties to the Christian social gospel; SDS, on the other hand, was not significantly influenced by that gospel."

Still, against its own inbred tradition of anti-union "liberalism," SSOC voted to adopt a program aimed at alliances with southern workers. The program was called SLAM—Southern Labor Action Movement. But the hoped-for alliance, some members charged, was scuttled by SSOC's own staffers who opposed it from the start.

234

As honest-for-anger radicals grew more and more restive of SSOC's liberal trend, they left in droves. They did not, however, leave the Movement. Rather, they formed SDS activist chapters of their own, or SDS-affiliated off-campus MDS (Movement for a Democratic Society) chapters, as did some former SSOCers in New Orleans.

Generally, SSOC "turf" was the deep South. It was strong on campuses in North Carolina, Georgia, Alabama, and Florida.

Despite the growing rift with SDS, some SSOC chapters briefly entered into hyphenated marriages with the radicals from the North. At the University of Georgia, as at the University of Florida, there was an SDS–SSOC chapter. Others were border state amalgamations—as in Louisville and Lexington, Kentucky.

SSOC doggedly fought SDS encroachment. At Florida State University (Tallahassee) and at the University of Alabama (Tuscaloosa), strong SSOC chapters ate the invading SDS "crazies" alive and literally threw them off their campuses. At one point, SSOCers proposed lynching some SDS deep South organizers.

But as SDS grew more radical and even revolutionary, SSOC continued to play the southern liberal. It abstained from confrontations with police. It even thought the election of enough good liberals such as Nelson Rockefeller might work the changes in America and the South its members sought. While SDS, under Maoist PL's prodding, was talking about "monopoly capitalism" and "imperialism," SSOC—really no more radical than a boll weevil—still hoped for change given a liberalization of the southern voter.

By the spring of 1969, the die was cast. SDS was on the move in Dixie. At its Austin, Texas, national council meeting that March, SDS voted to "Build SDS in the South"—an expansive program of southern campus conquest that (1) bypassed SSOC as a base and (2) divorced SDS from "liberal, racist, pacifistic SSOC."

Progressive Labor, then more than ever in control of SDS, had finally got its way. The "southern enemy"—SSOC—was now high on SDS's extermination list.

SSOC did the southern gentlemanly thing. It committed suicide. At a half-hearted and only half-attended conference of SSOCers near Edwards, Mississippi, in June, 1969, delegates voted nearly unan-

235

imously to dissolve. Thus expired the first and last indigenous radical student movement born and bred in the South.

Thereafter, SDS attempted to retain what southern chapters it already had and to build on those southern campuses where SSOC had formerly existed.

But the "red-neck, radical" South, while it may have its share of campus rebels, lacks them in the revolutionary Marxist–Leninist spirit of SDS. The Students for a Democratic Society hasn't found things easy-going the deeper it has penetrated south of the Mason–Dixon line.

Still, as one SDS national council resolution would declare, "There remains a pressing need for a revolutionary movement in the South; we can never make a revolution with only three-quarters of the country. . . . We [SDS] are in the South to stay . . . and so are our politics."

THIRD WORLD LIBERATION FRONT (TWLF)

The Third World Liberation Front grew up on the San Francisco State College (SFSC) campus as a kind of "international" spin-off from the Black Students Union (BSU), also founded at SFSC. The Third World Liberation Front, though turning much of its attention inward to better conditions for non-black/non-Caucasian Americans, is "world ethnic" in concept: an amalgamation of Latin-American, Mexican-American, Asian-American, Chinese, Filipino, Puerto Rican, and black students.

Despite its preoccupation at the moment with bettering the conditions of America's own "third world races," TWLF might properly be called the "international arm" of the American student movement.

TWLF's brown-skinned, yellow-skinned, and hyphenated campus membership causes it to agitate and work in behalf of better opportunities for its racial kin in America: the Chinese, the Filipino, the Puerto Rican, the Mexican-American—the whole slate of deprived and often discriminated-against non-Caucasians.

In its world outlook, TWLF sees all the inequities and inequalities of American society reflected and magnified in the economic and military imperialism practiced by the U.S. abroad in dealings with

236

the world's undeveloped, uneducated, and undercapitalized nations.

How TWLF came into being is perhaps best explained by a leader of San Francisco State's Latin American Students Organization (LASO). A son of South American and Irish parents, he explains:

"Most of us non-black Third World students were involved in what we loosely call the 'movement.' About the time that black consciousness became a pretty solid concept on campus those of us in the Third World who were not black had to turn around and orient our thinking to what was happening (to our own people) in our own communities."

Third Worlders thus became activists in behalf of elevating Filipino and Mexican-American workers; marched in support of California's Mexican-American grape-strikers; protested the "coolie wages" paid their own kind in establishments run by their own people (as the kitchen help in Chinese-owned American restaurants); pushed for stronger ethnic departments in their own schools and for alleviation of job discrimination faced in the American society by non-Caucasians.

TWLF grew from idea to inception during discussions on the San Francisco State College campus during the 1967–68 college year between the already powerful BSU and the heads of half a dozen on-campus ethnic groups, all of them small, powerless, and largely unheard. In the spring of 1968, five of these student ethnic organizations—LASO (Latin American Students Organization), MASC (Mexican-American Student Confederation), ICSA (Intercollegiate Chinese for Social Action), PACE (Philippine American Collegiate Endeavor), and AAPA (Asian American Political Alliance)—joined with the BSU (Black Students Union) to form the Third World Liberation Front.

On the SFSC campus, one of TWLF's first major confrontations was staged in May, 1968. It was a week's demonstration to support its demand for four hundred special admissions of Third World students, plus a guarantee of financial assistance for Third World students admitted under the relaxed qualifications program it advocated. Appended to the ten demands which the BSU handed the SFSC administration on November 6, 1968, were five additional demands from

237

TWLF. One of them called for the setting up of schools of "ethnic studies for the ethnic groups involved in the Third World."

At SFSC, Third World leadership dismissed the elevation of Dr. S. I. Hayakawa, himself a Japanese-American, to acting president of the college as merely "an Establishment sop."

TWLF is growing more active and increasingly more militant on campuses across the nation. On a number of campuses, splinter ethnic organizations are forming activist "fronts" of their own—either modeled after or associated with the Third World Liberation Front. On most campuses SDS is closely allied with TWLF, as is the BSU.

VOICES IN VITAL AMERICA (VIVA)

A relatively new (founded in 1967) but fast-growing moderate voice on campus, VIVA takes a nonpartisan, nonpolitical stand ("or no stand if we can avoid one," says one VIVA spokesman), aims to pose as the "alternative" between the militant Left and Right. While most Movement activists look upon VIVA as "rightist," VIVA considers its stance to be middle of the road.

VIVA advocates—to quote a memorandum directed to its chapters—"the need for a non-coercive academic environment, the redress of grievances without intimidation, and the need for every student to understand his responsibilities as a citizen. VIVA is not liberal, moderate, or conservative. We do not feel that the goals of VIVA are ideological in nature but applied common sense in a free society."

As the avowed voice of the campuses' "silent majority," VIVA pushes for open debate on grievances rather than open violence, sponsors the "VIVA Ombudsman" (to hear campus complaints, take them to the administration), organizes tutorial programs (*e.g.,* among American Indian children), conducts "Operation Mail Call" (a correspondence service between campus pen-pals and U.S. servicemen in Vietnam), and works for "free speech in an academic environment."

While philosophically opposed to campus violence, VIVA has on occasion resorted to activist techniques in its opposition to campus violence, whether on the left or right. VIVA national chairman Stephen R. Frank, while a student at Los Angeles City College, led VIVA-ites in tearing down barricades erected by student strikers.

238

Founded by five undergraduates on the UCLA (Los Angeles) campus in 1967, VIVA began as the Victory in Vietnam Association, which took the position that while "victory" in the Vietnam War did not necessarily mean "military victory," it did mean a freedom of choice "victory" for the people of Vietnam. Thus, for practical purposes, VIVA stood against any precipitous U.S. pullout—an opposite view from that of most Movement anti-Vietnam groups.

VIVA operates with a fund-raising, adult national advisory board (chaired by Mrs. Douglas Coppin), and an appointive VIVA national board of college and high school students (most of them VIVA chapter heads on their campuses) which elects the organization's Executive Council.

VIVA claims more than 125 active chapters across the nation, some fifty of them on college campuses, the rest affiliated with high schools. Its executive director is thirty-two-year-old Richard Thies. Headquarters is at Los Angeles, California.

YOUNG AMERICANS FOR FREEDOM (YAF)

Largest of student conservative activist groups, YAF (with a current claimed membership of 51,700 in 513 high school and college chapters) was born, literally, on the Sharon, Connecticut, estate of conservative author/TV personality/editor (of the *National Review*) William F. Buckley, Jr. There, on September 9–11, 1960, a group of ninety conservative youths, most of them from the campuses, met to mull over what they considered to be Richard Nixon's "sellout" to Nelson Rockefeller at the then-recent Republican National Convention. Though this was YAF's founding meeting, the organization was rooted in the Student Committee for the Loyalty Oath, created by two Washington, D.C., students—David Franke and Doug Caddy —in 1958.

From that Sharon, Connecticut, meeting came the "Sharon Statement," which remains YAF's credo. Among its thirteen conservative precepts are: (1) international communism is the greatest single threat to constitutional liberties; (2) the U.S. should stress victory, not coexistence, with the Communist world; (3) liberty is "indivisible," and political freedom cannot exist without economic freedom; (4) government should not go beyond what YAFers consider its primary function: to provide for the national defense, preserve internal order, and administer justice.

Senator Barry Goldwater became a YAF patron saint, one of its most vocal supporters (five YAF directors sat on the Youth for Goldwater national steering committee), and has been a longtime member of YAF's national advisory board. Other Board members have included California's late arch-conservative congressman James B. Utt, Senator Strom Thurmond, former FBI undercover informant Herbert A. Philbrick, columnist Eugene Lyons, and conservative spokesman Professor Russell Kirk.

YAF has spread nationwide from its first bastions of campus strength—New York, Texas, and Florida. *The New Guard,* its official monthly magazine (first issue: March, 1961), urges YAFers to counter campus liberal and radical groups, snap photos of protesters for local police, back conservative candidates on campus and off, and file suit against campus administrators who suspend classes in support of student strikes.

Taking to the picket lines themselves, YAFers have marched in support of HUAC (House Un-American Activities Committee), championed loyalty oaths for Peace Corpsmen, and in 1965 threatened Firestone Tire and Rubber Company with an aerial inundation of anti-Firestone leaflets at the Indianapolis 500 auto race (a longtime production-test event for the company) if Firestone went ahead with plans to build a synthetic rubber plant in Communist Rumania. Firestone eventually canceled its Rumanian plans, and YAF has always taken the credit for the company's decision.

YAF's earliest philosophy, by its own admission, hewed to the fundamentalism of Russell Kirk. Now, YAF claims a move toward the "libertarianism" of Milton Friedman, F. A. Hayek, and to some extent, Ayn Rand. However, both a spreading revolt in YAF ranks (launched at Stanford in November, 1969, but already infecting such former YAF strongpoints as Texas, Pennsylvania, and Southern California) and the disenchantment of YAF "liberals" at its 1969 national convention in St. Louis would belie any organizational liberalizing.

At Stanford, some YAF members burnt their YAF membership

240

cards, and formed a new conservative but libertarian group, the Free Campus Movement (FCM). "YAF," explained one dissident, "sees Bob Dylan as a dangerous radical. We think of him as just a great folksinger."

YAF's most recent national convention mirrored the growing hardening of its conservative stance. When liberal YAFers rose to speak they were countered by rightist cartoonist Al Capp who told the youthful delegates to get rid of the "outsiders" (yet nearly 250 of the 1,000 delegates sided with the liberals, so they were scarcely "outsiders").

Despite its denials, YAF is nearly 100 percent white (it has passed resolutions supporting apartheid in South Africa and white control in Rhodesia). It has few Catholics or Jews. It supported California's ranchers against the grape-strikers, symbolically suggests that U.S. B-52s drop nuclear bombs on North Vietnam, and has mirrored the "southern viewpoint" in integration and school desegregation.

YAF tabs itself "Rebels With a Cause"—meaning the conservative cause. Chapter leaders get the YAF monthly *Creative Politics* and "research" material that spans the conservative gamut from "The Hypocrisy of Social Security" (a pamphlet by Jameson G. Campaigne, Sr., member of YAF's national advisory board) to "The Untruth of the Obvious: The Minimum Wage Law." Its executive director is Randal Cornell Teague, who works from YAF's Washington, D.C., headquarters.

YOUNG DEMOCRATIC CLUBS OF AMERICA (YDCA)

Like the Young Republicans, the Young Democratic Clubs of America (also known as Young Democrats—YD)—which claims 250,000 members—is a two-tiered activist organization. Older off-campus YDers abide by strict party loyalty. Collegian YDers champion the candidate. During 1968's presidential primaries, the campuses flocked to the banners of Eugene McCarthy and the late Robert Kennedy in a move to "dump" YD's "national" candidate, then President Lyndon Johnson. The Vietnam issue also split YDCA. Off-campus hawks took an opposite perch from on-campus doves. The wounds have yet to heal.

Going it alone, some campus YDs joined the College Young Democrats (CYD), which held its convention in Boston a week before YDCA's 1967 biennial Miami convention. Disaffiliation by campus chapters and state YDCA organizations became epidemic. Two break-aways: Minnesota and Iowa, who decided not to renew their YDCA charters. Also stirring campus YDers to revolt was Allard Lowen-stein's anti-Johnson Committee for Concerned Democrats.

YDCA's 1969 Las Vegas convention, declared many campus YDers, was purposely staged during pre-Christmas examinations to exclude them. Most delegates were from off campus and over thirty. Elected president was twenty-nine-year-old David Sternoff of Belle-vue, Washington.

Collegians objected to the convention's "nonrelevant atmosphere" (Las Vegas' casinos), and its disregard for the youthful candidates the campuses had supported in the 1968 presidential campaign.

"It was as if the events of last year (the defeat of McCarthy, the assassination of Robert Kennedy) had never happened," said a turned-off Jeff Pressman, a UC/Berkeley acting instructor and a member of YDCA's national committee.

Liberal to radical campus YDers—who have joined SDS in pro-test, marched during the Moratorium days, are often violently anti-Vietnam and antidraft—have increasingly gone their own way on their own campuses. In "doing their own thing," they often run counter to national Democratic party policy.

Walter D. Toner, Jr., is executive director. YDCA headquarters is in Washington, D.C.

YOUNG REPUBLICANS (YR)

Known as the Young Republican National Federation, the 400,-000-member "youth arm" of the Republican party is a study in contrasts.

Off campus, YR is neither youthful (most members are rising young business and professional people in their late twenties and early thirties), obedient to the Republican National Committee (which it has repeatedly snubbed, despite the committee's annual $90,000 subsidy which keeps YR alive), nor representative of the moderate

242

Republican majority. Unabashedly ultraconservative and controlled by a secretariat called "The Syndicate," off-campus YRers champion Goldwater and Reagan, led the jeering of Nelson Rockefeller at 1964's Republican National Convention, and once suggested converting the UN in New York into a memorial to the late Senator Joe McCarthy. Only grudgingly and in recent years has YR permitted two Republican National Committeemen to sit ex officio on its conservative-dominated executive committee.

On campus, YRers tend to be more moderate, dovish on the Vietnam War, cool to the draft, and more prone to heed the ultraliberal Republican Ripon Society than their own off-campus conservatives. In April, 1970, a prominent YR national campus leader was found guilty of falsifying statements to his draft board.

Campus YR chapters have tended to disaffiliate from the conservative national group or set up on their own. Collegians charged that YR's 1967 national convention purposely excluded them by (1) being held in July, during school vacation; (2) meeting in "remote" Omaha, far from YR's moderate eastern campus strongholds, and, to make sure collegians wouldn't "pack" the convention, (3) charging $45 per person for admission to the convention's gallery.

Insiders charge that both the Young Republicans and Young Democrats have been "corrupted" by congressional patronage. One item: ten three-week European tours, annually awarded each organization's top leadership, to acquaint "young people" with NATO installations. The appropriations come out of the U.S. defense budget.

Young Republican National Federation headquarters is in Washington, D.C.

YOUNG SOCIALIST ALLIANCE (YSA)

As the youth arm of the Trotskyite Communist Socialist Workers party, YSA—organized in 1960—has long had an ubiquitous, but growing foothold on college and high school campuses. Its ubiquitous character stems from the fact that while youthful "Trots" seem, as campus insiders say, "always to be around, electioneering and campaigning," the YSA has never attained substantial power for itself.

Now, however, many believe YSA may inherit some of SDS's

243

disgruntled drop-outs. The reason: YSA's careful treading between Maoism and Moscow's Marxist–Leninism has made it a Marxist–Leninist "neutral" with no strong ties to either camp.

The Socialist Workers party (SWP) grew out of the Trotsky movement—a revolutionary Marxist–Leninist group that adheres to the "independent" Marxist credo of Leon Trotsky. Trotsky fled Russia after his break with Stalin, who insisted that all Communists pay allegiance to the Communist party of the USSR.

YSA–SWP, in their two major publications, the weekly *Militant* and *Young Socialist,* espouse most of the same issues as other radical Left organizations, including black equality, women's liberation, anti-Establishmentism, and withdrawal from Vietnam.

Unlike many other radical groups, however, the Socialist Workers party and YSA are active in fielding and supporting political candidates. In 1969, SWP ran candidates in New York City, Philadelphia, Seattle, and Cleveland. SWP mayoral candidate Syd Stapleton opposed Cleveland's black mayor, Democrat Carl Stokes.

YSA national chairman Larry Seigle, while conceding YSA's past organizational anemia, recently declared: "YSA is not the same organization that it was two years ago. We are significantly larger. We have muscle. We have experience. We have flexibility now that we didn't have then."

YSA, a vehement defender of Cuba and Arab revolutionaries, a staunch backer of the Black Panthers, and a participant in the GI and anti-Vietnam movements, recently won its first student government victory—at little Harpur College, in Binghamton, New York.

Unabashedly revolutionary, YSA poses as the "voice of reason" on the extreme left. YSA's campus membership is probably somewhere between two thousand and four thousand. YSA headquarters is in New York City. I believe that YSA is the only "left" campus organization with a future.

Index